To all those busy youth workers out there
who need to spend more time with
the youngsters you serve.

A resource for you:

Inspire

Volume 1

Inspire – A resource for busy youth workers © 2018 Paul Martin

Scripture quotations [marked NIV] taken from the Holy Bible, New International Version Anglicised Copyright © 1979, 1984, 2011 Biblica

Used by permission of Hodder & Stoughton Ltd, an Hachette UK company

All rights reserved.

'NIV' is a registered trademark of Biblica UK trademark number 1448790.

Artwork for cover adapted and modified from an original line drawing by Amy Walters. Permission is granted solely for use by Paul Martin in his Inspire series and may not be replicated elsewhere.

Acknowledgments

I would like to say a special thank you to Mum and Dad for all your hard work in checking through this manuscript to make it ready for publishing. Mum you always said I would write a book one day! Thank you for your support, encouragement and wise words that have kept me on track through the ups and downs of youth ministry.

Dad thank you for being the first to inspire me with all that God is doing in our time. Thank you for being a great role model for me and for always having time for me (as well as helping me out with those DIY emergencies!).

Thank you to Amy Walters for your lightbulb design which looks great on the front cover! Your vision and creative skills bring about the most inspiring results!

Thank you to Suzi Wheatley for all your support and encouragement in the early days when I first considered embarking on this project. Thank you for helping me to put my feet in the shoes of the volunteers who would be using my notes to teach the young people.

Thank you to Simon Genoe for being super encouraging with all that I do. It is an absolute privilege to be in ministry with you. You are an awesome friend and boss, incredibly inspiring and I am learning so so much from you!

Thank you also to Richard Lyttle for the use of the superb photo on the back cover. It takes a great photographer to capture me in the right light (what with me not being very photogenic!).

Inspire – A resource for busy youth workers - Volume 1

Contents

Introduction

How to use this resource

THE OLD TESTAMENT

1) Adam and Eve – Created in God's image............................13

2) Adam and Eve – Temptation..17

3) Adam and Eve – What Guilt does to you.............................20

4) Cain and Abel – Jealousy between brothers.......................25

5) Noah – A man under pressure...29

6) Noah – Faith in God's words..33

7) Noah – Obedience rewarded...38

8) Noah and the God who keeps his promise........................42

9) Noah gets drunk...45

10) Job – When things go wrong...48

11) Job – Judging others..52

12) Job Blames God..57

13) Job – God speaks on Job..60

14) Job – It's all sorted...65

15) Abram gets a big call from God..70

16) Abram – do lies get us out of trouble?..............................73

17) Lot compromises his principles...77

18) Hagar – The God who sees me...81

19) Sarah and God's impossible promise..................85

20) Abraham – Deal or no Deal?..........................89

21) Lot escapes with his life.................................93

22) Abraham takes his exams...............................97

23) Eliezer is given a mission.............................101

24) Isaac and the double miracle........................104

25) Jacob and the long con................................107

26) Jacob takes up wrestling..............................110

27) Jacob and his bro call a truce.......................114

28) Jacob! Joseph his son..................................117

29) Joseph is wrongly accused...........................122

30) Joseph's opportunity...................................126

31) Joseph and his big brothers.........................130

32) Moses the secret baby................................134

33) Moses murders someone.............................139

34) Moses the unsure leader.............................143

35) Moses hits a brick wall................................148

36) Moses experiences signs and wonders.........151

37) Moses disobeys God....................................157

38) Moses gets moaned at................................162

39) Joshua is called to lead...............................167

40) Rahab protects the spies............................171

41) Joshua is successful...................................174

42) Achan makes God well angry..................................179

43) Joshua forgets to pray..182

44) Deborah leads..186

45) Gideon chosen for mighty works.........................191

46) Gideon – is it ok to test God?..............................195

47) Gideon overcomes fear..200

48) Samson is born..204

49) Samson grows up...209

50) Samson doesn't learn his lesson.........................213

51) Samson rejects God's warnings..........................218

52) Naomi blames God...222

53) Ruth finds favour...227

54) Ruth makes her move..231

55) Ruth – Is God going to give me what I want?.....236

56) God becomes real to Samuel...............................240

57) Hophni and Phineas dishonor God......................246

58) Samuel gives Israel a King..................................250

59) King Saul is tested..254

60) Jonathan bravery in God's strength....................259

61) Saul doesn't learn...264

62) David and first impressions................................268

63) David beats the bully..272

64) David acts with integrity.....................................278

65) Saul goes off the rails...284

66) David – a heart for God..290

67) David's big mistake..294

68) David's Thankfulness...300

I dedicate this book to my wife Deborah
who has supported me in the ups and downs
of youth ministry for 17+ years.

Thank you for your love, support,
patience and commitment,
being so kind to me when I'm out
in the evenings doing something with the youth.

I love you my Sweetie.

Introduction

This book is all about raising up youngsters who know their God, who can understand his word and will let him impact their lives in a deep and meaningful way.

As you can see, this volume contains 68 sessions for church based youth workers to teach young people. These meeting plans have been used and re-used, tweaked and rewritten. I've tried and tested this material over the course of 10+ years with various groups of young people as a week in week out Bible teaching series.

INSPIRE is aimed at doing just what it says on the front: inspiring youngsters. Through mystery, suspense and discovery we can help our youth to understand and apply the Bible to their lives.

A wise man once said, "Give a man a fish and you will feed him for a day, but give him a fishing rod and teach him to fish and you will feed him for life." INSPIRE will provide you with the tools to train youngsters to "catch fish" for themselves; to gain a mind-set that can understand and correctly interpret the Bible throughout their lives.

I believe this is really important for our youngsters to make it in adult life. Some young people can feel alienated from the Bible, simply because they read and don't understand. This resource gives youngsters a greater confidence in understanding the Bible.

The "science" behind each session

Each week the teaching develops through four stages of interactive discussion:

Stage 1) Establishing what's happening
Stage 2) Identifying the key parts of the text
Stage 3) Applying what's there to today's situation
Stage 4) Understanding what God is saying today

These discussion questions are aimed at developing the way young people read and interpret the Bible.

Two volumes of this useful resource will take your young people chronologically through the Bible from Adam and Eve in the Old Testament, to Timothy in the New Testament. Each week has a meeting plan with icebreakers, text to read, discussion points and helpful answers for the leader to know what the questions are getting at. This is a very versatile resource that provides several years' worth of teaching material. Perfect for busy youth workers!

Here is an example of how these steps aid the young people's learning:

Stage 1: Establishing what is happening in the text.

We know the story, we've heard it all before, right? Er... not necessarily. So Noah's ark, the animals went in pairs two by two didn't they? No. In Genesis Noah was required to take 7 pairs of every kind of "clean" animal. From the start, the session aim is to establish what actually happened. This is the foundation the sessions are built on.

Stage 2: Identifying the key things of significance in the text

Often there are key words, statements or sentences that help to unlock pivotal questions about a text. For example, we read the statement "But God remembered Noah." Had God forgotten about Noah? A question like this then leads us on to a discussion about God's timing. So this resource highlights key details of the text, enabling us to discover something fresh. Frequently there will be clues in the Bible text that enable youngsters to discover why that particular information is there. Of course they may need you to help point them in the right direction!

Stage 3: Applying the text to today's situations

Bible study can't simply be an academic exercise. So we develop the discussion questions to ask "How might we respond in this situation?" And "Are there situations like these that we can find ourselves in today?" For example, if we are presented with an instruction from God that we don't understand at the time, what might we do? Of course this leads onto themes of discipleship such as trust and obedience in our relationship with God.

Stage 4: Understanding what God is saying today

The last stage of questions focus on what God is saying to us as individuals and as a group. Is it about trusting him? How may God be reassuring us? Is it to help us more fully enjoy God's protection and provision? This last stage is all about bringing clarity where there is confusion about what to do today. Is it an action to take? Maybe it is concerning guidance or moral decision making.

How will I know the answers to the questions?
In this resource the hard work is done for you. The research has been done so that your preparation time can be focused on communicating the Bible, rather than having to go through all the commentaries and dictionaries to understand what's going on.

Information in brackets after each question is there for two reasons:

Firstly to answer the question so that you can see what it's getting at. Since this is an interactive discussion resource, you may feel more comfortable re-wording some questions to your style. The answer in brackets helps you to "get" the question.

Secondly the answer is there to give you confidence in affirming people's replies and teasing out the truth of the text. It's not all about getting the right answer, but in understanding the Bible there has to be a correct teaching point coming out at the end.

What about the youngsters who don't like a discussion?
Not everyone is going to be super-chatty on every session. Therefore there are a variety of icebreakers, stories, scenarios and other things that aim to involve the whole group and enable people to be at ease; even the shy ones like me!

It is worth having a packet of sweets available for the first few times you lead these sessions (if not all the time!). The idea is that when someone answers a question they get a sweet. This isn't a sweet for the "right answer," but rather for a sensible, well thought out response to the question asked. Suddenly everyone wants to say something!

How to use this resource
This resource works well if you have a small group setting, such as on a Sunday morning or during the week. The size of the group doesn't really matter. This material works best for numbers from 6 and 30 youngsters and caters for ages from 11 to 17 years old.

It is advisable that leaders take around an hour preparation time each week, to read through the Bible text and the notes to familiarise themselves with the theme and the games. The games have been chosen so that there are minimal resources needed each week. You don't want to keep having to go shopping for every session!

The Bible is essential
Since this is a Bible resource, it works best if each youngster has a Bible to use. Have someone read out the text each week with youngsters following along. It's also very handy that they have Bibles open during the teaching so that they can base their answers on evidence found in the text rather than just guessing. This will enable them to have a basis for their answers as opposed to guesswork.

Volume 1 - From Adam through to King David
This resource is both text based and story based. Each session takes a look at a situation that a Bible character faces and aims to drill down into the text to relate it to things that we face today. There is so much that will help us today as we discover God working in our lives through their stories, their mistakes, their failures as well as their successes.

May your young people continue to develop in their understanding of the whole counsel of God, as they go through some of the key moments of Bible history. My hope is that they will grow stronger in their faith and discover more of how God wants to lead them in the future!

1) Adam and Eve – Created in God's Image

Icebreaker 1 – Chinese whispers (5 Minutes)
The leader whispers in one person's ear, that person passes it on:

"Fred rang to say he's sorry, but he can't make the midday train tomorrow. He's decided to catch the bus from Romford, which will arrive at 2. He said he won't forget to bring your surprise, can you remind him of your size."

Introduction (1 Minute)
Over the next year we are going to be studying the lives of some of the most important characters in history. There's so much insight that we can gain for help in living our own lives, by learning what the people of God did in the Bible. It's important to remember that these people were ordinary people just like us. They did some amazing things, but also made mistakes just like we do.

By keeping this in mind we can really understand how God related to people in the past and how he will relate to us today.

Discussion (10 Minutes)
Jenna Franklin has told her mother that she would like bigger breasts for her 16th birthday present. Her mother, who is a cosmetic surgery consultant, has herself had breast implants and has agreed to pay the bill of around £3,000.00.

However, the surgeon who would have performed the operation has announced that he considers cosmetic surgery inappropriate because Jenna is still developing physically. He also thought that a 15-year old lacked the psychological maturity in making such an important decision. He has announced that he will not operate until Jenna is 18.

Newspapers have reported that Jenna anticipates having lip-suction and dental work in her 20s and a face lift at 40. Around 25,000 teenagers receive cosmetic surgery each year in the United States. It seems that a similar trend is developing among young people in the UK to opt for the knife and implants to achieve the "perfect look and shape."

Q - Do you think Jenna is old enough to decide for herself if she wants cosmetic surgery?

Q - Jenna says she wants the surgery "to be successful, I need to have them." What do you think about that?

Q - Describe the pressures to be a certain shape that affect young men and women...

Q - Glossy magazines, adverts and films emphasise physical attractiveness. What else can make a person attractive?

Teaching 1 (10 minutes)
READ Genesis 1:1-27 & Genesis 2:4-7

Q - Does anyone have any comments on what we've just read? Have you noticed anything that you hadn't seen before? Any initial thoughts?

Q - How does Genesis say the plants appeared? (It's easy to think that God just made them appear, but here we see that he has established laws of nature and v6 tells us that he uses water to spring up from the earth to make the vegetation grow).

Q - Where does the Bible say Adam came from? (The dust. In the same way God uses what he has already established to form Adam ie. the dust).

Q - What image does God use to create Adam? (v27 His own. No other living creature is said to have been made this way)

Q - What do you think the words "image" and "likeness" communicate about Adam and Eve? (They were made having certain things in common with God. But being made like God is not just about our physical appearance).

Q - How does this make you feel about yourself knowing that you've been made in God's image? (God has made you in the form of his own beauty, there are some truly lovely things about you).

Q - In what way are we different from the other creatures on the Earth? (Get them to try and think how Adam and Eve were made)

Q - Verse 26 hints as to why we are different to the animals... The clue is where God says "Let us make man in our own image."

Q - Why "Us"? (God is Father, Son and Holy Spirit. 3 parts in 1 God).

As humans we have: ***a mind*** where we think, we feel pain, we love and stuff, ***a body*** that is physical that we can see and interact with others ***and a spirit*** inside us and will go to the next life when we die. In this way we are like God who is Father, Son and Holy Spirit.

God made mankind different from the animals in that we have a spirit. Animals don't know right from wrong. A lion will kill you and eat you without a second thought. They can feel pain, hunger, they can be loyal and intelligent, they can also be trained by us, but they have no in-built conscience.

There is no spirit inside them. They cannot go to heaven or hell. They simply have a body and a mind, and when they die they return to the earth. In this way we are special and distinct from the animal world.

Q - What attributes do you think mankind has that are like God? (Love, compassion, faithfulness, goodness, authority over the other creatures of the earth, power to rule, the ability to choose, etc.)

Q - Do you think a person can be beautiful simply by having these good attributes, without having a stunning outward appearance?

Q - Who would you rather be friends with: A) Someone who is outwardly beautiful but not necessarily inwardly beautiful, or B) someone who has a beautiful character, but not necessarily outwardly good looking?

Q - Same question again, but this time who would you rather go out with??

If we are honest we often give those who are physically good looking more attention than those who are good on the inside. It takes a deeper person to see people for who they are on the inside – their character. This is what makes a good friend and a good relationship.

Q - Here we have the first human being, made perfect by God. Why do you think God made humans as special? (Read Deuteronomy 7:6 He made us to have a relationship with him. And it is because we have a Spirit inside of us we can have a relationship with God).

READ Genesis 2:8-15 (5 minutes)
We're going to look at these verses more next week, but does this tell you anything about God's relationship with Adam?

Q - Try and put yourself in God's shoes... Have you ever had an Action Man or a Barbie doll or a small pet like fish or guinea pig? In what way are verses 8 – 15 similar to this? (God made a special place for Adam to stay, that Adam could take care of and enjoy. It was a special place of immense beauty in which Adam could make his home).

Q - How else does God interact with Adam in these verses? (He helps Adam in his search for a companion).

Q - What does this say about God caring for our needs? (Don't worry if you don't have a girlfriend/boyfriend and you want one. God will take care of that and find you what you need *when* you need it! - which might not be right away! Sometimes we think things happen instantly, but we see with Adam it took some time. There were lots of living creatures on the Earth! So take heart, he understands where you're at, and hears your prayers.)

Summary (1 minute)
So here is a fantastic picture of Adam interacting with God. Adam and Eve, made in God's image, made different from all the other living creatures, made with a spirit for a relationship with God. God shows himself here as one who interacts with us, and who thinks of our needs and provides for us in order that we may be satisfied in life.

Of course we all want to look nice, but whether we are stunningly good looking on the outside is not as important as developing good character on the inside. It's far better to build relationships with people who genuinely love and respect you for who you are on the inside.

Pray (As long as it takes)

2) Adam and Eve – Temptation Presents Itself

Ice Breaker 1 (2 minutes)
Leave an item that people will want to pick up somewhere in middle of the room (if you can source a remote doorbell button that would be ideal). Place a sign on it saying "do not touch." Say that you've just forgotten something and need to get it and leave the room... Come back a minute or so later and see if anyone has touched it.

Icebreaker 2 (10 Minutes)
Ask everyone to think for a couple of minutes and come up with two statements about themselves, one true and one false. They can be as wacky as you like, but if they've got unusual things to say about themselves which are true it could become very interesting. When everyone has had time to think, begin with one of the leaders, to give the youngsters a good idea of the sort of thing they can say. The leader has to give two statements about themselves and then the group has to decide which statement is true, and which is the false statement. Move around the group, allowing each person to make their two statements and everyone to select the true statement.

Have fun doing this, but at the end try make a point about lies. Sometimes they are more convincing than the truth; but they are always wrong. Satan is the father of all lies and Jesus is the way the TRUTH and the life.

Introduction (5 Minutes)
Last week we began looking at Adam and Eve. We learned about how God made them in his own image and although that doesn't mean physical likeness, it does mean likeness in character.

As humans we have: ***a mind*** where we think, we feel pain, we love. We have ***a body*** that is physical that we can see and interact with others. We also have ***a spirit*** inside us that will go to the next life when we die. In this way we are like God who is Father, Son and Holy Spirit.

So, Adam and Eve were made in God's image. They were made different from all the other living creatures and made with a spirit for a relationship with God.

Teaching (30 Minutes)
READ Genesis 2:18-25

Q – Why did God decide Adam needed a helper? (v18 He acknowledged that it wasn't good for Adam to be alone – God knows that we need others to be in relationship with – we get lonely)

Q – How did God go about getting Adam a helper to begin with? (vs 19-20 He brought all the living creatures to Adam for him to name them)

Q – Why do you think Adam didn't find a helper among all the creatures of creation? (There was no-one who he could communicate with, no-one with the same mind, body and spirit, so no-one he could be in equal relationship with.)

Q – What did God do about it? (vs 21, 22 He caused Adam to fall asleep and then created a woman out of Adam's rib – original cloning?! "The woman was *made of a rib out of the side of Adam;* not made out of his head to rule over him, nor out of his feet to be trampled upon by him, but out of his side to be equal with him, under his arm to be protected, and near his heart to be beloved." *Matthew Henry*)

Q – How did Adam respond to God's new creation? (v23 He recognised their likeness and felt her to be a suitable helper; he also saw the lifelong commitment it would be.)

READ Genesis 2:15-17 and 3:1-7

Q – What did God actually tell Adam he could and couldn't do? What would happen if he was disobedient? (He could eat the fruit from any tree in the garden, except the tree of the knowledge of good and evil. If he ate from that tree he would die.)

Q – Do you think that was fair of God? Discuss.

Q – What do we learn about the snake? Who was it? (The snake was clever and cunning – it was Satan).

Q – How did he begin his conversation with Eve? (v1 by questioning what God had actually said and casting doubt on it)

Q – Was Eve sure about what God had told them? (She knew that she could eat from all the trees except the one in the middle of the garden because they would die if they ate from that one).

Q – What did the snake say in reply, and why was this a temptation to Eve to eat the fruit? (He contradicted God and said they would not die, that they would know about good and evil and be like God. This appealed to her pride that she would be like God)

Q – How did Eve deal with Satan's temptation? (She gave into it)

Q – What would have happened if she had resisted the temptation Satan put before her? (She and Adam could have continued living in the garden in comfort and at peace with themselves and God)

Q - Think about when Jesus was tempted by Satan in the wilderness. How did He resist temptation? What did He do? (Matthew 4:1-11. He answered with the word of God and stood firm with faith in God)

Q – What can we learn from Adam and Eve's experience and how it compares with Jesus and how He dealt with temptation? (Discuss)

Round Up (5 Minutes)
Satan will always try to turn us away from God, he will do all he can to shake our faith. He is the master of lies and will delight in making us believe that God has lied to us. Remember Jesus said "I am the Way, **the Truth** and the Life". Also remember that we have a choice. Satan cannot make us give in to temptation any more than God would make us be obedient to him. We have free choice and that choice brings responsibility. We choose to listen to God or to listen to Satan's lies and we have to take responsibility for that choice. What can we do?

We can ask God to help us stand firm against temptation. Remember that line in the Lord's prayer, "Lead us not into temptation". God can give us the strength to say 'No' to Satan, but only if we want to.

Prayer (10 minutes)
Spend a few minutes chatting about things to pray for, encourage the youngsters to share if they have any particular difficulties/temptations they are facing and then have a prayer time together.

3) Adam and Eve – What guilt does to you

Icebreaker - Pass the Key (8 minutes)
Players sit in a circle, facing inwards; one person stands in the middle, holding a key behind their back.

The game begins when a player stands up, takes the key from their hand and sits back in the circle. The key is then passed behind their back undetected to another player, who must in turn secretly pass it on. The person in the middle must try to keep track of where the key is.

At some point the leader will say "STOP" and then everyone must hold both their hands in front of them, clenching their fists so the key cannot be seen. The person in the middle has three guesses at which hand contains the key. If they guess correctly, they swap places with the person with the key and the game runs again. Any players can do fake moves to make it harder for the guesser to keep track of the key.

After a couple of rounds add a further element to the game. This time, when the leader says "STOP" the guesser can ask up to three questions before making his/her three choices. For example they might ask "Do you have the key?" "Where is the key?" "Did you have the key at some point?"

Then ask... did being able to ask questions and see reactions make it easier? Why/Why not? Did anyone make guessing easier by looking guilty?

Discussion (10 Minutes)
Picture the scene. It's Saturday, around 3pm. You have rumbles in your stomach and you could really do with something to eat. It seems like ages until tea-time and you feel like you can't last out. So you go foraging around in the kitchen, where you come across your brother's stash of fun-size Twixes. He's not around to ask and there are loads in there. You're sure he won't even notice if one measly little bar is gone.

No-one's around and you know the Twix is just what you need. So if no-one notices you, it's probably not even like a crime at all??! (You think!). So you slip the Twix into your pocket and disappear upstairs.

You are now in your bedroom with the said Twix bar.

Q- What is going through your head right now? (What are the options you are considering? Is there much debate in your head as to what to do next, after all it is just a Twix? Or is it more than that?)

So you look at the Twix, and think of the biscuitty, caramel chocolate mix and you unwrap it. The shiny layers of chocolate look so tasty, so you decide to devour it on your own in your bedroom.

Q - How do you feel at this point? (Satisfied? happy? guilty?)

Q - Now the Twix is gone. If you had a time machine, would you go back and make another decision? (Discuss)

Q - Why is it that we are sometimes told *not* to do things? After all, aren't rules just boring? (Discuss)

Now, it's nearly dinner time, and you are watching the telly downstairs. Your brother comes home from playing sports. He needs to replenish his body sugar levels, so he goes into the kitchen for his stash of Twixes. Something's wrong. It's not as he left it. Fortunately he knows how many are left as he has one for every day left in the month. It's the 3rd today, so he should have 28 left!

Q - What would you do at this moment in time?? (eg. find a place to hide, or find your parents fearing for your personal safety?)

Q - What feelings are you experiencing at this moment?? (Anxiety, fear etc.)

Your brother is now looking for you. He confronts you and tells you that he's counted them, and there's a Twix missing! He tells you in no uncertain terms that he believes you did it.

Q - How do you respond? (Discuss)

Introduction (1 Minute)
Last time we saw how Adam and Eve were faced with a choice, a temptation. We saw that, because they chose to listen to Satan and disobey God, they were responsible for what followed. This week we're going to see what happened as a *result* of the choices Adam and Eve made.

Teaching (30 Minutes)
READ Genesis 3:1-20
Here, Eve is standing at the tree and Satan is telling her to eat some fruit.

Q - Did Satan *make* her eat the fruit? (No. She was faced with the choice. The only power the snake had was to try and persuade her to eat the fruit. The snake could not force her to eat it).

So with just the power of persuasion, just with words, the snake managed to make Eve do something wrong, that would affect the future of her life. He used the tree and its fruit to lure her.

Q - It says in verse 6 that the tree was beautiful. Would the outcome have been the same if the tree was unattractive and the fruit ugly? (Often we will find that at the time, the wrong things that we are tempted to do can appear very attractive).

Activity – Straight face
Find 5 volunteers who think they can keep a straight face no matter what. Get those in the group to ask the volunteers questions. The only reply the volunteers can answer is with the word "sausages." The one who keeps a straight face for the longest time wins a prize.

Q - What was the winner's secret to success?

Q - Now, take the example of the Twix bar - when it looked so enjoyable and you really wanted to eat it, how could you overcome such strong feelings? (Think about the outcome, think about something else, pray and ask God to help you find something else!).

Q - Did the fruit fulfil all that the snake said that it would? (No. Satan lied when he said they would be like God. He also told a half-truth that they would know good and evil. There were some very negative effects as a result of their disobeying God).

There's always the BEFORE and AFTER with temptation. Before, things look very attractive and promise to make you feel happy, excited or be something you will enjoy. And you can end up thinking of nothing else. But after, when you realise it was wrong and that you have made a mistake, you will probably wish you could turn back time. You've been tricked by a half-truth - yes the chocolate would be tasty, but you don't enjoy it as much as one you would have paid for. So you feel guilty.

Q - Describe the negative feelings Adam and Eve must have had? (v10 They felt guilty inside and shameful of what they had done. They were afraid of God).

Q - What does guilt do to us? (It makes us feel full of regret for what we've done. It's a horrible feeling we get inside, because our conscience reminds us that we've done a bad thing. It can stop us from sleeping and make us want to do things to help us forget about it. We just want to blot it out from our minds. It can mess us up on the inside and lead us to do further destructive things).

Q - If guilt makes us feel so bad, is guilt wrong? (Guilt is good as it is our gauge as to what is right and wrong. If we lose this we will lose control of our lives).

Q - Who and what were Adam and Eve afraid of? They were afraid that God would find out and be angry and He was. It made them want to run away and they were worried because of what might happen to them as a result of what they had done).

Q - What were they afraid would happen? (They'd messed up big time. This was the start of the world, and they didn't realise it at the time, but their actions had poisoned the human race. Our actions affect others, and when we do wrong others are affected).

Q - Adam and Eve knew there would be consequences, so they legged it. Do you ever run away from God when you've done something you know he isn't pleased with?

Q - How can we get rid of this guilty feeling? What can you do after you've messed up? (Confess it to God, and ask to be forgiven. Jesus will forgive you! 1 John 1:8-9)

Being forgiven is God's solution to the problem of guilt that we feel inside when we do wrong things. Guilt makes us feel all wrong on the inside. God is good, holy and pure and will judge all sin. But in his great love He has provided a way to take away all guilt and sin. Thousands of years later Jesus would come to Earth and through believing in him all guilt and every sin is taken care of.

Q - Take a look at verses 16-19. Do you think this is a harsh punishment for simply eating an apple? (These *are* very serious punishments, but we can always trust God to be fair).

Q - If God is always fair, this must mean that what they did was very serious. If it was more than just eating an apple, what was it that was so bad? (*Firstly* they disobeyed God. They decided to believe the snake instead of God and went against what God had asked them to do. *Secondly*, this was something more than an apple, because they were changed after eating it. Something irreversible had happened to them. They knew things they didn't before ie. that they were naked. God had made everything in the world good, but now it was no longer all good anymore).

As a result of the change that happened in Adam and Eve, things now had to change around them.

Round Up (5 Minutes)
So we see in verses 13-20, that as a result of what Adam and Eve had done, things were now going pear-shaped. The consequences of their actions were now being realised and the passing pleasure of eating a forbidden apple has turned into a nightmare. Often things that are wrong are wrong for a reason. God wanted to protect Adam and Eve from the bad things of the world, and provide a pleasant and restful environment for them to live in. Unfortunately, by disobeying God they destroyed many of the good things God wanted them to enjoy.
Often our actions have repercussions for other people's lives too. Eve's actions affected Adam's life and in turn their actions affected their children's lives and all of humanity.

When we risk getting involved in bad things we also put at risk our future happiness. God wants you to be happy, and he sent Jesus to set us free from the guilt and fear that attacks us as a result of what we do wrong.

Prayer (10 minutes)
Maybe there is something they feel guilty about and wish they hadn't been tempted. Maybe they made a mistake. Encourage them that there is forgiveness through Jesus and pray.

4) Cain and Abel – Jealousy between brothers

Ice Breaker - String Toss Game (10 Minutes)
Get a ball of string or yarn. Have each person answer a question (from the list of questions at the end of this study) when they have the string in their possession. They then hold on to the string and throw the ball to another person so they can answer the question. You eventually create a web of some sort. In the end, describe how we all played a part in creating the web, and that if one person was gone it would look different. When we all take part that is what makes the group what it is, unique and special.

Introduction (5 Minutes)
Last week we looked at the consequences of Adam and Eve giving in to temptation. They lost everything – their comfortable lifestyle, their innocence, their peace of mind and this was replaced with pain, hard work, eviction from the only home they had ever known and the knowledge that they had disappointed God. Their actions didn't only affect them; the consequences go on and on throughout the generations – we are still paying the price!

When we risk getting involved in bad things we also put at risk our happiness. God wants us to be happy, and He sent Jesus to set us free from the guilt and fear that attacks us as a result of what we do wrong. Today we see the birth of the first babies in the Bible and then things go a stage further down the slippery slope.

Teaching (25 Minutes)
Read Genesis 4:1-26

Q – What did the boys do when they grew up? (v2 Abel became a shepherd and Cain became a farmer)

Q – What was significant about the offerings Cain and Abel brought to God? (vs 3-4 Cain brought some food, but Abel brought the best of his flock)

Q – How did God respond to the gifts? (vs 4-5 God accepted Abel's gift, but not Cain's)

Q – Why did God respond like that? And how do you think God felt? (God gives us so much, and our response should be to give him the first fruits; not the worst fruits. Also all things come from God and of his own do we give him. God must have felt sad and disappointed with Cain's response)

Q – How do we respond to God's generosity to us? Do we give back to him generously, or do we give God what's left? (Discuss. Consider attitude of heart when giving back to God as well as the amount.)

Q – Cain felt rejected. How did he respond to God's words? (He didn't want to hear them, instead he left the way open for Satan.)

Q – Why did Cain kill Abel? Was there any justification for his actions? (Jealousy and Abel was making Cain look bad).

Q – What reasons can we have for being jealous of a brother or sister? (Maybe if we feel they get better treatment from us or when they are treated special because of something they have done well).

Q – What is the right response in these circumstances? (It isn't right to punish or blame them for doing well. It is best to celebrate the good things that happen in your family as your time will come too!)

Scenario
Imagine your younger brother has just passed his 11 plus. It's a big thing in your family as he is the first person to ever have passed his 11 plus (your parents didn't and neither did you). So as a reward your mum and dad buy your younger brother an expensive present and you all go out to celebrate at Pizza Express.

Q - How does that make you feel? (Hopefully really happy, but probably a little overlooked, and left out).

Q – What do you think the right way of dealing with those feelings is? (It is right to reward exceptional achievements, and we would always want the best things for our younger brothers and sisters since we love them. So try not to feel down on yourself instead enjoy the food and the fact that everyone wants to celebrate. If you get on with enjoying it, you will be demonstrating great love to your family and a good example for your younger brother to follow).

So just because someone else in the family gets a lot of attention it doesn't mean that you are being rejected.

Q – What emotion fuels Cain's jealousy? (It is his anger, combined with his jealousy that leads him to commit his violent actions)

Q – What did Cain do to compound his actions? (He wasn't honest with God.)

Q – Do we try to cover up or make excuses when we feel guilty and caught out? Are we any different from Cain? (Discuss)

Q – What was the result? Did Cain get away with murdering his brother? (No, he had to accept his punishment, which was that he would wander around the land and never settle. He would have no home and he would never grow good crops).

Q – Was that it? Had God abandoned Cain completely? (No, when Cain pleaded because he was afraid, God promised him protection, but he still had to take the consequences of his actions).

Q – What happened to Cain in the long term? (He moved to the land of Nod, married and had children, but through the generations they did not worship God and moved further and further from him, marrying more than one wife, killing, etc. So the consequences continued through the generations).

Q – What was going on with Adam and Eve? (They had another son, called Seth).

Q – Did Adam and Eve turn away from God because they had lost both of their sons? Abel being killed and Cain wandering the land and going away? (No, they acknowledged that their child was a gift from God).

Q – What happened about the time of Adam's grandson Enosh? (People started praying to God).

Q – What can we learn from what we've looked at today? (Discuss)

Round Up (5 Minutes)
Today we've looked at the beginning of family life. Family life is not easy, but Cain's reaction was perhaps a bit excessive!! He was jealous of Abel because God approved of Abel's offering.

Unfortunately he let this make him angry. His anger, mixed with his jealousy led him to commit the world's first murder. So Adam and Eve lost both of their sons; one to death and one to darkness and disillusionment. As a result of Adam and Eve's original disobedience, mankind is left to struggle with the problems of jealousy, misunderstanding and suspicion. The root problem of disharmony in today's homes is the same as that which afflicted the first human family, a refusal to let God be God.

Prayer (5 minutes)
Spend a few minutes chatting about things to pray for, encourage the youngsters to share if they have any problems they are facing either at home or at school and then have a prayer time together.

Questions for Ice Breaker
1. What was the first thing God created? (The sky and earth)
2. Can you name three of the disciples? (Peter, James, John, Andrew, Philip, Bartholomew, Matthew, Thomas, James (son of Alphaeus), Thaddaeus, Simon the Zealot and Judas Iscariot).
3. How many sons did Jacob have? (12)
4. Who was Moses' brother? (Aaron)
5. Who heard God call his name in the night? (Samuel)
6. What amazing thing did Jesus do at a wedding? (Turned water into wine)
7. Who was blinded by a bright light on the road to Damascus? (Paul/Saul)
8. How many commandments did God give to Moses? (Ten)
9. What number is the longest Psalm? (119)
10. Which is the only book in the Bible not to mention God? (Esther)
11. Who had a talking donkey? (Not Shrek! Balaam)
12. Who washed his hands when passing judgement on Jesus? (Pontius Pilate)
13. Who laughed when they heard they were going to have a baby? (Sarah)
14. Can you name the strongest man in the Bible? (Samson)
15. How many friends were put in the fiery furnace by King Nebuchadnezzar? (3 – Shadrach, Meshach and Abednego)
16. How many people did Jesus feed with five loaves and two fish? (5,000+)
17. Who walked on the water towards Jesus? (Peter)
18. Where was Jonah supposed to be going when he was swallowed by the big fish? (Nineveh)
19. Apart from the animals, who went on the Ark with Noah? (His wife, 3 sons, Ham, Shem and Japheth & wives)
20. Who found Jesus' tomb empty on Easter day? (Mary Magdalene and the other Mary)
21. Which disciple denied Jesus? (Simon Peter)
22. How many years did the people of Israel wander in the wilderness? (40)
23. How old was Jesus when his parents took him to Jerusalem and he got lost? (12)
24. Who was Jacob's twin brother? (Esau)
25. Who had a coat of many colours? (Joseph)
26. Who was Jesus' cousin? (John the Baptist)

5) Noah – A man under pressure

Ice Breaker 1 - Tongue-Twister races (5 Minutes)
Say 5 times "Irish wristwatch" or "Big bib on Bob the bouncing baby."

Icebreaker 2 – The Yes No game
Select a contestant and ask them a barrage of questions. When they say "yes" or "no" they are out.

Introduction (2 Minutes)
Last week we saw that in giving to God it is important to give him our best. To God, the reasons and motivations we have for giving a gift is even more important than the actual gift itself. A gift given to God that is meaningful to us is what God is looking for; rather than giving him something because we feel we have to.

Teaching (30 Minutes)
Read Genesis 5:28 – 6:22

Q – Little quiz question for you... how many generations was Noah from Adam? (See chapter 5). (Noah was the 10th generation from Adam).

Last week, we had a question which turned out to be a bit of a mystery. After Cain killed Abel, he was sent away. He was worried that people out there might find him and kill him. And we wondered where these people came from. The assumption is that God created other people after Adam and Eve.

Q - Look at verse 2-4 of chapter 6. Does this shed any more light on this issue? (Sons of God sounds like other men on the Earth.)

Q – It says "Sons of God" what do you think this means? Isn't there just one Son of God? (Sons of God probably refer to just that, human men made by God and put on the Earth, not Divine like Jesus. Jesus is different as he is God, and is his only Son).

What was different about these Sons of God is quite interesting. They seem to have been warriors of some kind – physically big. And so their children were also big (Called the Nephilim). See Numbers 13:3-33.

Q – How do you think God hoped these "Sons of God" would live their lives? (As good men).

Q – And how does the Bible describe the people who lived at the time of Noah. (Wicked and evil).

Q – So over 10 generations the world had been corrupted. How does God view all that's going on? (He regrets even creating man.)

Q – If God is omniscient (all knowing), why did he bother creating man in the first place? (God has given us free will to choose to love him or not. Even though he knew mankind would do evil, rather than force us to be good and to love and obey him, he gave us the opportunity anyway. And God being holy must exercise his judgement on those who are living evil lives. But there is one man who is good).

Q – What do you think upset God most, the people's sin or the fact that they were ignoring him? (He had created mankind to be in relationship with himself. If they had chosen him, their lifestyles would have been different. We can see this because of Noah's life).

Q – Why do you think God is pleased with Noah? (Because his character was different from those around him.)

The pressure to be like those around us is always very real. When someone is different it is noticeable. The people around at the time of Noah seem to have been violent, probably murderers, taking many wives, drunkenness and all sorts. These were people out of control, and a dangerous time to live in. In those days there was no TV, or posh houses to sit in, the people would have spent much of their time outside, living off the land and interacting with each other. And many people were becoming corrupted as a result.

Q – So Noah "found favour with God," do you think God has favourites? Are there any other people in the Bible that might be described as favourites of God? (At times it seems that God chooses certain people to use for his plan. So he promises things to them and does amazing things in their lives).

Q – What does it mean to be righteous? And blameless? Verse 9 (A person who is morally good. Being "righteous" has nothing to do with judging other people, but rather making sure our own lives are good. A person who believes what is good and does it. Blameless in that he didn't get involved with the bad stuff that was going on around him).

Icebreaker 2 - Plasticine Models (5 minutes)
Give everyone a piece of clay with these instructions:

'Please make a small model. Everyone should make every effort to make an identical model to everyone else. You may not talk or write notes to each other. You have three minutes.'
Do not say anything else. Observe how the young people go about choosing a leader and then copying them.

Q – How did you find that task? Difficult/Easy?

Q – Why was it difficult to try and create exactly the same thing as everyone else?

Sometimes it's right to do what everyone else is doing. But then there are other times when you have to break the mould and be who you are. Not to copy those around you by trying to fit into the shape people try to put you in. It's more important to do what is right. It takes wisdom and courage to decide against something others want you to do which is harmful to you or others, and go your own way.

Q – So Noah was righteous. How difficult is it to be "righteous" at School?

Scenario (5 minutes)
Q – How does the way other people are behaving around us, change the way we behave? (Eg. Say you have been looking forward to going bowling with your school mates for ages. You all meet up, but once inside one of your mates produces some alcopop drink. She shares it round and everyone has a swig. It gets round to you. What do you do? They say "Oh go on, it's only a sip." And "you can't get drunk on a sip" and "what's wrong with you? Is it because you're religious?" But you know as a 14 year old you are under age and it is illegal. (Discuss)

Q – Have you been in or can think of any situations where it's easy to compromise and just do what everyone else is doing, even though its wrong? (Discuss)

Q – Verse 11 tells us that the earth was corrupt. How do you think corruption starts? (Often it will start with something small, where you have to make a choice on some moral judgement. Say for example – I'm sure you can think of a better one! You are working in a shop. And you do a friend a good deal on an item of clothing. As a result they buy you a box of chocs. Then the next time they come in they ask you for a good deal on something and offer you some money. Maybe they even threaten to tell your boss about the previous deal? What do you do? If you give in it's easier the next time etc.)

Q – With this in mind what's the best way to avoid our lives becoming corrupted by friends and people around us who don't believe what we believe? (Discuss).

Q – When the Bible says Noah "walked with God," it's using picture language. What idea is it trying to communicate about Noah? (That he had a close relationship with God. That he was interested in God and wanted to communicate with God. And as a result, God found favour with him and communicated back with Noah and tells him what's going to happen next).

Q – How can we walk with God? (By taking time to talk with God and be interested in what he has to say. When we involve him in our lives and tell him about our day and ask for his help).

Q – Do you think it's possible to have a close relationship with God where he talks to us? (Discuss. Maybe someone has an example from their life where they felt God was speaking to them).

Q – Noah chose to live differently from those around him. How does this benefit him? (God entrusts him with a special task – to build an ark).

Q – Do you expect this made him popular? (hmm... we'll see next week. But doing the right thing won't always make you popular!)

Round Up (5 Minutes)
So today, we've seen that when everyone is living their lives doing what whatever they want ie. right or wrong. If you choose to be different and do what is right you will instantly stand out. It is then that pressure can be aimed at you to change to be just like everyone else. However it is possible to live "righteous" if we learn what it is to "walk with God," to live our lives in relationship with him. This is a life that pleases God and he's sure to look after us through the tough times and involve us in his future plan.

Prayer (5 minutes)
Spend a few minutes chatting about things to pray for, encourage the youngsters to share if they have any problems they are facing either at home or at school and then have a prayer time together.

6) Noah – Faith in God's words

Count to 20 (5 Minutes)
The aim of this game is to count to 20, but without interruptions. Without indicating who, one person will start by saying "one." Then anyone else can say "two" and so on up to twenty. However if two or more people say the same number at the same time, you have to start again at one.

Show clip
Evan Almighty "there's going to be a flood."

Introduction (5 Minutes)
Last week we saw how Noah stood out. Three words describe Noah best "he walked with God." We can all have that sort of relationship with God – it's our choice! To have that kind of relationship, we have to be willing to make sacrifices, to spend time with God. Going for a walk takes time. A good walk is not done in five minutes, nor is our walk with God something we can cut short because something better comes along. We need to invest our time with God and so develop our relationship with him and "walk with him". When we do that he will walk with us.

Teaching (20 Minutes)
READ Genesis 7:1-16

Q – Why did God say that Noah and his family could go into the ark? (v1 Because Noah was the best person alive at that time – note that God doesn't say that he was faultless, just that Noah was the best around.)

Q – What special instructions did God give to Noah about the occupants of the ark? (vs 2-3 He should take seven mating pairs of each type of 'clean' animal and bird and one mating pair of every other type of creature.)

Q – Why did they have to be male and female? (So that after the flood they could establish new herds/flocks, etc., by mating.)

Q – Do you know or can you guess which animals were "clean" and which were "unclean"? (Split the group into two and have one group open at Deuteronomy 14:4-20 and the other at Leviticus 11:1-31. Start a list of clean and unclean animals. *See next page.*)

Clean: Cud chewing animals with split hooves, cattle, sheep, goat, deer and gazelle, freshwater fish with fins and scales can be eaten, birds such as chickens, turkeys and pheasants, crickets, grasshoppers and locusts.

Unclean: camels, rabbits, and pigs, as well as creeping things like moles, mice and lizards as well as four-footed animals with paws; cats, dogs, bears, lions, tigers; sea creatures without fins and scales, catfish, lobsters, crabs, shrimp, mussels, clams, oysters, squid, octopi, any birds that eat decaying flesh like vultures, birds of prey, plus ostriches, storks, herons and bats.

Q – Why does God say that some creatures were fit to consume, but not others? (We know that God gave laws "that it might be well" with those who seek to obey him. We've already said that some of those on the "no" list are creatures that eat decaying flesh as well as other animals that might eat decaying flesh. Animals like bears, pigs and vultures do that, whilst hunting animals like wolves often go for the weakest in the herd, sometimes weak because they are diseased).

Sea creatures and bottom dwellers such as lobsters and crabs scavenge for dead animals on the sea floor. Shellfish such as oysters, clams and mussels similarly consume decaying organic matter that sinks to the sea floor, including sewage.

So many of these creatures have this in common: God labelled them as unclean since they would often eat flesh that would sicken or kill human beings. When we eat such animals we are eating things from the part of the food chain that includes things harmful to people. Maybe God made these "clean up" creatures for the very purpose of consuming the nastiness that comes through death and disease.

Q – With this in mind, why do you think God told Noah to take seven pairs of 'clean' animals and birds and only one pair of the other creatures? (It was likely that Noah needed the 'clean' animals for food for him and his family, so there needed to be more than one pair – that way they could breed more quickly. Also might have been the ones used for sacrificing to God).

Q – What if Noah found some road-kill one day and was very hungry. Do you think it would have been that bad if he'd eaten it? (We have to trust God's words are there for a reason. This is one of the ways we exercise faith. Obedience is really important in our relationship with God).

Q – God was very specific with Noah about when the rain would be coming and for how long it would last. Why do you think he was so specific? (Discuss. It could be that it was such a big and frightening thing that God knew that he needed to be really specific with Noah about when and for how long, so that Noah would have a better understanding and be able to trust God more.)

Q – Is God ever that specific with us about things? (It depends on what God is doing. Sometimes he is very specific, other times we just have to trust him without any indication of how long something is going to be/take).

Q – How did Noah respond to God's instructions? (He obeyed God totally, showing complete trust in him).

Q – Do you think Noah had much trouble rounding up the animals to get them into the ark? (Note that in verse 9 it says "they came to Noah". Isn't that amazing?? They just came. How powerful is God, to be able to do that?!! Not only did they just come, but exactly the right number and sex of each kind! Stunning isn't it??).

Q – Just think about it for a minute. Try to picture the scene. What do you think it would have done for Noah's faith? (It says twice in these few verses that Noah was 600 years old when all this happened. Notwithstanding that he had to build a boat when he lived a long way from the sea. Now God said he had to load in all these animals too. He must have wondered about how to find every species and mating couple of animal; then how to get them to the ark. But to see them come to him proved God's provision for what he has asked Noah to do. Here was the proof at last!).

Q – What do we see in verses 10 and 11? (The rain came just when God said it would. This is the first mention in the Bible of rain. Would Noah have even known what God meant by rain? See Genesis 2:5-6. Still he was obedient and built an enormous ship, miles away from water. God showed his faithfulness to Noah in doing what he said he would do).

Q – In this short passage we see it repeated that Noah was 600 years old when this happened and also that the rain came seven days after they entered the ark. Why are these details put in twice? (When things are repeated in the Bible, it means that they are important. These show us that God's word can be trusted. He said seven days and sure enough it was seven days. Noah was so old that it would have been impossible to do all this without God's hand. It shows the power of God in this situation).

Q – So much of this story is repeated within the passage, which emphasises there are some big things to learn from it. What do you think those lessons are for us today? (Discuss. Hopefully the group will talk about obedience to God, God keeping his promises; God's faithfulness – our need to trust God, etc.)

Q – Who closed the door? And what does that tell us? (God closed the door. He was in control. He made sure it was properly shut, thus he was protecting Noah, his family and all the animals).

READ Hebrews 11:1, 6-7

Q – What is faith? (Try to get the group to put the definition in verse 1 into their own words, to make sure they really understand what faith is).

Q – This chapter of Hebrews is often called the "Roll call of faith" because it lists great men and women of faith in the Bible. Why is Noah included? (He trusted God and obeyed him when he was asked to do something which seemed outrageous and impossible. How much faith must that have taken??!!)

Q – How can reading about Noah and his relationship with God make a difference to us today? (Discuss)

Round Up (5 Minutes)
This short passage of only 16 verses can teach us so much about God and what he requires of us his people. God is still that same now as he was then, and he still wants the same things from us as he wanted from Noah then. Noah is a wonderful example for us of a man full of faith, who was obedient to God and as a result we see God's blessing in his life.

In Noah's case these blessings were **protection** for Noah and his family from the flood, and **provision** in the here and now, as well as in the future. At the time, the animals came to Noah in the right numbers and types. God also provided for their future needs so that there were enough animals to breed and provide meat for the future. God also provided **relationship**, in which Noah and God could communicate together. God wants to pour his blessings into our lives, but he can only do that if we have a relationship with him. For that to work, we need to be able put our trust in him. What this means is that we are obedient to what he requires us to do in faith without knowing what the outcome will be.

Prayer (5 minutes)
Spend a few minutes chatting about things to pray for. Encourage the youngsters to share if they have any problems they are facing, either at home or at school and then have a prayer time together. Encourage them to get into the habit of talking to God about everything that happens in their lives so that they can be open and honest with God because God loves each one of us and cares passionately about us.

7) Noah – Obedience rewarded

Fizz Buzz
This is a concentration game where counting and knowing your times tables might help. Everyone sits in a circle and one person begins counting, 1, the next person 2, etc. However whenever a person is about to say a multiple of 2, they must say "fizz" instead. As people get counting and get the hang of that, start again and say that any multiples of 5 must be replaced with the word "buzz."

People will soon realise that when a number is both a multiple of 2 and 5 they must say "fizz buzz." Carry on until their brains have had enough.

Discussion Starter (10 Minutes)
In July 1976, Israeli commandos made a daring raid at an airport in Entebbe, Uganda, to rescue 103 Jewish hostages. In less than fifteen minutes, the soldiers had killed all seven of the kidnappers and set the captives free.

As successful as the rescue was, however, three of the hostages were killed during the raid. As the commandos entered the terminal, they shouted in Hebrew, "Get down! Crawl!" The Jewish hostages understood and lay down on the floor, while the guerrillas, who did not speak Hebrew, were left standing. Quickly the rescuers shot the upright kidnappers.

Unfortunately two of the hostages hesitated. Perhaps they stood to see what was happening, but they were also shot and killed. One young man was lying down and actually stood up when the commandos entered the airport. He too, was shot with the bullets meant for the enemy. If these three had listened to the soldiers' command they would have been freed with the rest of the captives.

Q - Put yourself in the position of the hostages. If you heard the warnings in your own language, what's the most sensible thing to do?

Q - How do you define obedience to someone (like your parents)? (Doing what they say you should do).

Q – What two actions do we do when we obey? (We listen to them and do what they say).

Q - How do you tend to act when you aren't sure of what the consequences of our obedience will be? (Discuss. Some people won't obey if they can't see why they should).

Introduction (5 Minutes)
Last week we discovered that Noah is not only mentioned in the Old Testament, but in the New Testament as a man of faith. We saw that God asked him to build a boat. But it was miles from the coast! We saw how it was God who guided all the animals into the boat saving Noah the job of herding cats and chasing chickens!

As Noah trusted God by doing what he said, God protected and provided for Noah and his family.

Today we're going to see what the Bible has to teach us about the benefits of obeying God.

Teaching (20 Minutes)
READ Gen 7:17-24 to 8:1-22

Q - Why did God send the rain? (To destroy the evil and wicked that was going on in the world).

Q – What word would you use to describe God's action? (Judgement).

Q – What does this judgement tell us about God? (That God is a good God. That he hates all evil, injustice and violence).

Q – Do you think Noah told the people what was going to happen? (Read Luke 17:26-28 and 2 Peter 2:5-6. It appears that Noah did tell the people that what they were doing was not right. He gave them opportunity to live and be saved in the boat; but they did not take it).

Q – What warnings does this give us? (That it's better to give our lives to God now in case we don't get another opportunity).

Scenario
What you do? You're in the boat the door has shut, it has started to rain big style and your friends are banging on the door calling "let us in!" Because they haven't taken the opportunity to get on the boat it is now too late; you can't let them in. In fact 2 days ago those same friends were taking the mickey out of you because your dad was building a boat in the middle of the land. How would you feel?

You would obviously want them to be saved. The people just needed to believe what Noah was telling them. So today, eternal life is received by faith for those who believe in Jesus before they die. There will be a time when it is too late.

Q – In verse 1 of chapter 8 it says, "But God remembered Noah," do you think he had forgotten about him? (No. God had done many things to protect Noah and wasn't going to forget about him now!).

Q – What might this phrase tell us about the passing of time? (Reflect for a moment what this might be telling us about how God responded to Noah's prayers. It communicates the passing of time before God did something).

Q - It took 40 days and 40 nights for the rain to stop. How long did Noah actually stay in the boat for? (Nearly a year – 7:17, 24 & 8:3-4)

Q – Did God lie in Genesis 7:4 when he said it would take 40 days and 40 nights? (No. Because he said it would only *rain* for 40 days and 40 nights).

Q – What does this tell us about God's timing? (God's timescales are always perfect, but sometimes we assume God will answer a prayer in a certain way, or at a certain time. Sometimes we don't understand all the facts and we can wrongly misinterpret God's plan.)

Q - Why did God save Noah? (Noah obeyed God).

Q – What does this tell us about how God will treat us? (When we listen to his word, and believe in him in faith, he will save us too).

Q – What's the first thing Noah does when he gets out of the boat? (He builds an altar and offers a sacrifice to God).

Q – Why does he offer a sacrifice to God? (He wanted to show his gratitude to God in a special way).

Q – Are there ways in which we can show special gratitude to God? (Discuss. See what they come up with. Maybe a special thank offering? Or giving time over to serve God in the church or on mission?)

Instead of going off and building himself a house straight away, he decides to build an altar to God and make a thank sacrifice to God.

Q – How does God respond? (In return for Noah's obedience and trust, God is pleased with Noah's response and promises never to destroy every living thing again like he did).

Q – What does this encourage us to not forget to do when God does something amazing for us? (Sometimes it's easy to forget that God worked in an amazing way on our behalf. We can get so focussed on what God has given us that we can forget God in it all. It can also sometimes be possible to forget that Jesus has saved us and given us the amazing gift of eternal life.)

Round Up (1 minute)
Today we have seen that God is also a God of judgement as well as a God of love. In love, God offers us the opportunity of being saved from disaster. At the cost of the life of his own dear Son he has done everything for us to accept his gift and avoid judgement.

Yet God is righteous too. If we don't accept his gift that frees us from judgement, we are still in line to be judged. Noah chose to believe God and obeyed him by building an ark, filling it with animals. God remembered Noah's trust and obedience that was rewarded with safety from God; but many others could have who didn't.

Have you asked God for his gift of Jesus, so that you might become right before him?

Prayer (5 minutes)
Have you ever thought about what it means to be a Christian? God loves you and wants you to be in heaven with him. It is by believing in Jesus that we are saved. Would anyone be interested in asking Jesus to save them?

Pray a prayer that they can pray in their heads and ask them to tell you afterwards if they made that commitment.

8) Noah and God's Promise to him

Icebreaker – Memory game (10 Minutes)
Play a game of "I went to the shop and bought ..." with the first person saying what they bought and the second person saying that item and a new item; the third person the first two items and a new item and so on. Keep it going until someone forgets something on the list. They are then out and the game continues until there is only one player left.

Sometimes our memories are not always very good, which is why we need to keep reading God's word, to remember his promises to us. Often he has a promise for us to carry with us for the day.

Introduction (5 Minutes)
Do you remember what we looked at last time we met? We thought about those who were not on the ark drowning; that they made their choice, even though Noah had told them about God and what would happen. They still wanted to do their own thing. We too all have that choice, either to follow God or to ignore him. No-one else can make the decision for us and we can only take that step for ourselves. It is not because it might please our parents or our friends have become Christians. It has to be a personal choice and decision to ask God into your life and then to follow him in all you do. Heavy stuff, but something we all have to think about.

Teaching (30 Minutes)
Read Genesis 9:1-17

Q – What did God tell Noah and his family to do when they left the ark? (v1 To have big families and fill the earth again).

Q – What did God give to Noah and his family? (v2 He gave them all the living creatures. He said they would all respect and fear man from that point onwards).

Q – What did God say about what Noah could eat? (v3 He said they could eat meat as well as veg!).

Q – Why did God say that they must not eat meat that still had blood in it? What do you think he means? (Discuss. Could it be that this represented uncooked meat which could be a health hazard?).

Q – What does God say about killing generally? (It's not allowed).

Q - Why is it not acceptable for humans to be murdered? (We're made in God's image and are special).

Q – Who did God make his agreement with and who was it for? (Noah and his sons and all the people who were to come after them, also every living creature).

Q – What was the sign that sealed God's promise? (A rainbow).

Q – What was the agreement God made? (He promised never again to destroy all living things by flood).

Q – Why was it important that God gave a sign to back up his promise? (It meant that they didn't have to live in fear every time there was a heavy rainfall. When they saw the rainbow they knew that God remembered his promise and was faithful and would keep it).

Q – How long was the agreement for? (Forever).

Q – When you see a rainbow do you ever think about God's promise and what it means? Is it still relevant today? (Discuss).

In groups
What other promises did God give? Get them into small groups and ask them to read 2 promises and to think carefully what they actually mean... Joshua 1:9; Jeremiah 29:11; Genesis 28:15; Exodus 4:12; Numbers 23:19; Deuteronomy 33:3; Proverbs 3:5-6; Isaiah 25:1; Isaiah 30:15; Isaiah 41:10; Isaiah 43:25; Isaiah 54:9; Isaiah 58:11; Malachi 3:17; Matthew 6:33Matthew 7:7-8; Matthew 18:20; Matthew 28:20; John 14:3; Romans 6:28; Hebrews 13:5.

Q – What happens when we read these promises? (Faith grows in our hearts to believe that God will break-through where we need him to).

Q – Does God always keep his promises? (Yes! 2 Corinthians 1:20 says that Jesus is the yes and as we come into agreement with his promises in prayer we are the amen! Then those things will surely come to pass).

Q - Are there any circumstances under which God will break his promises? (Wilful disobedience can disrupt God's plan for our lives).

Q – Do we keep our promises? How do we feel when others break their promises to us? (Discuss. Share any experience you might have had of a promise being broken and share how you felt when that happened).

Round Up (5 Minutes)
Today we have seen God making a promise to Noah, a promise that is still true for us today and sealed the promise with a symbol, the rainbow. That symbol is still a reminder for us every time we see one, that God will keep his promises.

We can trust God. He keeps his promises, always. But the question is, do we? How often do we break our promises, or other people break their promises to us? This always has an effect on those involved.

Promises are special and important. It's why they are called promises. So don't make promises unless you are sure you can keep them. Remember too, that you can stand on God's promises, since they are written for you in mind. He will never break his promises. When you are reading the Bible in your quiet time, look out to see if you can see a promise, and put your name on it.

Prayer (10 minutes)
Spend a few minutes chatting about things to pray for. Encourage the youngsters to share if they have any problems they are facing either at home or at school and then have a prayer time together. Pray, and where appropriate declare God's promises. Romans 8:28 tells us that all things work together for good for those who love the Lord, according to his work. God's hand is on our lives.

9) Noah gets drunk

Intro clip (5 minutes)
If you can find it there is a clip of Homer Simpson getting drunk. In the episode called "War of the Simpsons."

Icebreaker 1 – Create a Story (5 minutes)
Each person is allowed 5 words each. One person must begin by saying the start to a story (eg. One day it was raining and...), the next person then continues the story with their 5 words. Players must use no more and no less than 5 words. Stop when the story seems to be completed.

Icebreaker 2 – Broom Spin (5 minutes)
Get a young person to hold a broom, to spin around whilst looking at the top of the broom. When they have spun about 5 times, get them to walk in a straight line. Keep cups and objects out the way and have someone ready to catch them if they look like they will get into bother.

Introduction (5 minutes)
Today we are going to read about some stuff that happened to Noah when he drank too much wine. Just as in our "create a story game" the ending was unpredictable and anything could happen; so when people get drunk the outcome can often have a negative effect on us, we're going to see how.

Teaching (30 minutes)
READ Gen 9:18-29. Can anyone summarise last time's talk (Noah and the promise. The rainbow).

Q – What was Noah's occupation? (Farmer).

Q – What did he specialise in (apart from boat building!)? (Vineyards and wine making).

Q – So Noah gets drunk. Do you think he knew what the wine would do to him? (Yes and No. Sometimes we can feel a change happening to us when we've drunk a certain amount and feel a bit woozy).

Q – Is there a point at which if we cross we're likely to get drunk? (Yes).

Q – How do we know the point at which we are getting drunk? (May start to feel light headed, reaction time slows but knowing what that point is, is not always easy.)

Boiling a frog
People say that if you were to boil a frog you can't just drop it in boiling water, as it would hop out. So to boil a frog, you put it in a pan of cold water and heat it up. The frog won't be aware that it is too hot until it is too late.

Likewise if a person tries to gauge whether or not they have had too much to drink whilst drinking they will not know when to stop. The alcohol continues to have an effect for another 30 minutes after you have consumed it. So it is pretty impossible to know whether you have had enough until it is too late. The best solution is to know your limits, to decide before hand and stick to it (or choose not to drink at all!).

So Noah started drinking innocently, however it got out of hand. For us as young people, at first you might start off drinking with your parents and that seems ok.

However it might be whilst out with friends that you may be persuaded to secretly drink (under age). Then this may become a habit which leads to binge drinking with friends. This can cause severe intoxication, and lead to accidents. Imagine trying to make your way home after doing that broom spin!

It may just look like an innocent bottle of liquid, but if we misuse it, it can possibly even change the course of our future.

Q – What were the effects of the alcohol for Noah? (He got drunk and naked).

Q - Are the effects of alcohol always the same or does it make us behave in different ways? (Alcohol can make us behave in different ways, we may become loud or quiet, violent or soppy, depending on our personality and our mood).

Q – So Noah got naked. Do you think as young people that alcohol is likely to make us flirtier with the opposite sex and do something we will later regret? (For Noah it caused a problem, changing his future relationship with his son Ham).

Q – Does this highlight any dangers that alcohol can present us? (Yes, when we lose control of our actions, we don't always understand our surroundings, and can be taken advantage of. For Noah, he had 2 responsible sons who looked after him).

Q – Does alcohol make us do things we wouldn't normally do? (Yes, if we drink too much of it).

Q - Some people get drunk because it makes them act a certain way (ie. more confident, or bubbly etc.) is this a good reason to drink? (No. It's better to be yourself and work on your character, who you are, rather than to rely on a drug to make you into someone else).

Q – Do these verses in the Bible say whether Noah's actions were right or wrong? (It doesn't say either way).

Q - Are there any places in the Bible where it says that getting drunk is wrong? (Yes. Look it up in the back of the Bible) (Romans 13:13, 1 Corinthians 6:10, Ephesians 5:18, 1 Peter 4:3).

Q – What reason does the Bible give for why it is wrong? (It is because it leads us into bad actions and poor choices, whether that be immoral behaviour, danger, addiction or health problems).

Round Up (5 minutes)
Today we saw how Noah overstepped the mark from being a bit light headed to getting drunk. As we have seen, there is a point we cross when we've had too much to drink. For our protection we need to drink responsibly since alcohol can affect the way we view our surroundings. For youngsters peer pressure can be a deciding factor for getting drunk. Don't let it be! It is your body and your life! This is an important, but difficult thing to do. Doing the right thing isn't always the easy option!

Yet giving in to excessive drinking can carry consequences that affect our relationships, and even the future of our lives. We ought not to rely on alcohol to make us into fun people; we really can be fun without it. The Bible says getting drunk is wrong, since God wants to protect us and provide a good future for us. We put that at risk if we ignore this.

Prayer

10) Job – When things go wrong

Icebreaker – Card prize draw (10 minutes)
Two packs of playing cards (no jokers). A number of small prizes, at least twelve; have a range of prizes from small chocolate bars, to unwanted gifts, to tacky toys.

Description:
Everyone needs to sit in a circle. Place all the prizes in the centre of the circle, talk about each prize in turn emphasizing how desirable it is.

The leader deals out one pack of playing cards to everyone in the circle, don't worry if some people have one more card than others. The leader now uses the second pack of playing cards, calling out each card in turn.

As a person's card is called, they can choose a prize from the middle, once they have their prize they must put it down in front of them in full view. Keep calling out the cards until all the prizes have been chosen, then continue to call out the cards but now those whose cards are being called out can take a prize from someone else.

Once the leader has been through the pack those with prizes in front of them can keep what they have won.

Use to lead onto discussions on loss.

Introduction (1 minute)
It's very difficult to cope when bad things happen to us or those we care about. So whether it's an accident or when other people are responsible for causing disaster to happen to us, it can leave us feeling crushed and wondering what's going on. The book of Job has such a person who experiences exactly that.

Last week we saw how Noah drunk way too much of his home brew and things went pear-shaped for him. In the Bible the character to follow on chronologically from Noah is Job. Never heard of him? Well apparently at the time, he was the greatest man among all the people of the East.

Teaching (25 Minutes)
READ Job 1:1-22

Q – So Job is a good chap. Is there anything he does wrong? (It says he was blameless and upright and he even did his best to ensure his children were as well).

Q – Can you describe Job's life before the disaster? (He was happy, wealthy, lived a good life and followed God).

Q - Who can tell me where all this trouble starts for him? (In God's throne room).

Q – So did God make a mistake by mentioning Job to Satan? (No. God is in complete control of the situation. Satan could only do what God permitted him to do and no more).

Q – This scenario raises a very big question. How can God hand Job over to Satan who obviously wants to harm him? Aren't parents meant to protect their children? (Discuss)

The book of Job doesn't seem to answer this question directly. However when we see what happened to Job in the context of the whole Bible we can get a better picture. Sometimes when two people have a conversation there is an unspoken history between them that doesn't come out in the conversation.

The book of Job is thought to be the one that happened next after Genesis (chronologically). In Genesis we see Adam and Eve tempted by Satan who told them not to believe God about the harm that eating from the forbidden tree would do. Because they chose to believe Satan and to act on his words (effectively obeying Satan), they handed over rights to Satan by coming into agreement with him.

The ill effects of this fall weren't just limited to Adam and Eve, but to their children and children's children and so on. The curses that came to them affected all of mankind. They had handed over rights to Satan and Satan used this to poison mankind with sin and every kind of evil.

We know this because the Apostle Paul writes about Jesus being the last Adam and reversing the effects of the curse. In the Old Testament people made sacrifices to cover their sin. The life is in the blood, which had power over Satan's curses.

So in the Garden of Eden, because Satan caused Adam and Eve to come into agreement with him, he then had a legal right over those who hadn't given their hearts to God.

Maybe if this history had been spoken about, the conversation might go a bit like this:

The throne room dialogue
Satan: Of course Job praises you God. You've given him everything. But take it away and he will curse you.

God: No he won't. His love for me is secure. I know this because I know all things.

Satan: But you've put a hedge of protection around him. Take that away and he will curse you.

God: I protect him because I love him and he loves me.

Satan: He's mine!! Do I have to remind you that I have a legal right to every son of Adam and daughter of Eve??

God: Not to the ones that love me.

Satan: Prove it then!! Otherwise I'm right and I'm having what's mine!!

Proving Job's faith had eternal consequences. If Job's faith was not genuine, he would not be with God when he one day died. So Satan was accusing God of putting a hedge of protection around Job, so that Satan couldn't get at him.

Q – Do you think God was still protecting Job, even when Satan attacked him? (Yes. God was only allowing so much and no further).

Q – So bad things happen to good people. Is this a new concept for you? (Discuss)

Q – We can see that Satan is the direct cause of this disaster which befalls Job. This is a direct spiritual attack. Do you think spiritual attacks happen today? (Evil spirits do attack people in today's society in many different ways).

Q – Do all bad things have a spiritual cause? (No. Some disasters happen for no other reason than accidents happen).

Q – What do these verses tell us about God's power in such situations? (For the moment things look really bad for Job, a complete disaster. He could lose courage and give up. However we have to wait for the end of the story. Things may look bad, but this is only part of the picture).

Q – What does verse 7 tell us about Satan? (He can only be in one place at the same time. He isn't all powerful, and he isn't omnipresent, but God is).

Q – Does Job know what is happening to him? (No. It all has come as a complete shock. He doesn't know what is going on in the spiritual realms).

Q – How does he respond? (He praises God).

Q – On a scale of 1 to 10, how easy is it to say, "God gives and God takes away" and still praise him? (Discuss)

Q – Why is it difficult? (It's difficult, because we feel God could have done stuff to stop this from happening. However at the same time we see that God is working and still protecting Job).

Q – So Satan is not allowed to touch Job. What does verses 13-19 tell us about Satan? (He will try to do the very worst that he can, as he is evil. Evil is in the world because of Satan).

There are hardly any references in the Bible to Satan. The following texts give further detail about where Satan and evil spirits originated from: Ezekiel 28:12-17 & Isaiah 14:12-15 & Revelation 12:7-9.

Q – So Job didn't know why these things were happening. But unlike many people, he didn't just come to the solution that it was God's fault. Why didn't Job blame God for what happened? (He trusted God totally).

Summary (2 minutes)
We live in a physical world, but also a spiritual world. Satan is in this world and wants to kill, steal and destroy things in people's lives. However God is more powerful. Jesus came to destroy the works of Satan, and Jesus has power over Satan. Jesus gives us the power of prayer to overcome spiritual attacks in our lives. It is important to note that not all bad things that will happen to us are spiritual attacks. These seem to be occasional things and God will help us to see when our difficulties are caused by a spiritual enemy.

For Job at this point, he has more questions than answers. He doesn't know what's going on, or why all this has suddenly happened. If you've ever had to go through a disaster situation, you know that answers and reasons, or just something to help understand what is going on are of great benefit in difficult times. However, with no answers coming, with no reasons for these disasters he finds himself just trusting God.

11) Job – Judging others

Discussion Starter (15 minutes)
Ask for four volunteers, two girls and two boys, and tell them they are going to take part in a quiz to see whether males or females are the most intelligent! Ask each team one question at a time and keep a score. Take note - the key to this activity is to favour one team over the other!

Give the favoured team a couple of chances to answer the questions, hint at the answers for them, and give them points even when they get it wrong. In return, be really hard on the other team. Don't give them all their points, maybe time them out early, make sure that they answer 100% right and so on. Try to be obvious! Some of the people watching will get extremely annoyed and some will find it hilarious!!!

Who wants to be a millionaire?
Complete the following famous saying. The patience of ... ?
a. A cat
b. God
c. Esther
d. Job

Job lived in ... ?
a. Fuzz
b. Uz
c. Buzz
d. Cuz

Job had the following numbers of children:
a. 1 son and 1 daughter
b. 7 sons and no daughters
c. No sons and 7 daughters
d. 7 sons and 3 daughters

Job's sons liked to do the following:
a. Helping their Dad with the camels
b. Having a party
c. Fighting
d. Playing on an Xbox

After one of his children's parties, Job would ... ?
a. **Offer a sacrifice to God in case his children had sinned**
b. Eat all the left overs
c. Go into a huff because he wasn't invited
d. Tell his children off for sleeping in late

Who caused Job to be deprived of his wealth, servants and children?
a. God
b. His wife
c. **Satan**
d. The tax man

Why did Satan single out Job?
a. He was the only name he could remember
b. Because of the evil Job had done
c. Because of the good Job had done
d. **Because God was protecting him**

How were Job's oxen and donkeys taken?
a. In a whirlwind
b. By a flash flood
c. **By Sabeans (people from Arabia)**
d. By Spaniards

How were Job's sheep destroyed?
a. By Chaldeans (people from Babylon)
b. By lions
c. By Sabeans (people from Arabia)
d. **By lightning**

You may need to have other questions prepared depending on how long you want the quiz to go...

Q - Was that a good quiz or a bad quiz? Why? Why Not? (Discuss)

Q - We all like justice to be done. So why are some people treated unfairly? (Discuss)

Q - Why do some people have harder lives than others? (Discuss)

Introduction
So last week we looked at how Job had one disaster after another. He was a good man but it seemed like he was being singled out for bad times. We saw how Job's response to all that was happening to him

was that even though he didn't understand the cause of his problems, he was just going to trust God anyway.

Teaching (25 minutes)
READ Job 2:1-13

Q – So Satan visits Job a second time. How is this different from the first time that disaster hit Job? (The first time Satan took away all Job had, the second time he inflicted disease on Job)

Q - So what was Satan wrong about before? (He said that Job would curse God if everything was taken away from him, but Job didn't).

Q - What does verse 2 tell us about Satan? (He's not omnipresent, he can't be everywhere at the same time, so his powers are limited).

Q - Who does God blame for Job's tough times? (Verse 3. He blames Satan for causing the problem in the first place. Firstly Satan attacks Job's character, then he attacks Job's possessions and family, and when he doesn't get what he wants he insists on making Job ill).

Q - Describe for me some of the pain Job is going through? (He gets some sort of disease that is really uncomfortable).

Q - How do you think Job feels? (Discuss)
Here's a bit of what Job describes himself: READ Job 6:1-7 (See Good News version). He's suffering because he's in pain, he's sad for the loss of his children, his food has no taste, and he feels sick (probably losing weight), not a happy bunny.

Q - Have you ever been REALLY ill? Can you describe what you went through and how you felt? Did it stop you from doing anything?

Q - How do you think going through this might affect someone's view of God? (They might view God as not helping).

Q – Imagine you got ill and you prayed to get better and you didn't get better, does that mean that God doesn't heal people? (No. People still experience healing, the Bible also tells us that God does heal. There will be times when we will experience his healing immediately, at other times we have to wait and sometimes there is no answer and it is a complete mystery to us).

So Job's friends sit with him. They are really concerned for him but can say nothing because he is really having a hard time. However, time goes by and he doesn't seem to get any better. So they begin to wonder and think about why he is so ill. And then they start up a conversation with him that gets into a heated debate about God and why Job is ill.

Q - But first of all there's Job's wife. She has an opinion! Whose fault does she say is where all Job's hassles come from? (God)

Q - So his 3 friends Eliphaz, Zophar and Bildad (who all believe in God) start to offer suggestions as to why Job is having all this trouble and sickness. Can you guess what they say might be causing Job's problems? (Discuss)

This is what Zophar says to Job READ Job 11:1-20 (See Good News version)

Q - So what does Zophar suggest is wrong? What does he say Job needs to sort out? (He suggests Job is being punished for sins/wrongs that he is doing).

Q - Do you think this is a bit harsh? (Discuss)

Q - Who does Zophar say Job is offending? (God)

Q - How does this relate to Job? Is this a true picture of what Job is like? (No. He is righteous, good and refused to curse God for his troubles).

Activity
Show a clip from the X-FACTOR or Pop Idol where the judges are giving a particularly harsh opinion. It is so easy to judge - turn on the telly and away you go! The news, big brother, I'm a celebrity etc...

Q - Obviously we know the backdrop to all this, that Zophar has got it all wrong about Job. He was falsely judging what Job was like. Have you ever thought you knew what someone was like only to be proved wrong? Maybe at school? (Discuss a scenario of how it is easy to do – share a personal testimony about when you were wrong about somebody).

Q - Can you imagine what Jesus has to say about judging others? (See Luke 6:37)

Q - What's the name for a person who judges others, but themselves does things that are wrong? (A hypocrite - not a good thing to be - we have all sinned and fallen short of God's standard).

Q - Why should God be the only person to judge other people? (Well as God, it comes under his remit. He is completely fair, since he knows everything to do with our situation. He is completely Holy and therefore is not a hypocrite. He is completely righteous and knows what punishment fits what crime. Therefore justice will always be done by God).

Q - When will this kind of justice happen, now or later? (The day of judgement will come one day, and at times God will act to stop the ungodly in their tracks).

Q - Does God ever watch and punish us when we do wrong? (See Luke 13. God isn't someone who punishes us every time we do wrong. Our wrongs can form a barrier between us and God. But he has made a way for us to be forgiven so that we can instantly pull down that barrier).

Summary (1 minute)
So here is Job. He has lost everything, he is in pain and rather than getting better, things are getting worse. Along come his friends and accuse him of having a secret sin that is causing God to harm him. Yet this cannot be further from the truth. Job is a righteous man who is being attacked instead by Satan.

When someone judges, they choose to think that they know things like God does. Unfortunately as humans, we are limited and cannot hope to know the ins and outs of a person's life enough to be able to make a judgement. Yet we find ourselves making judgements all the time, but the moment we do that we fail God too.

Pray (5 minutes)

12) Job blames God

Icebreaker 1 - Sword drill (5 mins).
This is an oldie, but a goodie. Get each young person to have a Bible, and tuck it under their arm. You call out a Bible verse, and the first person to begin reading it out gets a sweet.

Icebreaker 2 - Wink Murder (5 mins)
Who's to blame?? Get some playing cards (one for each player) making sure that the King of Diamonds is included. Get the group into a circle. Choose a 'detective' and ask them to leave the room temporarily. Deal out the cards. The person who receives the King of Diamonds is the murderer. Alternatively you can just point at someone to be the murderer!

Once the murderer has been identified the detective comes back in and stands in the middle of the circle. The object of the game is for the murderer to wink secretly at people. Whoever is winked at should 'die' in a couple of seconds, with sound affects if possible. The detective has to try to guess who the murderer is before everyone is 'killed'. Who's to blame for killing everyone??

Discussion (8 minutes)
DeWayne McKinney is a man who has experienced great injustice. DeWayne spent almost 20 years in prison for a crime he didn't commit. It was his faith in God that helped him through and even gave him the ability to forgive those responsible for his wrong conviction. Twice stabbed in prison, DeWayne considered suicide as a way of escaping the hostile prison environment.

The Judge who originally sentenced him in 1982, met with DeWayne following his release and told him tearfully, "Someone in the system owes you an apology. We're sorry." Since then, the two had developed an "unexpected friendship." The judge told the LA times, DeWayne's story was "such a powerful statement about finding peace, solace and stability in the darkest moments of our lives."

Imagine you were in DeWayne's position: in jail for a crime you didn't commit.

Q - How would you feel towards those who had falsely accused you?

Q - Why do you think DeWayne decided to forgive the people who put him in there?

Teaching (10 mins)

Over the past 2 weeks we've checked out the disaster that hit Job and how things, instead of improving, got worse and worse. Then when things were at rock bottom, his friends judged him and said it was his fault that all these bad things were happening to him.

Somehow, Job manages to hold it together to have a heated debate on the whole subject of his suffering; that's pretty much what the book of Job is about. It's got 5 different people's opinions on suffering, including Job's. However, you'll have to read it at your own leisure to figure out who's right in it all, if indeed anyone was!

So Job's friends have been telling him what they think is wrong with him. This is Job's response...
READ Job 19:1-29. (The Good News version is recommended for this session).

Q - What did Job's friends say was causing Job's troubles and therefore who was causing Job's pain? (They were saying that Job's sin was to blame for his suffering and that God was punishing him as a result).

Q - Job answers back to all that has been said so far by Zophar, Eliphaz and Bildad. Who does Job blame for his troubles? (Verse 6 God).

Q - Is Job right to blame God in this instance? (In his head it makes the most sense to blame God for it, but as we saw from the beginning of Job, it's actually Satan who caused his suffering).

Q - In verses 6-7 Job accuses God of doing wrong. What do you think God might think of this? (We'll find out next week how God responds to Job's accusation. At times when it's difficult we may find all we can do is shout at God. He's big enough to cope with this).

Q - What about when people blame God for natural disasters? Is this kind of accusation justified? Why/Why not? (The world is subject to the effect mankind has had on it. Even the pollution from industry has taken its effect on nature. The temperature in the atmosphere rises, ice caps melt and even storms worsen. We hate death, especially when it seems so untimely. And in our grief, it's okay to ask why something so terrible has happened).

Q - What about when tragic things happen to people (eg. Princess Diana's death) people lay flowers with a note saying "WHY GOD?" As if "why did you not stop this?" Do you think it's always right to hold God responsible for things we don't understand? (God has allowed free will on Earth, and as a result, things like tragedies happen).

Q – Is it consistent to blame God for bad things and not thank him for the good things?

Q - How do you respond to things that really aren't fair? (You might respond by getting angry, and ask whose fault is it that this has happened? And direct your anger at them).

Q - So Job is being really honest with God here. Do you think God is okay with this? (Yes. God wants us to communicate honestly with him, we can't hide such thoughts from him, but he wants us to work them through with him).

Q - How does Job conclude his thoughts at this point? (v25 onwards). (He still sees God as his defender. Job still trusts him despite the fact he feels he's in God's bad books at the moment).

Q - What does Job believe the outcome will be of all that is happening? (Job trusts in the end God will see that justice is done).

Summary (2 mins)
Here we see that Job doesn't have all the answers. So what we get is Job's complete honesty in talking about the situation the way he sees it. And we see that such honesty doesn't distance him from God, even though he accuses God of doing wrong.

It's totally okay to be honest with God. In fact it's what God wants from us. When things aren't fair and we face injustice (like DeWayne) God wants us to come to the point of forgiving people and letting go of our desire to blame people. Whether we hold God responsible for our troubles or not, it is his desire to help us through it. Blaming God only distances us from him at a time when what we actually need is to come closer to God, in order that we can draw strength from him.

Job's still none the wiser about what is happening to him, but next week we're going to have a look at what God thinks about the whole conversation that Job has been having with his friends.

Pray (As long as it takes)

13) Job - God Speaks

Icebreaker (6 minutes)

Explain that you're going to give them a story to improvise. Each person takes a turn to say a sentence and we'll see where the story takes us.

You might want to choose two actors to go up the front for this game. To help kick start people's imagination here's a random scenario you might want to suggest:

Tell the two actors that you've chosen scene where one person is shopping for strawberry jelly only to find out that the store only carries raspberry. The shopper is allergic to raspberry jelly, because they were bitten by a spider whilst eating raspberry jelly as a toddler. The shopper is approached by a member of staff handing out free tasters of raspberry jelly. The member of staff speaks first.

Discussion (5 minutes)

Susie had been a Christian most of her life. She had a lovely family home, and a great relationship with God. She was the kind of girl that everyone loved to be around. She was funny, sweet, very loving and caring and the best friend you could ask for. As Susie grew older, she was desperate for more of God, more wisdom and more understanding.

Unlike her friends, Susie had a daily quiet time. God always met with her, until one day. "That's strange," she thought. "Must be me." On the days that followed, God seemed to stay quiet. She had no words, no pictures, no good thoughts, no joy. Her times with God were different, so she tried even harder.

Around the same time, Susie realized her boyfriend was acting strangely towards her. She confronted him and he told her he'd realized he no longer loved her. Susie was devastated and turned to God for comfort, but still he appeared to stay silent. Shortly afterwards, Susie received a phone call. Her best friend had been in a serious accident, she was lying in intensive care.

Lost and alone, Susie opened her Bible. Desperate and crying out to God, her quiet time became very loud - but still she heard nothing.

Susie began to blame God. "Why are you doing this? Why are you ignoring me? Do you care? Are you even there?"

As Susie cried, she remembered in the past telling God that no matter what the circumstances. He was still God and deserved her worship. She realized that it's easy to pray when God feels really close and things are good, but as soon as he'd tested her to see if she really meant it about worshipping him in all circumstances, she had struggled.

Q - Why might it feel that it is difficult to pray when God seems to be keeping quiet? (We might wonder if he's actually there and listening).

Q – Why is it important not to rely on feelings in our relationship with God? (Our feelings can change very quickly and although helpful, they don't always reflect the truth. God is still there whether we feel him there or not).

Q – If you knew that things will turn out ok, how would that help you through your troubles right now? (Maybe we would worry less about the future).

Introduction (1 minute)
We've been reading about Job and thinking about what it's like when disaster hits us. So far God has said nothing for some time and this has left Job questioning, with no idea what's going on.

Job has lost everything, he's got sores and diseases and he says that God has wronged him, that God is to blame. Job's friends agree that God has done this. However, they look on Job in judgment by saying that he is having all these troubles because of his secret sins.

Wouldn't it be great to have God say something about all this? Well this is what we find out this week, but what he says probably isn't what we want to hear at the time of our suffering. However, when we think about it, looking back after the event, it all makes a lot more sense...

Teaching (15 minutes)
Last week Job was getting pretty fed up with God, by saying that God had done wrong to him. So God responds. We're going to take a few snippets from what God says to gauge the essence of what is being said and piece the bits together...

Q – These are Job's last words on it all See Chapter 31:35-37. What do you expect God to say about it all? (Firstly God doesn't owe us an explanation!)

READ Job 38:1-15

Q - Where does God speak to Job from? (The storm).

Q – What do you think the storm might represent? (Often difficult times in our lives are like a storm that comes, bringing confusion hardship and also bigger than we can handle. Often it's in the middle of these times God speaks).

Q - In verse 2 what does God accuse Job of doing? (Making "His purpose unclear," saying confusing things about God, and questioning the reasons behind why God did things).

Q - What questions does God ask Job? (Basically who made the world? But also whose job is it to keep the world going?)

Q - What was God getting at by asking Job these questions? (That God made everything and as the Supreme Being, keeps everything in check and hasn't overlooked anything).

Sometimes we have questions, like "Why did this happen?" What we are getting at is that we want an explanation. Why didn't God do something we expected of him? Sometimes we are just asking the wrong question. Rather than answering why something happened God reminds Job of who he is. This isn't a boasting session, or a rant. God is saying that when we realise who he is, we would trust that he's not made a mistake or forgotten about us. But he is the Lord Almighty, who is just, pure and loving and who will make things right.

Let's look at another snippet…

READ Job 40 vv. 1-14

So God gives Job a chance to reply to the first lot of things that God has said. And Job realizes that actually, God is God and he can do what he wants to do. He is completely wise and doesn't do stupid things. There is a reason behind why he does everything.

Q - How does God describe himself here? (That he is awesome in majesty, power and splendor. And in all fairness, he has power to administer justice as he sees fit).

Q - God talks in verses 12-14 about being able to punish the proud. What do you think he's saying here? (Some celebrities and public figures have tried to challenge God and like Job his answer to them would be the same; "Will the one who contends with the Almighty correct him?" In other words, "How can these people assume such a high up position to attempt to cross examine God?" No one could get anywhere close to his purity, wisdom, power, justice or kindness).

So far we have seen then that God has a purpose in all of this, and Job's ideas about God were based more on his experiences than God's real nature. It is very easy for us to fall into the trap of limiting God to the extent of our experiences (good or bad) and then drawing conclusions about God from them. Better to read the Bible before deciding that we know who God is!

God is all powerful, knows what he's doing. He has a purpose and is constantly looking after the running of the Universe. Lets' piece that together with what else we know has happened...

Q - Who caused all this?? (Satan)

Q - What did God say Job would do, even if he had to suffer? (He would still praise God).

Let's take a quick look at a very interesting bit...
READ Job 40:15-24

Q – Any ideas what creature this text is talking about?? (Most possibly a dinosaur! Job was one of the first books of the Bible to be written).

Q – What clues are there to say it might be a dinosaur? (Verse 19 "He is the first of the works of God).

Q – Take a look at verse 17 "It's tail sways like a cedar." What is a cedar? (An enormous tree!)

Q – Why is God talking about a dinosaur? (He is describing the biggest of animals, but God is Lord over it).

Summary (1 minute)
God knew without a doubt that Job would get through this and that his faith would win through; through all the questions, discussions, false assumptions and sufferings. Job had to endure a time of disaster in order to prove the genuineness of his faith in God.

How do we know if our faith is true or not? One of the ways is when it seems like God has gone missing and doesn't respond to us in the ways we think he should. Job did not learn why he was suffering, but he did come to see that God was for him and not against him, that he was God, creator, sustainer of the universe and his friend.

As we go through experiences like this we discover so much more of God along the way, however sometimes it's only till afterwards that we actually understand what's going on. Through these conversations with God, Job got to learn who God was in a truly unique way.

Prayer (as long as it takes)

14) Job – It's all sorted
Icebreaker - Big Boss

Each person is now an employee in a big business and been given a role within the company:

1 Toilet Cleaner
2 Tea Person
3 Post boy/girl
4 General Dogsbody
5 Enquiries Clerk
6 General Office Clerk
7 Team Supervisor
8 Assistant Manager's Assistant
9 Assistant Manager
10 PR Consultant
11 General Manager
12 Manager
13 Managing Director
14 Area Director
15 Big Boss

The aim of the game is to obtain a promotion and work your way up in the company, to eventually become the Big Boss. If you are the Big Boss you will have to work hard to keep your job.

The game will depend on how many people you have in the group, so you may have to add or lose roles depending on the number of people. Make sure you have a toilet cleaner and a big boss, as businesses can't function without these two roles.

Make sure the youngsters are in a semi-circular arrangement. Give out a role to each person (written on a piece of paper or card), starting at one end with the "toilet cleaner." The person next to them should get the "tea person," next the "post boy/girl" etc., until each person has a role better than the previous one and the last person (at the other end) gets the "Big Boss" role. Each person should make visible the piece of paper with their role on it for others to see.

The game starts with the toilet cleaner who will call out their role, "toilet cleaner," then they must call out another role, "general manager." The person with the general manager role must immediately call out their role, and then the role of another person, but not the person who just called them out (in this case not the toilet cleaner). The next person who is called out must then call out their role and another. And so it goes on...

The game stops when someone makes a mistake.

Mistakes are:
1) If someone calls out a role that has just been called out.

2) Saying a role incorrectly

3) Pausing or hesitating.

4) Taking too long or missing that they have just been called out.

When someone makes a mistake they must stand up, put their piece of paper down on the seat they were sitting on and sit on the seat of the toilet cleaner. That person has been demoted and become the toilet cleaner. The person who is the toilet cleaner is now promoted to become the tea person, the old toilet cleaner must now take the seat of the tea person. Depending on who has made the mistake, this trend of moving up a role happens until the empty seat is filled. For example if it was the general dogsbody who made the mistake, the toilet cleaner would move to take on the tea person's role, the tea person, to the post boy/girl, and the post boy/girl t to the general dogsbody. All new roles will be filled, but no-one else moves up.

The game will then continue, starting with the toilet cleaner who then says "toilet cleaner to…"

Once you have played a number of rounds, whoever is Big Boss at the end is the winner.

Teaching (30 Minutes)
Read Job 42:1-17 (Using the Good News version will make getting to grips with this text easier!)

Q – How does Job start off talking to God at this point? (vs 1 & 2 He acknowledges that God is all powerful).

Q – What does Job mean in verse 3, can you put it in your own words? (I was talking out the back of my head. I didn't know what I was talking about. He was saying he was sorry for having doubted God, for not having understood the greatness of God. He realises his own audacity at challenging God to answer his questions).

Q – What has Job learned about trust and faith through all of this? (He has learned that the essence of faith is trusting that God is working, even when we don't understand why things have happened.

He sees that looking for someone to blame, is a bit simplistic since there are factors beyond our understanding involved).

Q – In verses 7 to 9, after God had sorted out Job, what does he do? (He turns to Job's friends and sorts them out).

Q – Why is God angry with Eliphaz and the others? (God says they have not been wise in their counsel or spoken the truth about him.

Q – Does this say that people who are mean to us will get their comeuppance in due time from God? (Discuss)

Q – What does this tell us about God's forgiveness? (Discuss)

Q - We find the words of Eliphaz and his friends in the Bible, though they aren't always representing Job very well. What danger does this present for us if we take out odd Bible verses and use them on their own? (We might be getting the wrong end of the stick. Some Bible verses can be used on their own as they can often sum up a wider concept that is being communicated ie. John 3:16. However, to ensure we are using that text right, we need to understand the verse within the other bits).

Q – Why do you think God said they had to ask Job to pray for them? (It's like God was affirming Job's righteousness in all this. But also Job needed to forgive his friends in order to move on.)

It's really difficult to know how Job would have felt about it all afterwards. On the one hand, the pain of losing his grown up sons and daughters would have been immense. If only his friends had understood, the time he needed them most they let him down badly. On the other hand Job would have had a life changing meeting with God that few are privileged with. This was also the beginning of a new relationship with God, starting again on a new footing. Job was now confident that he need not fear similar things happening again to him in the future.

Q – Job did pray for his friends. What does this tell us about Job? (That he cared about them and had forgiven them for what had happened).

Q – Consider something someone has said or done to harm you. Maybe they have made life for you much harder than it needed to be. Maybe you feel they are controlling you unnecessarily. How hard is it to forgive these people? (Discuss)

Q - God obviously didn't promise that forgiving others was easy, but he said it is still necessary to do. Why do we have to forgive others?

Here's a list!

1. It helps us put the issue behind us.

2. Holding something against someone else because of what they did makes us hard-hearted.

3. Forgiving someone helps us to heal inside.

4. Not forgiving someone hurts us more than the other person.

5. We make mistakes too and need to be forgiven.

6. Forgiving someone mends friendships.

Q – Looking at verses 10–17 what happened after Job had prayed for his friends? (His brothers and sisters all came to see him and consoled him and gave him presents. Then God blessed Job and restored his prosperity and also gave him more children. He ended up with twice as many animals and seven sons and three daughters.)

Q – This is the end of the story about Job. Sometimes we will find that we won't always get the answers that we want from God. He's not always going to explain everything. Is there anything we can learn from looking at Job "the man"? (His faith in God was proved true. He got somewhat swayed by the thoughts of his friends and brought into an argument that led him to assume things about God's role that weren't right).

Q – What can we learn about God through this? (God was determined to prove Job's faith in order that Satan would not have an opportunity to take Job from him. As the sustainer of the Universe, God is there in our struggles and is working for our good. He's not left us alone. Though we can't know the end, he will not let us down).

Q – Does knowing this help your relationship with God? (We know during the times when we don't understand what is going on, when it even appears that God has left us, we can trust him to take care of things, enabling the best outcome to happen).

Q - Do you think Job is a good example for us? (Yes. We see his human-ness as a follower of God and that we aren't expected to have it all together. He doesn't let go of God and sees that God hasn't let go of him).

Q – Why does looking back on events in our lives help us to understand what has gone on? (At the time we often won't understand, because certain things that God has planned haven't happened yet. So months or years after the event can give us a greater perspective on what God was doing during those times).

Round Up (5 Minutes)
Job's counselling session with God brings him to the awareness that we don't know what God the Almighty has to deal with. We know that Satan is loose on the earth and seeks to find ways in which he can try to legally or illegally, steal from, kill and destroy mankind. He also tries to make us think that God is responsible for the destruction Satan causes.

God is completely good. He does not bring disease and sickness upon us. He sent Jesus to destroy these works! We are in a spiritual battle in which we cannot always see what is happening in the background, in the spiritual realm. When disaster strikes it can be easy to blame God on the premise that he didn't stop something terrible from happening. There is a day when all things like this will end. God has planned it. We need to trust that he knows what he is doing.

There is also a lesson about forgiveness here. Job forgave his friends and prayed for them. There are no promises in this life. No guarantees that things will turn out perfectly the way we plan them. What is important is our relationship with God and whether we can trust him to only be working for our good according to his purposes.

Prayer (As long as it takes!)
Spend a few minutes chatting about things to pray for, encourage the youngsters to share if they have any particular difficulties they are facing and then have a prayer time together.

15) Abram Gets a Big Call from God
Icebreaker – Guess a minute (5 minutes)
Tell the youngsters you are going to see who can live without a watch. Their task is to guestimate how long a minute lasts by counting in their head. Have them all sitting down. You will have a stopwatch and tell them when to start. When they think 60 seconds is up, they must stand up. The winner is the one to stands up closest to the time of 60 seconds on the clock.

Discussion Starter (10 Minutes)
Take a couple of minutes for each person to think about the most interesting person they have ever met, famous or not. Say "Tell us about the person and the job that they do." Go around the group and share each person's experience.

Introduction (5 Minutes)
Q - Who have we been learning about over the past few weeks? (Job).

Q - What are the main lessons you have learned through studying the life of Job? (When going through times of suffering we have the tendency to blame God or suspect we've done something to offend him. But the best thing we can do is to trust that God has a good outcome in store for you).

We are now going to move forward a few generations to a man called Abram. I'm sure you've heard about him before (Abram). We're going to look at his life and his relationship with God over the next few weeks. Abram was born in a place called Ur. Can you say Ur?? It is found is Southern Iraq. Abram was a direct descendant of Shem, (one of Noah's sons) and an ancestor in the line of Jesus Christ.

Teaching (20 Minutes)
Read Genesis 12:1-9

Q – What did God ask Abram to do in verse 1? (To leave his home, his family).

Q – How do you think Abram felt being asked to move, without clear instructions as to where? (v2 Discuss.)

Q – How do you think you would feel if you were asked to do something like that, without clear instructions about where and how? (Discuss.)

Q – What would it take to be able to obey God in this situation? (Faith first of all that God had said it. A trust in God that his plan was for good, that he would guide you as you went along.)

Q – What does the fact that Abram felt God tell him to do something say about his relationship with God? (He believed God was real and he expecting God to speak to him).

Q – Do you think God is more likely to speak to us if we expect him to? (Yes. If we read his words we will understand more that it is him speaking, when he does speak to us directly).

Q – Ask yourself this: Is your relationship with God close enough to hear God speak to you and have you the faith to do what he says? (Discuss how we don't have to be a spiritual superhero to hear from God. What does it take to do what God says?).

Q – Along with this big ask, what did God promise Abram? (v.2 That he would become a great nation, be blessed, famous, be a blessing to others, be protected and cause all the people in the world and future generations to be blessed.)

Q – What do you think this all means? (Discuss).

Q – How would future generations be blessed through Abram? (The nation of Israel would come from Abram's grandson. This nation became the people of God. Jesus, God's son was born from the line of Abram and faith in Jesus is compared to the faith that Abram had).

Q – This was all a big promise. Do you think Abram understood any of it, some of it, or all of it? (Discuss.)

Q – What was Abram's response to what God said to him? (v.4 He packed his bags, rounded up his family and started the adventure of following God and finding a new home).

Q – Who or what did Abram take with him? (His wife, his nephew, his servants and everything he owned).

Q – Abram and his group set out for Canaan, and when they got there they went through the land to the great tree of Moreh at Shechem. What happened there? (God appeared to Abram and promised to give him and his descendants the land of Canaan).

Q – Why does God chose certain times to appear, or speak very clearly to us in a very memorable way? (When he has something life changing or specific about what he wants us to do with our lives, he will sometimes make it a time we will never forget. He makes this extra clear, so that in times when it seems that what he has said won't come to pass, we will keep going and not lose hope).

Q – What was Abram's response to hearing God? (He built an altar and worshipped God).

Q – What did Abram do next? (He went all through the land setting up altars as he went).

Q – Why do you think Abram did that, was it an appropriate response to God? What does it tell us about how he viewed God and his relationship with him? (Discuss. He was establishing it as a place of worship, dedicated to God).

Round Up (5 Minutes)
What an interesting guy Abram is. Like his ancestor Noah, when God spoke to him, he acted immediately and obediently. He listened to God, did what God asked and received God's blessing and guidance.

Abram's response to God as the first of the promises was fulfilled was to build altars and worship God; he moved around the land building altars at all sides, almost like claiming the land as God's. This response was also a worship to God who was blessing him. Abram is a great example and witness to us as a man who had faith in God. He obeyed God with the big decisions of his life without question and responded to God in worship.

Think about it for a minute. Do you have faith in God? Would you obey him as willingly as Abram did?

Abram obeyed God. He did not have a clear destination, but he did have a clear promise "I will bless you and I will make your name great". Doubtless it was this promise which fired his faith and started him out on a journey which, with hindsight, is one of the epic journeys of history. When God calls us to do a new thing or to accomplish something special for him, God's call is not always accompanied by a reason, but it is always accompanied by a promise. It is always easy to understand a promise, but not always easy to understand a reason.

Prayer (As long as it takes!)
Spend a few minutes chatting about things to pray for, encourage the youngsters to share things that are happening that affect their lives both at home or at school. Encourage them to pray, out loud if they want, or if not the leader should close in prayer.

16) Abram Do Lies get us out of Trouble?

Icebreaker - Alibi (10 Minutes)
You announce that a murder has been committed. State the time and location and incident (eg. last night at 7:45pm a man was shot dead).

Two people are chosen to become the primary suspects in this murder. They will be asked what they did last night, so they need to invent an alibi. "I was on my own watching telly" is not a good alibi. So they need to think of something that they did together. They can expect to be quizzed individually to see if their alibis hold up.

The two suspects will then leave the room to make up their alibi.

Once the suspects have been sent out of the room, those that remain must think up 10 questions that they can ask the group to see if they can find holes in their alibi.

Specific questions are good for establishing information to place on a time line on a flip chart, and open questions that cannot be answered by a "yes" or "no" are best.

The young people who did not leave the room can ask 10 questions to each suspect, both can come into the room together, but one must listen to music on some headphones so that they don't hear what's going on. Alternatively the other suspect can be supervised outside the room, so that they don't hear what's being said inside.

Can you find a flaw in their alibi?

Introduction (5 Minutes)
Last time we saw how Abram had a life changing moment which would affect the rest of his life. We saw how God told him to leave the place where he'd grown up and get going... somewhere. God didn't give Abram clear instructions for where he was to go. This took trust on Abram's part and as we will see God rewarded Abram for this trust.

Today we are faced with all kinds of tricky decisions or problems that may leave us feeling out of our depth (eg. when we're in trouble and don't know what to do, or when we have to choose what exams to take, or where to do our work experience, who to hang out with, who to go out with) all sorts of things. So we're going to see how Abram responded when faced with some big decisions and a problem that he couldn't handle on his own.

Teaching (30 Minutes)
READ Genesis 12:10-20

Q – Most people who travel go from A to B. They have a start point and an end point in mind. Abram didn't know where he was going. What things necessary for survival might influence your travel? Describe what it would be like.... (You might be a bit like Captain Picard of the Star Ship Enterprise discovering new places, people, animals etc.)

Problem 1
Q – Abram comes across a few problems on his travels. What was his first problem? (v10 There was very little food).

Q – Why was this problem for Abram? (He had lots of mouths to feed).

Q – How many mouths did he have to feed? (Ch 12:5 His wife Sarai, nephew Lot, servants and animals).

Q – So Abram didn't know where he was going. What might be a good sign from God for Abram to find the right place? (Ample food, supplies and an appropriately safe place to live).

Q – Food supplies are Abram's problem. How does he decide to resolve this problem? (He goes to Egypt).

Problem 2
Q - This decision is not without its difficulties. Tell me what Abram's second problem is? (They choose to go to Egypt for food, but Sarai his wife is very beautiful. Abram is now concerned that the Egyptians will want her and try to get rid of him).

Q – Do you think Abram had anything to be nervous about? (He would have felt powerless, afraid and out of his depth to do anything against the Egyptians. When we feel out of our depth, it can seem impossible for us to change what's happening to us).

Q – Can you think of a situation you have been in when you have felt powerless or out of your depth or worried about what people might do to you? (Discuss).

Q – So Abram was worried about his wife, but also about his life. What reason did Abram have to not be worried? (God had promised him some amazing things. God wasn't going to let things take his plans off course).

Q – What does Abram do to solve this problem? (He lies).

Q – Does this seem like a satisfactory solution to the problem? (No. This plan backfires making Sarai seem available and results in her being taken away).

Q – What happens to Sarai? (The king takes her to be his wife).

Q – How do you think she would have felt? (Was she frightened for her future without her husband and wider family? Maybe she felt honoured at being the attention of the king. Remember these were different times and a different culture! She was probably wondering what would be expected of her and just wanted to leave).

Q – As a result of his lies, Abram no longer had a wife. However, looking on the bright side, he was still alive. Do you think things would have been different if Abram had trusted God and told the truth? How do you think things would have been different? (Discuss. See God's promise in verse 3).

Q - Although Abram lies to get out of his problem, it all seems to be okay in the end. Is lying ok then? Since all's well that ends well? (No. Abram had an opportunity to trust that God would come through for him as he had promised. Sarai may never have been taken in the first place and all that unnecessary stress would have been avoided).

Q - Although Abram had a lot more property, did his lie end well? (No. He was banished from the whole of Egypt!).

So the way Abram chose to remedy this second problem turned out to be the more stressful and scary option, because he had lied. Things are a lot more straightforward when we tell the truth and trust God to look after us.

Q – What does verse 17 tell us about God? (Even though Abram's journey into Egypt was a bit of a failure, God was right there with him in all the problems he had. God will use his power to help us in order that we can stay on track with his plan).

Round Up (5 Minutes)

Abram didn't know where he was going, but this experience in Egypt was one he would hopefully learn from! But God was guiding him. We see God's guidance a bit like giving someone directions piece by piece. Rather than telling him the whole lot in one go, Abram had the freedom to go where he felt led. Food was a motivating factor, so he went where his needs led to being provided for. But God was ready to guide him if he went off course.

For example, if I gave you directions to the bike shop in town, I might say, "Go left out of here, down Main Road, past the roundabout, then left at the traffic lights. It's there on your left, but if you go past the bowling place, YOU'VE GONE TOO FAR!"

Egypt was too far for Abram. God wanted Abram to stay in Canaan, as that would be the land he promised to him. At times God orders our circumstances so that we might stay within his plan.

In the future you will encounter choices that you will ask God about. It could be a job, place to live, or subject to choose. "Which one is the right one?" you might ask. It may be that God will inspire you to choose the right one, or it may be that God doesn't say anything; in which case he wants you to choose. If you choose a way that he doesn't want you to go, he will lead you causing your circumstances to bring you back on track.

When we face tough problems, our problems can become God's problems when we bring them to him. So trusting God when things don't seem to go as we hoped is far better than trying to get out of it with lies, and whatever you do, it will go well with you.

Prayer (As long as it takes!)

17) Lot compromises his principles

Icebreaker 1 - The Yes No game (5 Minutes)
One contestant volunteers to answer a barrage of questions asked by the rest of the group. The contestant must not say "Yes" or "No" or "Don't know." The people asking the questions must ask one at a time and allow a chance for each question to be answered.

HINT: Asking questions in quick succession will give the contestant less thinking time and will cause them to crack under the pressure!

Icebreaker 2 – Two true one false (5 Minutes)
Get each person to share 3 things about themselves. Two of the statements must be true and one a plausible false statement. Everyone else has to guess what the false statement is.

Introduction (5 Minutes)
We started our Bible studies with Adam and Eve, going on to Cain, Abel, Noah, Job and Abram. This is interactive, so keep your minds alert as we're going to find out together God's words for us from the Bible.

Q - We now pick up the story of Lot, who do you think he's related to? (He is Abram's Nephew).

So Abram has left home and is on his way to a land that God has promised him. He and his family ended up in Egypt and to keep himself from being killed, he lied about Sarai being his sister when actually she was his wife.

Teaching (15 Minutes)
READ Genesis 13:1-18

Q – What began to happen between Abram and Lot's herdsmen? (They started to argue because there were so many of them).

Q – Why do you think they began to argue, why couldn't they live together happily? (Discuss)

Q – Are you more likely to argue when you are living closely with someone? If so why? (Discuss. Consider how we get on with our families, if we have to share a bedroom, etc.)

Q - So Abram didn't like the arguing and made a suggestion for solving the problem. What did he come up with? (v9 For them to stay friends but go their separate ways, for the sake of having more space).

Q – Why do you think he gave Lot the choice of where to go, because Abram knew he probably wouldn't get the better half? (Abram placed the need for a peaceful solution in his family above his own needs. When we are not selfish and honour God with our decisions, God will honour us in return).

Q – Did Abram put any pressure on Lot as to which way to go? (No gave him a completely free choice).

Q – What did Lot see when he looked into the Jordan Valley? (v 10 he saw a lot of water there and felt it was like the Lord's garden. It was fertile, rich, would get good crops and so would succeed).

Q – Lot chose to go to the Jordan Valley. Was he being selfish? (Discuss)

Would you Rather???
Here's a couple of choices for you. Get up and stand on one side of the room or the other depending on your preference.

- Visit the doctor or the dentist?
- Eat broccoli or carrots?
- Watch TV or listen to music?
- Own a lizard or a snake?
- Have a beach holiday or a mountain holiday?
- Be an apple or a banana?
- Be invisible or be able to read minds?
- Be the most popular or the smartest person?
- Make headlines for saving somebody's life or winning the lottery?
- Go without television or fast food for the rest of your life?
- Eliminate world hunger or bring lasting world peace?
- Stranded on a deserted island alone or with someone you don't like?
- See the future or change the past?
- Be three inches taller or three inches shorter?

So Lot had made his choice. He looked at the land and saw the water and lovely vegetation and thought that was the better choice.

Q – Did Lot make the right choice? If not why not? (v13 tells us that although the land surrounding that area was good, those who lived there were far from good).

Q - So Lot compromised his principles to get what he wanted. How do you think that would have affected him and his family? (Lot put himself and his family in danger by living so close to the cities which were evil. Although the location was nice, the more important thing was their safety and wellbeing).

Q - Have you ever wanted something so much and then when you got it, you discovered you would have to compromise something you believed in to keep it? (Discuss)

Scenario (10 minutes)
Imagine you've had the hots for a boy for some time (or a girl if you're a boy). You've seen them around at school and fancied them for ages. You have thought about them lots and admired them from afar. Well it turns out a mate of yours has mentioned it and this boy you fancy has asked you out. Think how you would feel at that point.

Imagine that you meet up on your first date and go to the cinema, the new James Bond film. You are both enjoying the film together when during the film his hand starts to wander, ever so slightly but deliberately touching slightly more than you think he should.

What do you do? You wanted to go out with this boy and you can't believe you are on a date with him, but you are a Christian and you don't like where this might lead in the future.

Q - What do you do? Do you:

A) Think you'll let him touch you and see how things go?

B) Make a joke of it, treat it like a mistake and hold his hand for the rest of the film?

C) Do you tell him to stop, risking your chance of any future dates with him? (Choose an option and discuss)

You may want to use a slightly different scenario for a younger group:

You are on a first date with a boy/girl at McDonalds. Some of his/her friends come in and they join you. The conversation begins to go downhill, either becoming rude or talking in a way and using bad words that you would not normally use. Do you:

A) Laugh and join in, so that you feel included?

B) Stay quiet and ignore it all by looking at your phone?

C) Tell him that you need to go and then leave, risking your chance of any future dates with him?

Q – Do we always make the right choices? How do we know what the right choice is? (Sometimes it's our conscience, and sometimes we realise it when we read the Bible, and sometimes it's when we listen to those who love us, like our parents. They might say it in the wrong way, but you know they are right!)

Q - What happens if we make a bad choice? (When we realise we've made a bad choice we need to think about how to get out of it. Yes it won't be easy and we may upset some people along the way, but in the long run it will protect our future happiness).

Q – Lot made a lousy choice, but when they went their separate ways where did Abram go? (v12 The land of Canaan).

Q – What was Abram's experience? (v14 onwards. God honoured Abram after he gave the choice to Lot saying that he would give him all the land he could see).

Round Up (3 Minutes)
We see here that sometimes we will find ourselves having to choose between what we want and actually what is good for us in the long run. The way we can make the right decisions is to ask God for his help and ask for him to help us to make the right choice. On the surface one option may look very attractive, but as Lot found out there was a problem with his choice.

Lot did nothing to correct his situation, and placed his family in danger and risked his future happiness. We need to go deeper than the surface and consider what God really wants for us. Decisions made without his guidance are likely to come at a cost.

But whatever situation we find ourselves in, God is there and ready to help us out.

Prayer (As long as it takes!)

18) Hagar encounters God

Ice Breaker 1 – Moose head (10 Minutes)
Everyone stands in a circle. One person is nominated to go first. They point to someone else in the group but say their own name. That person must then point at someone else and say their own name.

The game continues until somebody hesitates or says someone else's name instead of their own name. They then make an antler shape with one of their hands by sticking their thumb on the side of their head and spreading their fingers out.

Once somebody gets two antlers they are a 'moose head' and cannot play anymore. However, they stay in the game with their two antlers, or sit down. No one is allowed to point to a 'moose head' but if they do, it is as if they have said the wrong name, and they then get an antler. The game continues until only one person is left in.

Introduction (5 minutes)
Christians believe that sometimes God arranges for key events to happen in our lives. Something positive that happens that changes the course our life, taking us in an unexpected direction.

For example it might be a time at Summer Camp when God made it clear he was speaking to you. Or it might be when you found you had to trust God and take a step of faith for something, and it turned out amazingly. Maybe it was a Christian friend who met up with you and encouraged you with a word from God, and helped you to realise stuff you never thought of before.

This is called a "divine appointment" when God sets up a memorable meeting, a turning point in your life. Have you ever had such an occasion, or do you know of someone else's story about a divine appointment?

Well they do happen today and the Bible is full of these moments where a person's life is changed when God sets up the appointment.

Prayer (12 minutes)
Hand out a piece of paper and get the youngsters to write their name on one side and on the other what things they hope for the future. It might be to use a particular talent they have, or it may be that they want something particular from God. It might be for a future job or role they have in mind. Or other hopes they have for their life or just a general thing.

Tell them that whatever it is they can bring their futures to God. Just write it down; in doing this they can see what they are particularly asking God for.

Get them to fold the paper up, with only their names showing and put the bits of paper in the middle of the room as a prayer asking God for their hearts desire. Put a bit of PVA glue on each bit of paper. Read Psalm 37:1-6 (re-read verse 4). Remind them that our relationship with God is a two way thing - we give our lives to him, including our hopes and dreams, and God will sprinkle the dust of his vision for your future on top. Sprinkle some glitter on top of the pile of paper.

As you sprinkle the glitter tell them that just like we can't tell exactly how the glitter will fall, so things may not always work out the way we plan, but God's plan is the better plan and we must trust that he knows what he's doing.

Have a couple of people pray asking God to shape our hopes and to speak to us in his time about what he wants to do with our lives. At the end (once the glue has dried) return the bits of paper to each person.

Teaching (15 Minutes)
Turn to Genesis 16:1-16. Here we pick up in the middle of a story about Abraham. God had promised him twice that he would be the father of a great nation, but he and his wife could not have kids. READ Genesis 16:1-16.

Q – Have a look at the start of the story, how were things going for Abram and Sarai? (Not so good, they wanted children, but couldn't produce any.)

Q – What did Sarai do and why do you think she suggested it? (She was obviously desperate to have a family, but as she couldn't have any, she thought the next best thing would be for her servant to have one for her; like a surrogate mother)

So because of Sarai and Abram's decision, Hagar as the slave/servant had to become the surrogate mother for their child. And so after Abram and Hagar sleep together, Hagar has a bun in the oven.

Q – How does this affect Hagar? (She gets a bit over confident and begins to treat Sarai badly, because she knows she is important as she is carrying their baby. In those days you were seen as having God's blessing if you had loads of kids).

Q – What was Sarai's response to Hagar? (Is to be mean to Hagar and Sarai has more power over her).

It's so easy when disagreements can develop into a bit of a war. And every time you see that person you give them evil looks, say something nasty, or ignore them.

Q - Anyone had this happen to them? (Discuss how it feels to be in this sort of situation).

It's at times like these when you need extra help, as we can see with Hagar living with that day in day out is really difficult to cope with. And with life being too much, she runs away.

Q – We read in Genesis 12 that Abram and Co. had come from Egypt. What Nationality was Hagar? So where was she running to? (She was going back to her original home. She was so distressed, she wasn't planning on coming back. So if there's any moment in her life that she needs God its now).

Q – Some people think that God only shows himself to important people. What does this angel appearance to Hagar (who is just a slave girl) tell us about God? (He is a God who sees us. And we don't have to be an important person for him to have a special plan for our future. He is omnipresent, with all of us at the same time. He hears our thoughts, feels our feelings and sees where we're at).

Q - Now that Hagar was pregnant with Abram's child, what new hopes does Hagar have for her life? (That she would have a significant role and that her life would now have more meaning from now on).

Q - However Sarai was causing her trouble. How did this affect Hagar's view of her own future? (She would have thought it was all hopeless. Her child would be taken away and she feared that she would be cast aside as a "nobody").

Q – So it had all gone pear-shaped for Hagar, she was upset and confused and ran away. Why do you think God let this happen? Do you think God was late in sorting out her difficulties? (God was actually waiting for her where they met).

Q - What does this tell us when we go through hard times and nothing seems to be getting better? (That God has a time that is right to sort out our difficulties. Without these hardships Hagar would never have ended up facing God).

Have you ever waited for a bus and worried that it was going to be late and got all stressed, and then it has arrived and you've been on time? Sometimes we can get like that about God thinking he's not going to answer, but God's answers are always on time.

Q – Do you think we mistakenly think like Hagar sometimes, that we aren't worth it to God? What reasons might we have for thinking that way? (Sometimes we tend to assume that God isn't interested in us and that he is far busier with other things; but actually, he sees us, and knows all about us and our hopes and dreams for the future).

Q – When have you met God or had a thought and afterwards realised it was God speaking to you? (Tell us about it).

Q – Did Hagar have to do anything to receive this blessing? (Yes she had to return to Sarai and Abram, even if it meant enduring some more hassle).

So Hagar was greatly encouraged. She knew now that God saw her where she was at, and he also knew her hopes for the future and included them in his plans.

Q - Does this encourage you about your hopes and dreams? How? (That God knows them and what they mean to us! He also knows where we are in the journey towards those things. He will shape them to turn out for our good).

Round up (2 minutes)
This is a life changing story where God takes a slave girl, someone whose life was not expected to go anywhere except to be a servant for life. But God had a divine appointment for her where she would be honoured. Sometimes we can wonder where God is and think that God doesn't care, but actually his timing is always perfect.

He is the God who sees us and knows what we hope for our future. We can trust him with our hopes and know that he is for us and that his plans involve our hopes and dreams and are ones that will be just right for us.

19) Sarah & God's Impossible Promise

Ice Breaker 1 – Chinese drawings (5 Minutes)
Tell the youngsters that they are going to be asked to do a drawing of something. I will tell the person on my left what to draw. They will draw it and show it to the next person. They will then do one for the next person and so on, until we get round the group. After the first drawing has been drawn a few times, I will give the person to my left another drawing to draw. When the pics get to the end, the person on my right will have a try at guessing what was originally drawn. (Pic ideas: hammer, cup, pineapple, laptop, first aid kit).

Introduction (2 Minutes)
So much has happened since Abram leaving home. Last week we heard about Abram's mistake when he and Sarai made Hagar their surrogate mother. This wasn't the way God wanted his promise of a child to be fulfilled, as we find out today.

Teaching (30 Minutes)
READ Genesis 17 & 18 1-16

Q – What does God promise Abram and Sarah, and when? (A baby, this time next year).

Q – How old was Abram when he left home? (75 years old).

Q – So how long was the wait for a son? (25 years).

Q – What has changed in the bit we read? (Their names).

Q – Can you try and pronounce the bit that has been added? (In the Hebrew it is pronounced "Kh." It's almost like the breath of God, as if God is breathing his life in to them).

Q – What difference does this make to the meaning of Abram and Sarai's names? (It adds the dimension of being a father and a mother of many).

Q - How does God describe himself v1? (God Almighty. The Hebrew word for this is El meaning God, El Shaddai, meaning God, the nourisher of his people).

Q – Why does God call himself this? (It describes an aspect of his character. That he lovingly cares for us. That he won't ever change his ways, to him a name means something, it tells us about the person).

Q – How do Abram and Sarai respond when they hear the news that in a year's time Sarai will have a baby? (They laugh. Kh Kh Kh ha ha ha. It's like God is breathing his joy and life not just into their names, but also into their lives).

Q – Why do you think they laughed? Do you think Abram and Sarai laughed for different reasons? (Abram laughed out of amazement/joy. Whereas did Sarai think it was a joke?)

Q – So now we'll call him Abraham! What plan did God have for Abraham's descendants v7? (That he would be the God of Abraham's descendants and that they would be his people).

Q – What did God want from mankind then and what does he want from us today? (God wanted to be in relationship with mankind. To have a people who would be called his own and who would worship him as the God that he is. It's the same today).

So God Almighty who made the sun, moon, stars, the galaxy, Earth, everything… this great big God wants to talk to us and be involved in our lives. And if you think about it, we're pretty insignificant in comparison to God, yet he is still interested in our lives and the difficulties we face along the way. Do you believe it? If you do, it'll make the world of difference to your life. Even though we're insignificant in comparison to God Almighty, he sees it as part of his job to provide nourishment for us.

Q – Verse 11 This is the first instance we see of circumcision. What's circumcision all about? (It's a medical procedure done on the foreskin of a man or boy's genitals. The significance of it was for Jewish people to know they were God's people, set apart according to the agreement, or covenant between God and Abraham).

Q – Who had to be circumcised? (Every male)

Q – Do we still have to do this in today's world as God's people? (No).

Q – Why not? (When Jesus came, things changed. What things changed??)

The old agreement or covenant made with Abraham and future generations with its rituals and requirements was done away with when Jesus died on the cross. Do you remember when he died and the curtain in the temple was torn in two?? (Mark 15:33-38).

In the Old Testament, the priest had to go into the temple, and through to the Holy of Holies, which was curtained off by a giant curtain that was (3 inches thick) Here he would make a sacrifice, a goat or bull, a pigeon or dove. This was how they obtained peace with God in the old covenant.

However, when the curtain was torn in two, it signified the fact that the old covenant or agreement that brought people to God was being replaced with a new covenant.

Now by believing in Jesus and receiving him into our lives we can come to God and be forgiven. In the old covenant they had to be circumcised to show they belonged to God and sacrifice animals to have peace with God.   But when Jesus died that curtain was torn in two, to show that Jesus' death was our sacrifice to replace the old agreement between us and God with a new agreement. So we don't need circumcision anymore!

Q – But here we see the start of Abraham's agreement with God. God had promised Abraham that his descendants would become a great nation. As we've discussed before, this was an amazing promise since his wife was unable to have a baby. God even gives them the name of their future son…? (Isaac, which means… "laugh").

Q – How many times does God tell Abraham that "in a year's time his wife will have a baby?" (Two)

Q – Who told him the second time? (The Lord, an angel? Or Jesus?)

Q – How do you think Abraham would have felt hearing this a second time? (He would have felt more confident that God had said it and that he hadn't just imagined it. It would have been like a confirmation of God's word to him).

Round Up (5 Minutes)
Sometimes when God speaks to us he will make sure we know it's him by saying it through different ways and confirming what he's said. Like Abraham you may have a feeling God is saying something to you, for example that he really wants you to learn the guitar or something. Then, if a friend or someone you know also says the same stuff to you (without knowing), it could be an indication that God wants you to take notice that it's him who said it. If that is the case, you ought to get on with it!

God wants to direct us for the future and it may well be the case that God has given you an ability that he wants you to develop. Maybe it will be of significance for your career or future life.

Today we have seen that God had plans for Abram and Sarai's future that involved them putting their trust in him to breathe into them his life and create inside of Sarai their future hopes and dreams. God confirmed these dreams to Abram and made him laugh at the excitement of what lay ahead.

Prayer (As long as it takes!)

20) Abraham - Deal or no Deal?

Icebreaker 1 – Bartering with Skittles
Give everyone ten Skittles or sweets each, making sure that everyone has a good mix of colours. The aim of the game is to get ten sweets of the same colour as each other by swapping with other people. If you have a prize for the first person who gets ten sweets of the same colour, it introduces an interesting dynamic; people will want to get the colour they need without helping others to get the colour they need! Watch out for some good bargaining going on. And of course they can eat the sweets once the game is over.

Introduction
Sometimes if you want something from your parents, they can take some persuading. Imagine you're out shopping and you'd like a new top, a cool poster, trainers or whatever. So you ask if you can have it and your parents are like "well I don't know." And you can see that they are going to take some persuading.

So you might try to do them a deal... You have no money, but you're not afraid to work for it. You'll do washing up for a week, you'll take the dog for a walk, wash the dog, you'll agree to be shown how the washing machine works (or where it is located).

In addition you might try to convince them that it's coming round to winter, and you need something to keep you warm and how the top would go well with other layers (keeping winter bugs away). You might say that if you get the poster it will help you to take more pride in your room, and so helping you to keep it tidier. You might explain how you are really enjoying your place in the school football team and that it keeps you fit and healthy, so trainers are a small price to pay for good health!

Basically you try to get them to agree to spend the money and get the item for you by persuasion.

Q - Tell us about a time when you did that and what you had to do in return.

Q - What about God? Do you think we could persuade God to do something, by promising to do something for him? (Discuss)

Teaching (25 Minutes)
READ Genesis 18:17-33

Q – Who was the Lord talking to when he asked the question? (Remember from last week? See the beginning of chapter 18. He asked the three angels who had just visited Abraham and were on their way to Sodom).

Q - Why do you think God asked them the question? (Discuss. Was it really a question? Did he expect an answer?)

Q - What did God say about Abraham and his children? (They would be a great race and a powerful nation and would be a blessing to all nations).

Q - Why had God chosen Abraham in particular for this job? (God knew that he could trust Abraham to teach his children to live God's way and be fair).

Q - What had God heard about the people of Sodom and Gomorrah? (He had heard many complaints about how evil they were).

Q - What was God going to do about it? (He was going to go down into the city and see for himself).

Q – Are there any lessons we can learn from God's way of dealing with the gossip he had heard? (Discuss. Consider whether we just accept what we have heard or whether we find out for ourselves the truth).

So Abraham approaches God and asks God what he was going to do about the place of Sodom and Gomorrah.

Q - Why did Abraham care about those people? After all they were evil? (Abraham cared for the good people of that city and his Nephew Lot and family lived down that way).

Q - How does Abraham begin his approach to God? Was he demanding? (He appealed for a reason and asked if God would do the right thing. Discuss this approach to God and consider how we approach him when we want to ask for something).

Q - Abraham began by asking if there were 50 good people would God save the city. How did God answer? (God agreed that if 50 good people could be found he would save the whole city because of them).

Q - Remember the scenario where you're in the shop trying to persuade your folks to get you something. How does it make you feel when they don't say "no" straight away? Maybe they begin to discuss the details of your little deal (eg. so you will wear layers when it gets cold??) (Discuss)

Now that God had agreed if there were 50 good people he wouldn't destroy the city, do you think it made Abraham feel bolder to ask for more? (Discuss. It always makes us feel good if we think we've been listened to, so Abraham persisted).

Q - How do you think you would have acted in this situation? How do we respond to answered prayer, does it make us bolder? (Discuss how we respond when God answers in a positive way).

Q - What happened as God continued to grant Abraham's wishes? (Abraham continued to ask for more and more, becoming more daring).

Q - Why do you think Abraham persisted in this way, what was his point, what was he trying to achieve? (Discuss. Was he just trying to push to see how far he could go or was there a real point in what he was doing?).

Q - How persistent are you in your prayers? Would you be bold enough to challenge God in this way? Do you think it is right to pray in this way? Does God bless such persistence?

Q – Have you ever given up praying for something?

Q – So Abraham stopped asking his questions. What happened next? (God left and Abraham went home).

Q - What are the characteristics of Abraham's intercession? (He was bold [18:23] he pleaded [18:24] he argued [18:25] he was humble [18:27] and he persevered [18:32])

Round up (5 minutes)
As we can see here that prayer can be a conversation. If you went to your parents and asked "Can I have a computer tablet for Christmas" they may take some notice. But if you never mentioned it again they may think you weren't serious.

However if you talked it over with them and told them how the tablet would be useful to you, that it was the thing you wanted more than anything else, and that you have seen an affordable version that is compatible with your current computer setup, they may take you more seriously, it's been thought through.

Jesus said we should pray and not give up (Luke 18). And persistent praying is just this. It's not repeating "Dad can I have an iPad" over and over again, it is the other way, it's in conversation, using persuasion, thinking it through, talking it through

Today we have seen Abraham trying to do a deal with God, he interceded for the people of Sodom and Gomorrah; appealing to God not to destroy the whole city if a few righteous people could be found. His prayers took on the characteristics of all great intercessors, boldness, pleading, argument, humility and perseverance. Do we pray for people in this way, do we care enough? Or more importantly do we believe that God answers such prayers? If we pray only half-heartedly, then can we really expect God to take us seriously?

Prayer (As long as it takes!)

21) Lot escapes with his life

Icebreaker - This is my friend (5minutes)
Begin the game with people clapping twice (in unison), and patting their knees twice. Clap clap, pat pat, clap clap, pat pat. During the claps someone must say their name, and then someone else's name, whilst being in time with the rhythm of the clapping. So on the first pair of claps say their name, then after the knee pats on the second pair of claps say someone else's name. That person then must say their name in time and then someone else's - on claps not pats.

Introduction (2 Minutes)
Last week we read about how when Abraham prayed it was like buying something down the market (he tried to haggle with God). Can you remember what the deal was? And we discovered that sometimes praying about stuff means we have to persevere and "intercede" almost to persuade God to help us receive what we ask for.

Discussion (8 Minutes)
Can you think of any computer games where you can do whatever you want? (Grand Theft Auto, the Sims etc.)

Q - What sort of bad things can you do in these games? (Shoot people, run innocent people over, punch people, go out with people, pick up street ladies, go to dodgy clubs etc.)

Q - Do you think it is ok when playing these games to do the bad things? Even though it's only a computer game. Do you think it affects us in any way as people? (Discuss)

Q - So obviously we wouldn't do these things in real life. Discuss what the difference is between doing them in a game and doing them in real life?

In real life there are laws which need to be obeyed (ie. not committing criminal offences, and common decency) therefore this means we need boundaries or rules in living, so that we don't harm others, or wreck society. However when people don't live with the same set of principles, it makes the world a horrible place to live in. The people of Sodom weren't playing a computer game, they were living by their own rules and doing evil stuff.

Teaching (30 Minutes)
Read Genesis 19:1-29

Q – Where is Lot when the angels arrive? (At the city gate in Sodom).

Q – So why were the angels there? (Genesis 18:21 said that God had heard the complaints about the evil people and that he would go down and check it out for himself).

Q – Does Lot realise who they are? (No he probably didn't, but as strangers to Sodom, he bows to them, showing his respect for them).

Q - So Lot meets the 2 angels. Where do they suggest to stay and why? (The city square. Why? 1) To check out the city, 2) It could be to test to see if Lot cares for them).

Q - Why does he beg them not to spend the night in the city square? (The people of Sodom were evil, and Lot wanted to protect them as he knew they would be in danger).

Q – If the place was so dangerous, why do you think Lot was living there? (Going back to Gen 13:8 Lot chose the valley near Sodom, because of the lush vegetation and landscape of the area).

Q – Why do you think he continued to live there, since there were not even 10 good people in the city, surely it couldn't have been a good place to live? (Discuss)

Q – So the men of the town knock on Lot's door. What do these verses tell us about the people of Sodom? (That their deeds were evil. They were violent, they wanted to rape people, and they didn't care about others, basically evil.)

Q – So all of the men of the town wanted to have sexual relations with Lot's male visitors, why does Lot offer his daughters instead? (He was trying to indicate that homosexual sex is against the creator's instructions, so he offers his daughters to show that relationships should be with the opposite sex).

Q – So is it wrong to be gay? (Discuss. Some people have sexual feelings for people of the same sex. It isn't wrong to feel like this. However, according to the Bible to act on those feelings and have sexual relations with someone of the same sex is wrong (Romans 1:21-27). Ultimately it is for God to judge on that one and we have to love people without condemnation. Is it wrong to have feelings? Just because we feel a certain way doesn't always mean it is right to act. A married man having loving feelings for a woman who isn't his wife wouldn't be right to begin a relationship with her. In fact Jesus said that to even think about doing that is wrong doing before God).

As young people your bodies go through changes and as you develop through adolescence your hormones and feelings fluctuate. This can be a confusing time understanding who you are. So if you find you may have feelings for someone of the same sex, this is not necessarily an indication that you are gay, but simply that your body is developing into adulthood. So to decide you are gay during your teens is not something you have to do. It may just be a developmental phase you are going through.

The media often pressures us to make decisions about things that we aren't ready for yet. It is wise to consider that time can really clarify things about who we are.

Q – So once Lot discovers that Sodom is going to be destroyed, what does he do next? (He tells his future sons-in-law).

Q – Why do you think Lot's sons-in-law reacted like they did? (Discuss)

Q – Do you think people believe the whole judgement thing today? (Many people believe God is a God of love, which he is. Yet they don't see the other side of him; a holy God, who is all good and pure and hates evil).

Q – Do you think God will come again in judgement? (READ Matthew 10:11-16. When Jesus was sending out his disciples to tell the gospel, he spoke of a judgment day to come...)

Q – So does Lot leave immediately? (No).

Q - It says in verse 16 "But Lot delayed." Why do you think he delayed? (It seems that Lot got attached where he had lived).

Q – Who else seemed attached to Sodom? (Lot's wife).

Q – The angels commanded Lot and his family not to look back, How do you think living in Sodom had affected Lot's wife? (Being in the environment of the people of Sodom and their evil ways had influenced Lot's family. Lot's wife was chosen to be saved on the condition that she didn't look back. For her to take one last look for memories sake proved that she still didn't want to leave).

Q – READ verse 27-29. What changes does this have to the landscape? (The place became a land of burning waste of salt and sulphur, nothing planted, nothing sprouting, no vegetation growing on it Deuteronomy 29:33).

The area of Sodom and Gomorrah cannot be located on a normal map. It is actually located in the same area where the Dead Sea is. The Dead Sea was not a part of the landscape before this event. Archaeological evidence suggests that around 2000BC a catastrophe took place, possibly an earthquake. This area is the only place on earth where you can find pure monoclinic sulphur in a round ball, which suggests the truth of Biblical version of events. The destruction caused by God's judgement changed the landscape forever.

Round Up (5 Minutes)
Today we have seen that through Lot's involvement with the people of Sodom he and his family were adversely affected and put in danger. We saw an example of what the people were like and how evil they were. It seems very strange that Lot would live there, yet as they left, Lot's wife was still attached to the place.

Lot escapes with his life, but loses almost everything. The place that once looked lush with vegetation was now a barren wasteland, the result of some bad choices.

Prayer (As long as it takes!)

22) Abraham takes his exams

Chinese Whispers (5 minutes)
Start at one end and get the youth to whisper the following. "I ate a banana in the garden it was sub-zero, I was such a hero," and "She saw a red lorry and a yellow lorry on the beach beside the sea." And see what it comes out like.

Introduction (1 minute)
At the age of 75 Abraham had been in the middle of a slightly confusing situation. He and his wife were old and couldn't have children. And into their situation God spoke and said that their descendants would number like the sand on the sea shore. Miraculously God did what he promised and Sarah gave birth to a son Isaac.

This week Abraham again finds himself in a confusing situation, where God asks him to do something which seems to be the opposite of what God had promised him. Testing often helps what we have learned. It stays with us as an important memory. Today we're going to see how it affects Abraham...

Teaching (20 minutes)
Genesis 22:1-19

Q – How many sons did Abraham and Sarah have? (One. Isaac. One son of the promise, but there was also the arrangement where Hagar became a surrogate mother bearing baby Ishmael).

Q - What did God ask Abraham to do? (Take Isaac to the land of Moriah and offer him as a sacrifice to God).

Q - How important do you think Isaac was to Abraham? What was special about Isaac? (He was very important, since Isaac was his only son. He had been promised to Abraham by God and he had waited 25 years for this to happen. Isaac was now growing up and was probably a youth around 12 years old).

Q - How do you think Abraham would have felt having to kill Isaac? (He'd wanted a son for so long, and now he had his wish. He obviously loved his son. Besides the trauma of having to inflict pain and kill Isaac, this also would mean Abraham would have no descendants as God had promised).

Discussion (15 minutes)
Q - Tell us about exams - run us through everything you have to do to prepare for an exam. Before and on the day...

- You need a plan what you are going to study and when to do it.
- Need to understand your subject.
- Have to study the right things.
- Revise again and again re-reading stuff, highlighting, spider charts etc.
- You must know your timetable of exams.
- Get up and be ready in plenty of time.
- Eat a banana to help your brain work (brain food).
- Catch the right bus and do some last minute study on the bus
- Be in the right room at the right time

All this is all before sitting down to take the test. Basically if you want pass well you have to be ready. And if you don't prepare well, you might end up writing an answer like this...

This is a real answer in an exam question. See if you can spot the mistakes, "Ancient Egypt was inhabited by mummies and they all wrote in hydraulics. They lived in the Sarah Dessert and travelled by Camelot. The climate of the Sarah is such that the inhabitants have to live elsewhere."

Q - Why are exams useful?
Exams form a big part of the way teachers and others can find out what you know about your subject, and what level of expertise you have in say... Geography. And it's also a great way of finding out if you have really learned and understood anything!

So here Abraham was faced with the greatest test of his life, an exam from God. Would he do what God asked? Would he trust that God had a plan? Or would he work a way around having to kill his son? This exam would certainly show what his level of commitment to God was. In all ways the stakes are very high.

Q - Why then does God have to test us?

Testing
Christians sometimes go through exam-like testing, where we are met with a situation that challenges us to trust God, even when our circumstances are telling us that God isn't going to help us. It benefits us by enabling us to become stronger (to carry more) and tougher (to withstand more).

Personal Testimony (5 minutes)
Share a time when you personally went through a time of testing.
Ever failed the module but passed the exam? God is there to help us through times of testing. He doesn't leave us all to do it ourselves.

Abraham was faced with the choice of his son or God. Abraham's test was that he was being asked to give up his only son in order to show his obedience to God. Isaac was his most treasured possession, his own dear son.

Q - There's a verse in Luke 12:34 that says "For where your treasure is, there your heart will be also." What do you think that means? (Some things in life we want so much that they become more important to us than God. When that happens our soul begins to worship this other thing rather than God himself.)

Q – Can you think of a situation where you might feel a challenge from God, where God asks "Is this person more important than me??" (Perhaps you might begin dating someone and in your interest for them, you have forgotten God. Obviously God wouldn't ask you to kill them!).

Q – How do you think you would do in a test like that? (Discuss).

Q - What do verses 7 and 8 tell us about Abraham's faith? (He was still trusting in God's promise that he would have many descendants. He didn't quite know how God was going to save his son, but he knew he would return back down the mountain with Isaac.

Q - Imagine you were Isaac, carrying this wood up the mountain with your dad. How would you feel? (Discuss)

Q - Now imagine you are being tied to the altar, what would you be feeling then? (It's like um... what's going on, I thought we were going to use an animal as a sacrifice; you said something about a Lamb? This is rather unexpected... ok this is no longer funny.)

Q - Tell us how it pans out. (Just as Abraham is about to kill his son, God gets an angel to go "stop!" and he provides and alternative sacrifice instead.)

Q - Verse 14 is one of the most amazing promises in the Bible, yet a lot of people never even notice it. What does it mean? (It means that whenever we go through the tests of our lives, God will give us what we need).

Q - What will happen if we trust God and believe him when we go through times of testing? (It means that whenever we face the tests of our lives, when we trust God for the solution, HE WILL PROVIDE WHATEVER WE NEED).

Type of Christ (If time allows)
Q - This is a true story. It also reminds us of another story in the New Testament. Any ideas? (It tells us about God who was willing to give his Son for us as a sacrifice.)

Round Up (5 Minutes)
So Abraham takes his exams. Tests are never easy. They challenge us and can be really tough going. We can cry out in the pain, "This is too much!!" Tests are hard and can stretch us to the limits of our character; that is the nature of them. Just because things are difficult it doesn't make them wrong. When we're in the middle of the situation we don't always see the end in sight. Stepping into the unknown and doing what God is telling us to do is faith. It is passing the test. One day you will look back and see what God was doing, even if at the time it is confusing.

In Abraham's confusion God had given him Isaac. God wanted to see if Abraham was willing to give him back, or whether Isaac had become more important to him than God. In the challenge Abraham trusted that whatever God would do, he would keep to his promise and maybe God would even raise Isaac from the dead? However it doesn't come to that. God provides for Abraham. He also promises to provide for his people who trust him during the examination.

Prayer (As long as it takes!)

23) Eliezer is given a mission

Discussion (5 Minutes)
Today we are going to look at Isaac's love life and how he finds a date.

Q – Where's the best place to find a date? (School ball/event, the playground, clubbing?)

Q – Many people think that going to a night club is the place to find their future partner. Is this a good idea? (Discuss how issues like: physical attraction, what too much alcohol might do, etc might have a bearing on the consequences of a long term relationship)

Q – What criteria do you think is important when fancying someone? (Looks, body, personality, similar interests, same nationality or faith etc.)

Q – What's the best way to communicate if you fancy someone? (These are not recommendations, but you might want to discuss these options: Valentines card/present, text them – maybe warn them about the risks of this, email them, flirt with them, call them, tell a friend and get them to ask).

So today we are going to see how Isaac meets his future wife and how God was involved in the process.

Teaching 1 (10 Minutes)
Read Genesis 24:1-11

Q – So what's this whole thing about the servant putting his hand under Abraham's leg? (When they made a promise, to show how serious it was, they had to touch the other person's leg. This demonstrated that they would keep the promise. Nowadays we just shake hands on it or sign a contract).

Q – Why does Abraham commit Eliezer to make this promise? (v3 He doesn't want Isaac to marry a Canaanite woman, but Hebrew woman).

Q - Why is it so important to Abraham that Isaac doesn't marry a Canaanite woman? (The Canaanite people followed other gods, and Abraham wanted Isaac to follow the LORD God Almighty).

**Q – Was Abraham just being prejudiced (that he just didn't like Canaanite people), or do you think he had a good reason for

wanting a Hebrew woman for his son? What might that be?
(Abraham knew that if Isaac married a Canaanite woman she would take him away from the LORD and worship other gods, who were idols and not real gods. See 1 Kings 11:1-8)

Q – What things that a non-Christian person might do that can cause a Christian person to go downhill spiritually (or lose faith)? (Discuss)

Q – Read 2 Corinthians 6:14 how does this relate to dating and marriage between Christians and non-Christians? (When one of you is not a Christian, they will be pulling in a different direction from you. Certain interests that non-Christians don't have a problem with may leave a Christian feeling compelled to join in because they are dating that person. Even a strong Christian may find it difficult over time).

Q – So today, should Christians go out/marry non-Christians? (Discuss).

Some people say "What if the person they go out with becomes a Christian?" This is a possibility, there are some who have become Christians this way, yet equally there are some who have lost their faith or divorced because of the difficulties this has caused. We cannot expect people will change, but have to accept people as they are when it comes to marriage. The Bible gives a warning to keep us from this kind of hurt and shows us the best way to live. If we decide to go against what the Bible says, we risk it all turning out pear shaped. However God wants the very best for us and has instructed us for our good.

Abraham as a father wanted the best for his son. And his future happiness warranted this important promise with Eliezer.

Teaching 2 (10 Minutes)
Read Genesis 24:12-32

Q – How does Eliezer go about finding Isaac a fiancée? (He goes to Abraham's homeland to find a Hebrew woman as instructed. Then he prays and asks God to show him the right woman).

Q – What was the sign that showed Eliezer that the woman was the right one for Isaac? (He would ask for some water, she would give him water, but also be generous and ask if he wanted water for his camels to drink).

Q – Does God answer with this sign? (Yes)

Q – Can we expect God to show us the person he wants us to go out with? (Discuss. Yes in the bit we read we see Eliezer praying and asking God to help him. God answers him and we can expect God to do the same for us. Yet when we do ask God we need to wait for the right person and allow God to direct us in his own way, and obey what he shows us.)

Q – How does he treat Rebekah? (He gives her respect. He checks her out carefully so as to honour the promise made to Abraham).

Q – What does Eliezer do to seal the deal? (He gives her some gifts in gold).

Q – So he has just given the gold away, how do you think he knew she was the right person? (Sometimes we don't have the exact picture of what that person is going to be like and we have to go by faith, trusting that God has shown us. Her response to him was very positive. If she had not been so, she would have been the wrong person).

READ Genesis 24:32-51

Round Up (5 Minutes)
Today we have seen how God was interested in Isaac's love life, and how he is also interested in our futures too. Abraham's promise with Eliezer meant that he would be directed to the most suitable choice for Isaac. God tested Eliezer to see if he was up to the challenge of finding the right woman for Isaac. He followed Ab's instructions and prayed to God for guidance, but was the marriage successful? We'll find out next week...

Prayer (As long as it takes!)

24) Isaac and a double miracle

Icebreaker (5 Minutes)
If you've ever been at a wedding, or seen one on EastEnders or something, you may well be familiar with the words of a traditional wedding.

The man will say... "I David, take you Victoria, to be my wedded wife. To have and to hold..."

(Can anyone complete the sentence correctly?? Give them a chance to recite it. If they are wrong, just tell them they are wrong, but not where they were wrong and give someone else a try. Once someone has recited the whole thing correctly go to the introduction).

"...from this day forward, for better, for worse, for richer, for poorer, in sickness and in health, to love and to cherish 'till death do us part."

Introduction (5 Minutes)
Last time we looked at the whole "love at first sight" thing that Isaac and Rebekah experienced with each other. If you remember, Isaac was Abraham's son (whose wife Sarah couldn't have children). Ab was the guy who rescued Lot and who prayed for the people of Sodom and Gomorrah. Before Ab, was Noah (who built the ark because of the flood) and before him was Cain (who killed Abel) whose parents were Adam and Eve.

Anyway, Isaac and Rebekah got married, and this is where we pick up the story...

Teaching (20 Minutes)
READ Genesis 25:19-26

So Isaac and Rebekah are married, a really exciting time where two people start the rest of their lives together.

Q – How did things initially turn out for Isaac and Rebekah?
(They came across a problem. Rebekah wasn't able to have children).

Sometimes we think that when we get married, we will live happily ever after with no problems anymore. We expect to have normal healthy bodies and things like that, but it can't always be guaranteed. In our modern day wedding vows, the husband and wife promise themselves to each other and although we don't want to think of bad stuff happening, we are prepared to keep going whether sick or healthy, in good times and bad. At times this can be really difficult.

Q - What does Isaac do to get them through this? (He prays for his wife).

Q – Do you think he prayed just once and it happened? (No. It took about 19 years for Rebekah to get pregnant).

Q – How do we know that it took about 19 years? (Verse 20 says that Isaac was 40 years old when he married Rebekah, and verse 26 that Rebekah gave birth when he was 60).

Q - The word in Hebrew used for when Isaac "prayed" is "agonised." How does this reflect Isaac's desire to have a son or daughter? (It showed it was so important to them both to have children that he prayed intensely from the heart).

Q – What's the difference between praying regular prayers and the way Isaac prayed? (Discuss)

Q – Has there ever been a time when you have really prayed to God like really desperately? Do you think God answers these types of prayers more? (Discuss)

At times life can be really, really difficult; some of you have experienced this. When we come to depend on God for the outcome, we can feel safe that it will be for the best. This doesn't mean just praying for "whatever may be may be," but rather praying that God would step in and change the natural outcome of things. God is a powerful God who changes things.

Q - Do you remember the promise given to Isaac's dad? What was it?? (Genesis 22:15-18).

Q - How was this now significant to Isaac? (Isaac was part of the promise. He was the only son Abraham had with Sarah, and as a result was also going to have descendants. His name also sounded like "he laughed" a great reminder of how his dad responded when told he would have a child. There was hope for Isaac too!).

Q – So after some time, how did God answer Isaac's prayer? (Rebekah became pregnant with twins. A double blessing!)

Q – It's always exciting to feel the baby kick, but for Rebekah, things were a little out of the ordinary. How does she act? (She goes to ask God for the reasons why all the struggling??).

Q – Have you ever gone to God with something you didn't understand that was happening in your life? (Discuss)

Q – What can you do to hear God speak to you?

If you've ever tried to listen to God, you'll know that he speaks in different ways. Sometimes it's simply a case of working out how he is speaking. Often he will speak during your prayer time where you feel inspired. That might be by a verse you have read or a picture that comes to mind when you are praying which communicates with picture language an encouragement for you. Whatever will happen he wants to give you his peace to reassure you that he hears and that he is there.

READ Philippians 4v8

As you begin to think on Jesus and things to do with God, the Holy Spirit will take a hold of your thoughts and then speak to you. Don't just read it the Bible, but think it through too and write down what inspires you!

Q – So God gave Rebekah insight into what was going on. How did God say he would bless them?? (Their children would be leaders of 2 nations. Just think, giving birth to two Donald Trumps! Wow two for the price of one!)

Round Up (5 Minutes)
This story spans 20 years. Often when we read about people's lives in the bible we assume it all happened in quick succession. At times the stories recount stuff that happen in the space of a week and other times it's a lot longer. Isaac's love for his wife spurred him on to pray until he agonised over their childlessness before God. God heard and answered with two sons of great nations. Sometimes when we go through difficult times whilst depending on God through it all, it can be that God also has great blessing lined up for us in the future too.

Prayer (As long as it takes!)
So prayer is powerful. What can we pray for you this week??

25) Jacob – The Long Con

Ice Breaker – Who am I? (5 Minutes)
Get someone to volunteer to think of a famous person. They must then answer questions as if they were that person, with either a "yes" or "no." The rest of the group have 10 questions to ask and at the end of the 10 questions, have to guess who that person is impersonating. Eg. "Are you a man or a woman?" or "Are you on the telly?" "A film star?" "Musician?" Each question can only receive a "Yes" or a "No" answer.

Introduction (2 Minutes)
This next story we're going find out about, is when the boys Jacob and Esau have grown up. If you've ever done a trade with your brother or sister, or with a friend, you will know the importance of doing a deal and honouring your part of the bargain.

With this story there's a start a middle and an end; unsurprisingly. We've got a bit to read, but it's just like an episode of the old TV series "Hustle." Jacob is after something money can't buy, a birth right. Jacob was younger than Esau by just a few minutes (remember the birth last week?). This meant that Jacob being the younger one wasn't in line for the perks that went with being the eldest son of a Hebrew household. As I say there's a bit to read, but you're going to want to know how this baby turns out... well he's not a baby any more...

Teaching (40 Minutes)
READ Genesis Gen 25:27-34. Then READ Gen 27:1-41 in characters. Allocate someone to narrate, an Isaac, a Jacob, an Esau, and a Rebekah).

The Con – part 1 (Genesis 27:6-34, Genesis 26:12-13)
Q – Back to the start of the story, what was it that caused all this trouble in the first place? (The soup. Esau had been hunting and was well hungry).

Q - If you've been hungry after a game of footy and needing food you'll know the feeling. Can you describe this? (Feel weak, lactic acid in legs – like jelly, needing energy, sweaty, starving and grumpy).

Q – If you was this hungry and your brother had just come back from KFC with a chicken tower meal with an apple pie and large Pepsi, and large fries. The food smells great. Mmm... Dinner isn't due for over an hour. There's nothing in the fridge and you

have no money. Would you then trade the food for your favourite PS4 game or designer top?** (Discuss).

Q – What was the birth right? (The oldest son received everything the father owned).

Q – How much do you think the birth right was worth at the time? (At the time Isaac wasn't majorly rich or anything. So probably just to be in charge of the household when Isaac died).

Q – So Jacob is cooking when Esau got back. Do you think Jacob pre-planned to trade for Esau's birth right? (Discuss. Bearing in mind what Jacob's name means "trickster," and the fact that he came up with the idea immediately indicates some forethought).

Q – So Esau had been out hunting. Do you think his hunting trip had been successful? (Probably not, as it seems there wasn't an immediate alternative to eat).

Q – Look at verse 32, do you think Esau was actually going to die? (No, he may have been exaggerating; like we do "I'm starving!" a drink of water would have kept him going).

Q – So did Esau value his birth right? What was his attitude towards it? (No. He didn't negotiate with Jacob; "Tell ya what, I'll swap it for a pair of sandals." Esau readily gave it up, like it didn't mean anything to him).

Q – Over the years how does Isaac's money situation go? (He gets rich, which means Jacob will get rich when Isaac pops his clogs).

The Con – part 2 - Genesis 27:1-41
Q – So Isaac is now very old and frail. He's ready to give the blessing. Instead of giving a blessing, what do modern day parents prepare before they die? (A will and testament).

Q - Who does Isaac think has the birth right? (He thinks Esau still has it, being the oldest. No-one has told him of the transaction).

So Esau hasn't come clean about the "soup-gate" incident. Although many years have passed since he gave away his birth right, now the time is nearing for Isaac's death. Suddenly it means a lot more to him.

Q – What does this tell you about Esau's attitude? (He was someone who lived for the moment, rather than considering the long-term implications of his actions).

Q – How does Jacob's attitude contrast to the attitude of Esau? (More than anything, his attitude was directed towards being a part of God's plan. He's looking to the future and a life of blessing).

Q – So who comes up the idea of conning Isaac for Esau's blessing? (Rebekah).

Q – Was this blessing rightfully Jacob's? (God had promised Rebekah that Esau would serve Jacob and Esau had given up the right to the blessing; yet Isaac didn't know this as Esau was his favourite son).

Q – Did Jacob just want honour? Or was he after the family riches too? (Jacob recognised that he was also a son of God's promise just like his ancestors Abraham and Isaac. He wanted to be a part of this exciting plan God had for him. Esau on the other hand didn't have same regard for God's plan as his brother. READ Heb 12:16-17).

Q – So Jacob gets his father's blessing. Are these just words or something more significant? (The blessing was more significant than just words. It was like he was foretelling (or prophesying) God's plan which God had guaranteed would happen. God would honour these words because Jacob valued them, unlike Esau).

Q – How does Esau respond when he finds out? (He throws a wobbly, and tells his dad about the deal. Basically he gets what he deserved; he cries when he realises what he's lost).

Round Up (5 Minutes)
What we have learned today is about the value of God's gifts to us. God's blessings and plan for our lives are really important, and we should seek after and value these highly. If we are fixed on just getting blessings in the form of money, food, gadgets or other things; that is what we will probably end up with. Yet God has got so much more for us when we choose to become a part of his plan and want more of what he has for us. Jesus said, "The thing you should want the most is God's kingdom and doing what God wants. Then all these other things you need will be given to you." Matt 6:33

Prayer

26) Jacob Takes up Wrestling

Icebreaker 1
I packed up my saddle bag and in it I put... (5 Minutes)
Jacob set out with his family and servants and all his possessions to go back to Canaan. What do you think he packed? We'll play a round or two (depending on time) of "I packed my saddle bag and in it I put ...." With each person adding an item as it goes round and everyone remembering everything that has already been packed, in the right order.

An example of this would be, "I packed my saddle bag and in it I put: a wool blanket."

"I packed my saddlebag and in it I put: a wool blanket and a toothbrush,"

"I packed my saddlebag and in it I put: a wool blanket, a toothbrush and my teddy bear," etc.

Introduction (5 Minutes)
Last week we looked at "The Long Con" and we saw Jacob conning his brother Esau out of both his birth right and their dad's blessing. Now there was nothing for Esau. Effectively although he was the younger son, Jacob had God's favour originally reserved for the older son. As you can imagine Esau wasn't best chuffed with this and would have killed Jacob if he could have got his hands on him. So with his mother's help Jacob escapes and goes off to live with his uncle Laban.

Today's story takes place some 20 years later; but not 20 easy, quiet years. No Jacob has worked hard, been conned into marrying the wrong woman, you have to read it!! So Jacob ends up with 2 wives.

Meanwhile, things have not been good on the domestic front. Leah (the unattractive wife of Jacob) has given birth to lots of children, but Rachel has not been able to have any children. Eventually, with the help of a servant, Jacob has a massive family. Leah has six sons, her servant two sons, Rachel's servant has two and eventually Rachel has a son (Joseph) and later on another one.

So the scene is set. They're on their way home to face Esau. Jacob is scared, but God has told him it's time to go. They are nearly there; they'll meet up with Esau the next day. But what will 20 years have done for Esau's rage?

Teaching (30 Minutes)
So here we are, after 20 years away from the land of Canaan, Jacob is on his way home. The one thing he fears is the displeasure of Esau. He sends messengers on ahead to say he is coming. Then, however Jacob learns that Esau is coming to meet him, with 400 men! Jacob is scared out of his mind and calls out to God to help him...

READ Genesis 32:22-32

Q – Why do you think Jacob got up in the night and packed his wife, servants and children off across the ford at Jabbok? (Possibly to protect them. If they are separate from Jacob, then maybe they won't be attacked).

Q – What else did he send over the stream and why? (Discuss. He sent all his possessions. So he was absolutely on his own. Again, less chance of being attacked).

Q – What happened when Jacob was left alone? (A man appeared, who wrestled with him).

Q – How odd was that, for a guy to suddenly appear from nowhere and start a wrestling match with him for no reason? What do you think Jacob thought about it? (Maybe he was just taken by surprise and then didn't have time to think; maybe to begin with he thought it was someone sent by Esau).

Q – How long did they wrestle for? (Still wrestling at daybreak, no-one winning, a tiring night!).

Q – What did the stranger have to do win? Was he playing fair? (Discuss. He pushed Jacob's hip out of joint.)

Q – Why did the man want to go? What was significant about daybreak? (It was morning; they had been wrestling all night, daybreak meant it would be light and Jacob would see his face).

Q – What did Jacob want before he would let the man go? (He wanted a blessing from him).

Q – What happened and what was the significance of it? (The man asked Jacob his name and then said he would be called Israel from then on because he had struggled with God and men and overcome. The new name represented a new beginning for Jacob).

Q – What was the outcome? (Jacob got his blessing).

Q – Do you think we can talk to God in such a way, that it could compare with wrestling? (Persistent prayer, where we don't give up. At times it might seem difficult, long and a struggle, until there is that moment of breakthrough - like the wrestle).

Q – What did Jacob do when he had received his blessing and the man had gone? (He built an altar and called the place Peniel).

Q – What did that mean and what was the significance? (It meant he had seen the face of God and lived. They believed if they saw God's face they would die, so this was an amazing thing).

Q – What was Jacob's legacy from this event? (He had a limp to remind him of this occasion for the rest of his life).

Q – So, good story, but what can we learn from it? Is there a truth we can learn from it; is there a promise; is there a lesson for us? (Discuss. Think about how God talks to us; how we know what he wants for us. Some things don't always come to us in an easy package. Jacob was motivated by the reward; a blessing from God. Through this hard, tiring and painful time, God was with Jacob. Jacob was brought to a place of helplessness and sometimes we too have to be brought to that place before God can bless us).

Q – Jacob's name was changed. He changed from being a deceiver to being "A Prince with God." Can God change us? (Sometimes people put labels on us. However God is able to refine our characters, in order that the good parts of our character shine through. Our desire should be to become the person God wants us to be and if we allow him, he will change us and our attitudes to become the person he wants us to be).

Q – How do you think God changes us? (Through circumstances and through prayer).

Q – How can we cope when things seem too difficult, or we feel too weak? (Look at 2 Corinthians 12:9-10 to see what Paul says. God gives us the strength we need, we just have to depend on him and let him work through us).

Round Up (5 Minutes)
Well, Jacob had quite a life; changing from deceiver to a prince with God. We have seen him conning others and being conned by his uncle, but here we have seen that before God he can do nothing, except let God change him into a new man. God wants us to be centred on him and not be centred on ourselves. It's sad isn't it that in order to

overcome our self-centredness, God sometimes has to not only wrestle with us, but show us our weaknesses. We need to learn that the key to spiritual power lies not in our strength, but in our weakness.

Prayer (5 minutes)
Have you prayed for something and not felt that an answer has been forthcoming? (Sometimes God does answer "Yes," "No," or "Wait"). If you haven't had a peace about something that you have been bringing to God, maybe it is time to persist with those unanswered prayers?

Don't give up until the answer comes!

Get the youngsters to write a note to themselves with the Bible verse references for today to read later on at home. Also have them write down anything they feel they may need to ask God for and to persist in prayer before God.

27) Jacob and his bro call a truce

Introduction (5 Minutes)
Last week we saw how Jacob would not let God go till God blessed him. In an unusual wrestle with God, Jacob struggled and kept persisting with God till he got the blessing he wanted.

Pairs with Skittles (10 Minutes)
Using around 16 plastic cups place pairs of coloured Skittles under each cup. Whatever pair of colours you place under one cup, make sure that you have an identical pair under another cup. Then youngsters must turn over one cup, and then another cup. If the pair under one cup is identical to the pair under another cup, then that person gets to eat those Skittles. If the pair doesn't match they replace the cup and it is the next person's turn.

Teaching (40 Minutes)
Over a period of time, memories of past events fade somewhat; a bit like Chinese whispers. Years before Esau was so angry at Jacob, he wanted to kill him. All this was because Jacob stole his brother's blessing by tricking their old dad into thinking he was his hairy rug of a son Esau. Now they are about to meet again and time can be a good healer. Jacob has already sent a message to Esau with a gift. Esau was coming with 400 men.

READ Genesis 33:1-20

Q – Jacob separated his kids among his wives who followed him. Have a look at verses 1 and 2. Discuss why he did this. (Jacob was making sure that if Esau was going to attack he had an escape plan for some of them).

Q – What do you think Jacob meant by all the bowing down to Esau? (Since Jacob was the holder of the birth right, according to custom Jacob was the superior. Here he was showing a humble attitude towards Esau. And his family were doing the same).

Q – How did Esau's actions show his changed feelings towards Jacob? (The running and hugging thing showed that he'd accepted Jacob's apology).

Q – Esau offered help to Jacob, why didn't he take it? (Things had changed in Jacob's attitude; his name had changed to Israel. He no longer felt the need to trick others or even take from his brother).

Q – It had been over 20 years since the brothers had seen each other because of the intense dispute that had arisen following Jacob's dastardly dealings. 20 years is long time that they have missed out together. Think of all the hurt feelings and regret both would have had over that time. Do you think it was worth leaving things unresolved for so long? (Discuss)

Q – Is it okay that we get angry with others? (Yes, but doing it in a way that doesn't hurt others is important).

Q – When we read about other people's disputes, they can appear silly and we wonder how it's taken them so long to forgive each other. However, when it happens to us it's a different story. How are arguments that involve us different? (Discuss. A possible scenario could be when a friend stole your boy/girlfriend).

Q – Why do we find it so hard to forgive? (The person has hurt us and we think we are right and the other person should pay).

Q – So how do we tend to punish people we don't forgive? (We might start a fight, or be in a mood with them and have a bad attitude towards them. This is called bitterness).

Q – How does bitterness affect us? (Bitterness makes us angry inside, we hold a grudge and generally become grumpy. It does us no good at all, and actually makes what the person did to us much worse).

Q – List the things that Esau had to forgive Jacob for... (Tricked him out of his birth right, stole his blessing, ran away, and wasn't sorry to start with).

Q - Do you think it was easy for Esau to forgive Jacob? (Jacob had taken everything from Esau and left him with nothing. He had taken his status, his father's blessing; pretty much everything of significance. So it must have been painful to put that all behind him).

Q – Are there any people in your life that you currently are finding it hard to forgive? (Have a think. This is practical stuff that affects our lives).

Q – Do you think you will forgive them one day? (It's worth doing it sooner rather than later. Think of the time that passes by. You may as well do it now) READ Matthew 18:21-35.

Q – Does this mean we then have to be best buddies again straight away? (It may take time to build up the relationship again, but forgiveness starts immediately).

Round Up (5 Minutes)
So Jacob was changed. As a result his relationships began to change too. Sometimes we can be a big part of our own problem. When we change our attitudes, our problems also resolve quicker. It takes character to swallow our pride and forgive someone who has done us wrong, but in the long term it makes us stronger and healthier people.

What exactly do we have to do to forgive someone? Do we have to forget what they did to us? Some things are very hard to forget. Forgiveness is not about forgetting the wrong. Forgiveness is refusing to have hard feelings against that person any more. When we forgive, we are not saying what happened didn't matter; but rather that even though it happened, we choose not hold it against that person any more. We release our feelings of hate and everything else negative up to God. And we ask God to forgive that person too.

This is not an easy thing, yet we will find out next week what the side effects are when we hold on to negative feelings.

Prayer (As long as it takes!)

28) Jacob! Joseph his son

Icebreaker 1 – Happy families with a difference (10 Minutes)
Have a pack of "Happy Families" cards. Give one card out to each person. They must not show this card to anyone. Get them all to stand up and move around, and without talking they must find other members of the family on that card. For example Mr. Bun must try and communicate using his hands to other members of the group to find Mrs. Bun and the others. Once they have found their family, they can sit down.

Introduction (5 Minutes)
Last week we learned about forgiveness. We talked about Jacob going home to the land of Canaan and meeting up with his brother Esau after 20 years. Jacob had expected Esau to still be angry with him after all that he'd done to him, but Esau had forgiven him and was pleased to see his brother again after all that time. It's good to be reminded of how important it is to forgive others when they hurt and upset us; bearing a grudge does us no good whatsoever. We're now moving on again a few years; the family has settled back into Canaan and we now find Joseph, Jacob's youngest son at this time, as a teenager.

Teaching (30 Minutes)
READ Genesis chapter 37:1-36

Q –Joseph was living at home with his family, what sort of work was he doing? (Like his brothers, he looked after the flocks for his father).

Q – Was Joseph a good brother, and if not why not? (He was righteous. He was just a good guy, unlike many of his brothers. Unfortunately Joseph was annoying. He was maybe even more unpopular when he opened his mouth).

Q – Have you ever noticed that some people that you come into contact with seem to be into more negative stuff than you? It might be depressing music, horror films, unhealthy things they are into online? How does it feel hanging around with people like this? (Discuss)

Q - Why did Jacob love Joseph more than his other sons? (He was born when Jacob was old, but also he was the son of Jacob's favourite wife, Rachel.)

Q - How did Jacob show that he loved Joseph more than the other sons? (He made Joseph a special robe with long sleeves).

Q - How do Joseph's brothers respond to Joseph when they see this favouritism taking place? (They were jealous and hated him and couldn't speak politely to him. It made for bad family relationships).

Q – Is it right for parents to have favourites? How would you feel if it was happening to you? How would you react? (Discuss. It's easy to wrongly conclude that your folks have favourites. It's best not to assume anything!).

Q - What did Joseph do that made matters even worse? Should he have bothered telling his brothers about it? Are there times when it's better to keep things to yourself? (Joseph had a dream which implied that his brothers would bow down to him one day. Telling his brothers made the situation much worse. Perhaps there are times when it's better just to keep our mouths shut. Discuss).

Q - Having had a poor reaction to his first dream, what about his second dream? What happened in this dream to make things even worse? (The second dream included his parents bowing down to him and only made his brothers more jealous.)

Q - Even though Jacob reprimanded Joseph, did he dismiss the dream completely? (No, he thought about it and wondered what it could mean).

Dreams
When you hear something from God, it's important to know if this is private (just for you), public (for others to be encouraged by), or corporate (for a group of people). It's okay to tell others about your dreams, just in the right place. In some settings, people may be sceptical and make fun of you and others won't understand. Other times you may have a friend interested enough to hear more. Knowing people and trusting them is important.

Q – Has anyone had a dream lately that seemed to be telling you something? (Spend time chatting about anything people share. It's important that any interpretation is based on more than just people saying "I think it means this." What is the general gist of the storyline in the dream and what do they key elements/objects or situations of the dream represent?).

Q – So Jacob sends his sons off to herd the flocks. He then asks Joseph to go and see if they were okay. Do you think Joseph is maybe becoming his dad's spy? (Discuss.)

Q - What happened when Joseph got to the place where his brothers were supposed to be? (They aren't there, so Joseph asks a man where they have gone and is told they have moved on to Dothan. So Joseph goes down to Dothan and finds his brothers there).

Q – Joseph's brothers recognise him as he is coming towards them. Were they pleased to see him? What was the plan they begin to hatch? (They weren't at all pleased to see him coming towards them and decide that it will be good to kill him and throw his body into a well. They planned to tell their father that he had been killed by wild animal).

Q - Did all of the brothers want to kill Joseph? (No, Reuben wanted to just put him down a well).

Q - Why was Reuben anxious for them just to throw him into the well? (He thought that he would be able to come back and save his brother and send him back to his father without the others knowing).

Q - What did the boys do to Joseph before they threw him into the well? (They took off his special robe which his father had made him).

Q - What happened while the brothers were having their lunch? What did they decide to do as a consequence of this? (They saw a group of Ishmaelites travelling toward Egypt and Judah. They suggested selling Joseph to these travellers and then they wouldn't be guilty of killing their brother. After all he was their flesh and blood.)

Ironically it was Joseph's dreams that caused the start of all of this!

Q - Did the other brothers think Judah's idea was good? How much did they get for selling Joseph? (Yes, they got 20 pieces of silver for him).

Q - Who was sold for 30 pieces of silver? Are there any similarities in the stories? (Jesus was sold by Judas for 30 pieces of silver. There are definite similarities in the stories and Joseph is often seen as a forerunner of Jesus).

Q - Reuben obviously wasn't there when they sold Joseph, what happened when he came back and found that Joseph was no longer in the well? (He was devastated, he tore his clothes and went to ask his brothers what had happened).

Q - What did the brothers do to make Joseph's disappearance seem convincing to their father? (They killed a goat and dipped Joseph's coat in blood so that their father would think that he had been killed by a wild animal. They pretended that they had found Joseph's coat).

Q - How did Jacob react to the news? Do you think they then would have regretted their actions when they saw how devastated Jacob was? (Jacob was heartbroken he tore his clothes and was inconsolable no matter how his sons and daughters tried to comfort him. He said he would be sad about Joseph until he died and he cried for his lost son. The boys must have felt guilty when they saw how badly their father took the news. All actions have consequences. We need to think about it and consider the possible consequences before we do anything. We also need to consider how our actions will affect others).

Q - What happened to Joseph when he arrived in Egypt? (He was sold to Potiphar, who worked for the king of Egypt).

Q - Do you think Joseph deserved what he got? Do you think Joseph was to blame for what happened? (Discuss).

Round Up (5 Minutes)
Joseph knew right from wrong and lived it out. Unfortunately he had some growing up to do as he was a bit annoying. He dropped his brothers in it by reporting their evil deeds and then made it worse by bragging about the dreams that he had from God. Not a way to make yourself very popular! With his dad Jacob showing obvious favouritism toward Joseph it is understandable why his brothers did not like him and could not say anything good about him.

However, this does not make it right to plot any harm against someone! They were just keen to get Joseph out of their hair and selling him seemed a good idea at the time. Not only would they rid themselves of their father's favourite child, but they also got some money into the bargain.

Yet they didn't think of the consequences of their actions. They were shocked at how Jacob reacted when he thought Joseph had been killed by a wild animal. He was never the same again. To make matters worse they were unable to do anything that would console him. They had done the deed and they had to live with the consequences. They could not undo it.

It is not, and cannot ever be right, for a parent to have a favourite child and to show that to other children. Yet this was the atmosphere that the brothers lived in.

What can we learn from this? Sometimes our actions can have very unintended results. On the one hand you have Jacob's favouritism, which showed up in the brother's hearts as jealousy. Joseph was the second youngest of the brothers and each of them felt they did not compare to him in their father's eyes. They were jealous of their father's love. This jealousy of Joseph turned to them feeling rejected by their father. Joseph enjoyed his father's favouritism and possibly believed he was superior to his brothers. This produced an atmosphere where Joseph was hated and he wasn't doing a great job improving the situation by being his dad's spy.

When things like fear, jealousy, and rejection start to make a home in our hearts, we then become vulnerable to the devil beginning to work in us. It may start with thoughts, but always ends in deeds. Maybe this will show up in rebellious actions against our parents, addictions or other things that will steal the joy of life from us.

Jesus gives us the antidote to protect us from this evil ever taking hold of us. This antidote is called forgiveness. People will act in a way that will hurt us. The devil will put lies in our minds to try to lead us into fear so that he can bring harm to our lives and those we love.

Is it time to forgive someone in your family for things you feel they have done or said? Don't let the enemy get a foothold in your life.

Prayer (As long as it takes!)

29) Joseph is wrongly accused

Icebreaker 1 – Cheat (5 Minutes)
If you've ever been falsely accused you'll be able to relate to today's talk. How does it feel to be wrongly accused? Normally it's not a nice experience, but here's a game you'll enjoy...

Play a quick 5 minute game of cheat – using playing cards.
Basically the aim of the game is to get rid of all of your cards. One player starts by announcing for example that they are putting down three 7s. These cards are placed face down in the middle, so no-one can see what they are.

If someone doesn't believe they have put down what they have announced, they can say "cheat." If the player has not cheated the accuser must pick up the entire pack of cards in the middle. However, if the player who put the cards down has cheated, that person must pick up the cards.

When a card is laid down (eg. 7), you can also put down other cards of that value (7), or a card one value below it (6) or one value above it (8).

The winner is the first person to get rid of all their cards. This game can go on, so you may need to stop it at an appropriate point.

Icebreaker 2 – Count to 21 (3 minutes)
The aim of this game is to count out loud as a group to 21. Any person can say a number, but if two or more people speak at the same time you have to start from 1 again. See if you can get to 21 without people interrupting each other!

Introduction (5 Minutes)
Last week we saw Joseph getting a rough deal, being sold into slavery by his brothers. Today we see where Joseph ends up...

Teaching (40 Minutes)
Read Genesis chapter 39:1-23c

Q – So where exactly does Joseph end up? (He is taken to Egypt where he is sold by the Ishmaelites to Potiphar).

Q – What Job did Potiphar do? (He was Captain of the Palace guard)

Q – Was Potiphar an important man? (If he was working today in London, he would probably be the Chief of Police at Buckingham Palace).

Q – What did Potiphar think of Joseph? (He saw that God was with him. Things were very successful when Joseph was around).

Q – How do you rate Joseph's attitude at this point? Imagine you had to be a slave or had to do a job you really hated. What can we learn from the way Joseph goes about his work? (Even though Joseph was a slave, he tried to work hard and to the best of his ability, with God helping him to do a really good job).

Q – Things were going so well, what ended up being Potiphar's only concern? (Verse 6 Everything was so well run, all Potiphar needed to concern himself with was this: When was dinner time???!!)

Q – Have a look at the story. Is there anything to indicate the passing of time? *Hint: Is Joseph still a boy?* (The end of verse 6 tells us Joseph was now well built and handsome. Time had passed an he was growing up)

Q – Who begins to notice Joseph? (Mrs. Potiphar)

Q – Do you think Joseph was tempted by Potiphar's wife? (Discuss. Joseph may not have fancied her, or there may have been some attraction. But basically he was a bloke and she was a woman, and it's not too difficult to understand that she may have been difficult for him to resist).

Q – How does he deal with her at first? (At first he doesn't notice her, so when she propositions him it's a bit of a surprise. He then explains how he must be responsible, since his master trusts him)

Q – Why does she go on at him? (Because she thinks she can get Joseph to give in to her advances. Also because he is only a slave, she feels it is okay to harass him).

Q – What subtle plan does she use in verse 10 to attract Joseph to her? (She talks to him every day, to befriend him and build a relationship with her through conversation).

Q – What further steps did Joseph take to avoid further temptations? (He refuses to even talk to her as friends. Sometimes when temptation comes our way through relationships, the only thing we can do is to set boundaries. If we find we are tempted when alone together with a certain person, it is better to spend more time in groups. Think ahead so you won't be tempted in the first place. A lack of wisdom in this area can bring disaster!).

Q – Next we see them all alone and Potiphar's wife tries to seduce Joseph. How does he respond? (He runs away, leaving his coat behind).

Q – Running out the door seems a bit extreme, or maybe not. Why do you think Joseph does that? (He probably felt that if he stayed he might do something he'd regret. Also if he went to his own room she may have followed him, so he ran outside).

Temptation can be a difficult thing to resist. We're faced with 2 choices. In some situations giving in to temptation is the easy short-term option. God wants us to resist temptation in order that he can protect us from the problems that arise through giving in.

Q – What would have happened if Joseph had given in and slept with Mrs. Potiphar? (He would have dishonoured Mr. Potiphar's marriage. Mrs. Potiphar would still continue to harass Joseph. Would he then have to give in again? More chance of Joseph being caught too! That would mean certain execution. But ultimately he would have dishonoured God and his future wife to be).

So Joseph made the right choice. He got away, yet it cost him his job.

READ 1 Corinthians 10:13. Whenever we are tempted, if we want to make the right choice God will help us to do the right thing. Joseph had the route of escape, which at the time seemed a bit extreme, yet God made the opportunity available to get out. We ought not to complain about the route of escape, even if it might seem a bit silly.

Sometimes we will suffer for telling the truth. But in doing this we honour God and he will reward our obedience.

Q – What lies does Potiphar's wife tell? (She accuses Joseph of attempted rape).

Q – How do you think Joseph felt about the whole situation? (Joseph would have felt let down. As a slave he probably wasn't given the opportunity to give his side of the story, yet he was put in prison)

Q – What can we do when we face injustice like this? (Firstly Joseph was honest and obeyed God, because of this he was also trusted. Potiphar could have had Joseph executed, but instead it seems that he was lenient with him; maybe deep down he believed Joseph).

Q – How do we see Joseph benefiting from being honest and kind later on? (Even in prison he makes friends in high places and gets upgraded to prison officer and becomes successful again).

Q – If we lie a lot, how does this affect our chances when we are accused? (There's a lot less chance of being believed when we are falsely accused. If Joseph had been known as occasionally telling fibs, he may well have not been so highly regarded and been executed; however, his respect for people and his honesty of character with God's help saw him through).

Round Up (5 Minutes)
So far Joseph has not had a very good experience when it comes to his coats; they always seem to be getting him into trouble!!

Yet seriously, no matter what happened to him, his trust of God and integrity of lifestyle made sure he saw no harm. At times we will be mistreated, tempted, mistrusted and falsely accused. These are all part of life. Yet if we follow Jesus, believing in him and living a life of honesty and kindness to others, we will certainly be rewarded.

Prayer (As long as it takes!)

30) Joseph's Opportunity

Icebreaker – Rock, Paper, Scissors Champions (6 minutes)
Get youngsters into pairs to play "Rock, paper, scissors." Maybe get pairs to play the best of 3. Whoever wins goes through to play the other winners of that round until you have your finalists. You can announce them like they are champion boxers, play their entry music using their smart phone, feel free to do a pre-match interview with each player. They can play the best of 5 and give a small prize to the winner.

Discussion starter 1 – Weather Symbols (10 minutes)
Get the youngsters to draw a weather symbol to communicate how they are feeling today. Sunny relates to feeling happy, a thundercloud relates to feeling upset and cross (etc.). Get people to show you what they have drawn (if they are happy to) and ask how what they have drawn symbolises their feelings.

Discussion Starter 2 – Dreams (5 Minutes)
Has anyone had any memorable dreams this week? Maybe they've had recurring dreams or nightmares? Do they just forget their dreams or are there any that stand out? Do you think God still speak to us in dreams today? Discuss for a few minutes. Share any dream experiences you've had.

Introduction (1 Minute)
Do you remember where we got to in story of Joseph last week? He was sold by his brothers and taken to Egypt. Mrs. Potiphar took a shine to him and tried to seduce him when Mr. Potiphar wasn't there. Joseph did the honourable thing and ran away, however Potiphar believed his wife and had Joseph put into prison. But he didn't really believe his wife, otherwise he would have had Joseph killed.

Teaching (10 Minutes)
Today our story has moved on a few years. Whilst in prison Joseph had done well and had worked his way into a position where he was helping in the prison and was a favoured prisoner and when two of the Kings officers were put in prison he was able to talk to them. They both had dreams whilst in prison and Joseph was able to interpret their dreams and these interpretations came true. This resulted in the baker being hanged and the cupbearer being restored to his position. And now we move on a further two years.

READ Genesis chapter 41:1-43

Q – What were the dreams that the King had? (He dreamt about seven fat cows and seven thin cows and seven good ears of corn and seven thin ears of corn and how the thin ate the fat).

Q – Do you think these were God given dreams, or just a lively dream that occurred because the king ate a late night pizza with extra cheese? (The dream has a definite story to it. The structure of it appears to have an imagery that needs to be decoded by an interpretation. It's God.)

Q – Can people who aren't followers of God have God given dreams? (Yes. God uses them to point people to him).

Q – How did these dreams affect the King? (He was troubled by them).

Q – What did the King do about it? (He sent for the magicians and wise men in Egypt and asked them what his dreams meant).

Q – Were they able to help him? (No, no one had any idea).

Q – What was the next amazing thing that happened? (The cupbearer remembered his promise to Joseph. He told the king what happened to him years before when the baker was imprisoned).

Q – What did the King do when he heard about Joseph? (He had him fetched from the prison and brought before him – after giving him a new wardrobe, and having him cleaned up and shaved).

Q – Why do you think the King was so quick to call for Joseph? (He was desperate for help and as no one else could help him, anything was worth trying).

Q – How do you think Joseph felt when he was fetched out of prison, cleaned up and taken before the King? (Discuss. Sometimes we can find ourselves in really scary places. These are the times when we have to lean hard on God, but it is our time to shine!)

Q – Have you ever felt like you've been in a scary position, where it is a moment of opportunity, but also that you have to make the most of it? (Eg. Seeing the head teacher about an idea you have).

Q – When the king asked Joseph if he could explain the meaning of his dream, what did Joseph say? (That he couldn't do it, but that God could do it).

Q – Why was this a great attitude to have (that God could do it but he couldn't)? (He was giving God the glory for what was about to happen).

Being put on the spot to do something that you know that you can't do (but that God can do), takes a trust. Trusting for God to step in when there is no other option can be both scary and exciting. Just know that God's strength works best when we are weak and know we can't do it.

Q – When the king had explained his dreams to Joseph, what did Joseph say they meant? (Joseph said that it meant there would be seven years of good harvests followed by seven years of famine and that the two dreams were basically one and the same thing).

Q – Why did Joseph say the king had two dreams that were the same? (He said that this showed God had firmly decided that it would happen).

Q – Did Joseph stop talking once he had explained the dreams? (No, he went on to give the king some advice about how to deal with the famine. He advised him to choose a wise man to gather 1/5 of all the food that was grown during the seven good years and store it to provide food for the seven years of famine).

Q – Why did the king think Joseph's idea was a good one? Why did he think Joseph was the man for the job? (He had no hesitation in following Joseph's advice because what Joseph said rang true in the king's mind. He also saw that Joseph was a man for the job by saying that God's Spirit is truly in him).

Q – How do you think Joseph felt about this? (Discuss. What an enormous change of circumstances, from prisoner to second-in-command of Egypt!)

Q – When Joseph was in his chariot, what did the people walking ahead of him shout? Do you think this struck any chords in his mind? (Bow down; perhaps he remembered his own dreams).

Q – So what can we learn from this passage that is relevant for our lives today? (Discuss. We see Joseph totally trusting God and being willing to speak out boldly in God's name. There will be times in our lives when it is right to speak out boldly, that can be a very scary thing to do, but like Joseph we can do it in the knowledge that Jesus is with us and will give us the right words to say. He will protect us.)

Round Up (5 Minutes)
Joseph is becoming a more likeable young man as his story unfolds. No longer is he a tell-tale and boastful, rather he is a hard worker, faithful, and willing to speak boldly for God. He has become a real example to each one of us.

He didn't wallow in self-pity when things went badly for him. Joseph demonstrated that it is important to do everything with care and honesty. Joseph knew that his duty before God was to be with God (friendship) and through industriousness (hard work) let God work through him. He served to the best of is ability; because the things he did, he did for God. As he proved he could be trusted with running a prison, so God made a way for him to run things in Egypt as a second-in-command to the King.

Did Joseph have a 5 point plan to get where he got? No. He simply had integrity, which meant serving others in a smelly prison. Unlike some people who pick and choose when they will make the effort, when they will honour God, Joseph did it in the worst times and God honoured him with the opportunity for the best of times.

So the challenge for us is this:

Do you only make the effort in the things you enjoy? Some people when they are required to do the rubbish jobs, or study things they aren't interested in, they don't show as much care in what they do.

However we honour God by putting to use our gifts in whatever scenario they are required, we can see that God will reward what we do. He will increase the strength and depth of those abilities that we have and also enable greater opportunities for using those gifts. Life will become an adventure not to miss out on and God will take us to places we never dreamed possible!

Prayer (As long as it takes!)
For wisdom to know what gifts I should use that I am strong in and what abilities that I am weak in that God wants me to develop in. For knowledge to know how to use my gifts when I am faced with different tasks and opportunities each day.

31) Joseph and his big brothers

Icebreakers
Introduce the game "Crime fighter," then once people have got the idea play a simple game of catch using a foam ball and at the same time, just to make it a bit trickier!

Crime Fighter (12 Minutes)
Chose the number of cards needed according to the number of players. Be certain that the Ace of Spades is in the deck. All players draw cards. The player who chooses the Ace of Spades is the criminal.

The criminal recruits other criminals by winking at them. When the criminal catches the eye of someone and winks at them, the person has to wait for a few moments, so as not to give the criminal boss away and then say "I have committed a crime". That person then gives his or her card back and is out of the game.

The object of all other players is to a) not get outed and b) try to identify the criminal boss.

Play continues until the criminal recruits all players without being identified by other players. If a player misidentifies the criminal boss, he is out.

Introduction (5 Minutes)
Last week we see Joseph interpreting the King's dreams, and as a result of Joseph's interpretations he is made ruler over Egypt. Now the dreams come true and famine occurs in the land. It's now Joseph's job to resolve the needs of the people in the famine.

In Canaan, Jacob and family are experiencing famine conditions. So he tells his sons to get off their butts (42:1) to go to Egypt and find some food for the family. However, because Benjamin is Jacob's only son left from Rachel (who died when giving birth to Benjamin), he prevents Ben from going on the trip in case something happens to him.

So Joseph's brothers go to buy grain in Egypt and come to Joseph who is governor and is selling grain. However, the brothers don't recognise him. So Joseph decides to play a few games with them, instead of telling them who he is straight away. First he accuses them of being spies. So in order to prove that they are not spies, he takes Simeon as a hostage and tells them to return with Benjamin (their youngest brother). Joseph then sells them the grain they need. Unbeknownst to the brothers, Joseph secretly gives them back their money.

When the brothers get back to Jacob they tell him what happened and of the governor's demands to bring Jacob's youngest son Benjamin. Jacob is very upset. He doesn't want Benjamin to leave his side as he is so precious to him than anything. Well the brothers go back to Egypt knowing they had to take great care of Benjamin.

Again they return to Joseph bowing down before him. So Joseph invites them for dinner. However, Joseph sets a trap for them. While their sacks were being filled up, he secretly asks his chief servant to place a silver cup in Benjamin's sack. So when the brothers are set to leave on donkeys, Joseph sends his servant to catch up with them to check their luggage. The silver cup is discovered and the brothers are brought before Joseph once more. To the horror of his brothers, Joseph decides that the punishment must be for Benjamin to become his slave. Let's read on what happens next...

Teaching (20 Minutes)
READ Genesis 44:18-34, 45:1-28

Q – What did Joseph want as a result of meeting his brothers again? Was it revenge? Or was it something else? (Discuss. He wanted to be recognised by his brothers and reunited with his dad).

Q – What did this mean to him to see them again? (He was obviously very emotional about the whole situation and seeing his brothers again brought him to loud tears. See 45:1).

Q – Imagine your brother or sister was kidnapped by a travelling circus company and forced to learn how to juggle whilst standing on a giant ball. Obviously this may sound like a great idea to start with, think how you would miss them being around after a few months or so. Do you think this might make you appreciate them more by not seeing them for a long time? (Discuss)

Q – So is it alright to cry? (Discuss. When a situation causes you to be upset or joyful and the tears start to appear; don't fight it. It is so much better not to bottle these things inside, because showing our emotions is a very healthy thing. The hurt and the grief flow out with the tears, as inside we heal up and deal with what's happened).

Q – How easy is it to show our emotions in church? (At times it can feel quite difficult because we're around people we know and feel self-conscious and fear that people may think we have a problem. However when we go away to somewhere like camp or Soul Survivor it seems a lot more easier to do this).

Q - Should it be easier to show our emotions in general life? (Discuss)

Q – How did Joseph's brothers feel when they realised that the governor was Joseph their brother, whom they sold as a slave? (They were very afraid).

Q – Why were his brothers so fearful? (They didn't know Joseph and were afraid that he would use his position of power to take revenge on them).

Q – In Chapter 45, take a look at verses 5-8. How does this show Joseph's perspective on the events of his being sold by his brothers? (He saw the bad stuff that happened as part of God's guidance in order that he could save his brothers and God's people).

Q – How does Joseph show that he still loved his brothers? (He sorts out a change of clothes, wagons for transport, etc. homes and land for them all).

Finally READ Genesis 50:15-21
Q – Now that Jacob has died what are the brothers now concerned about? (That Joseph is still secretly angry and will pay them back evil, now dad has gone).

Q – What is Joseph's response? (He told them not to be afraid. Even though they had planned evil for him (because they were annoyed with him), God had planned that he should save lots of people).

Q – What happens if we say we forgive, but still hold bad feelings against that person? (Bitterness can form inside us on an emotional level and cause us harm on a physical level. It can also block our relationship with God, since God has forgiven us of many things that we have done against him, Matthew 18:21-35).

Round Up (5 Minutes)
We see here that God had engineered plans for Joseph to save his people. Because of the famine they had to leave Canaan, and stay in Egypt. Many years later Moses would come along and rescue them from the nasty Egyptian Pharaoh.

At times when bad things happen to us and we are separated from the people we love, God hasn't abandoned us. Even at times when the circumstances of how we are separated may seem wrong, God can still cause good things to result.

Prayer - Table Tennis Ball Drop (10 minutes)

Have two boxes made up. Have one with a toxic logo on it and the other with a picture of a bird flying high and the word freedom on it. Place a good number of table tennis balls in the toxic box.

Say something like: Maybe you have hard feelings against someone who has done you some harm? Maybe you see them and judge them? It might be time to let go of your hard feelings against them as all they are doing is producing a build-up of toxin inside of you. God wants you to be free, but you have to decide to want to forgive.

Whilst you play a quiet song, give the youngsters an opportunity to think of people they need to forgive. And for each person, to pick up a ball from the toxic box and place it in the freedom box, as an outward sign that they want to forgive that person and need God's help.

32) Moses the Secret Baby

Icebreaker - Splat (7 Minutes)
Have the youngsters stand up and in a circle, with one person standing in the middle. The aim of the game is to last to the end without being splatted. The person in the middle will point to a player in the circle and say "go." The two people standing either side of that person must then try to splat the other by pointing and saying "splat."

The person in between must try to duck in time. If the person ducks before either player says "splat," they are safe. If this happens, whichever player either side is "splatted" first, they are out. However, if the person in the middle doesn't duck before a player points and says "splat," then they are out.

Duel
When you have just two people left, have them stand back to back. Get them both to take two steps forward. Have the person (who was standing in the middle) to stand in between the two. This person must flip a coin catch it and say "go." If the coin says heads they must silently crouch down, if it says tails they remain standing.

On hearing the word "go" the remaining players can choose to turn, point and say "splat," or to not. If they turn and say "splat" and the person is crouching their opponent is splatted and they are the winner. However if they turn to say "splat" and find the person in the middle standing, they get splatted themselves and are out.

Introduction (2 Minutes)
Over the past four sessions we have been looking at the life of Joseph. He's one of the most inspiring characters in the Bible. Although he was not very wise as a boy, he was one of the few people who were able to stay close to God at the peak of success as well as in the middle of trouble.

Even though he was incredibly gifted, he was known for his faithfulness in fame and his ability to forgive his brothers who betrayed him.

Now we are going to move on a hundred years or more in the story of God's people. Remember that they had left Canaan and settled into Egypt and enjoyed the good life while Joseph held high position in the government.

Teaching (25 Minutes)
READ Exodus 1:6-22

Q – After Joseph and his brothers died, what did the Israelites do? (They had lots of children and became very strong in the country. Egypt was filled with them).

Q – Why was the new king afraid? (He didn't know about Joseph and he felt the Israelites were increasing in number and that was threatening to him. He also thought that if there was a war they would join the enemy and escape).

Q – What did he do about it? (He encouraged the people to make life hard for the Israelites and put slave masters over them).

Q – What work did they make the Israelites do? (They had to build cities which were to be supply centres for the king).

Q – Were they effective in controlling the Israelites? (No. They grew in number and spread out).

Q – How did the Egyptians respond to this? (They were afraid and became even meaner to the Israelites. They made them make their own bricks and mortar for the buildings and to work in the fields and they showed no mercy).

Q – Why do you think God allowed this to happen? (They were living under a cruel regime, and it was time for the Hebrews to leave Egypt. God had a plan for them to have their own land. If God had sent a rescuer when everything was fine, they would not want to or know their need of being rescued).

Q – What did the king tell the midwives to do? (Kill all baby boys that were born to the Israelite women. The girls were allowed to live. Why?)

Q – Were the midwives obedient to the king? If not, why not? (They were more afraid of God than the king! So they let the babies live).

Q – What excuse did the midwives give? (They said the women gave birth before they got there).

Q - Here's a question... Was it OK to lie? Exodus 20:16 (However for the saving of lives against an evil dictatorship, it was necessary).

Q - Can you think of any other scenarios where it would be okay to tell a lie in order to save people? (Discuss).

Q – How did God reward the midwives? (They had families of their own).

Q – What was the king's next ploy for reducing the number of Israelites? (He told all the people to put any Hebrew baby boys into the river Nile so that they would drown, but girls could live).

Q – How do you feel the Israelites felt about all this? They were being treated cruelly. Their baby boys were being killed. Do you think they felt that God was protecting them? (Discuss. We're not always saved from going through difficult times, but protected within them, i.e. they continued to grow in number and be stronger even though facing such terrible times).

Persecution
In Indonesia, the government required everyone to carry a card that identifies their religious status. Although the government said it allowed everyone to follow either, Islam, Christianity, Buddhism, or Hinduism, yet Muslims still received preferential treatment.

Since 1996, Muslim extremists have burned down many church buildings in which many Christians have died. In 1997, a mob rioted in Banjarmasin. They set fire to a church and when they left, the people hiding inside came out to extinguish it. The mob came back and set fire to it again, and so the people tried to put it out again. This continued on until the military finally came and assisted them in putting out the fire. The mob was gone though. That same mob targeted another church except this time, the fire got out of control burning down not only 14 churches, but several homes and a large shopping centre. Hundreds of people were trapped inside the centre and died. There have been many more mob attacks on Christian churches since.

READ Exodus 2:1-10
Taking a risk in faith

Q - So what did Moses' family do first of all to protect their child? (They hid him for three months).

Q – Why was it not possible to continue hiding the baby? (Discuss. Did the baby get noisy? Would people begin to notice?)

Q – What did the mother do to try to protect her baby? (She got a basket and covered it in tar and put the baby in the basket among the bulrushes on the River Nile).

Q – Do you think she had a plan? Or was she just hoping? (Discuss. She was willing to do all she could to keep her baby alive, a mother's instinct).

Q – What precaution did she take to further protect her baby? (Her daughter stayed close by so that she could see what was happening).

Scenario
Imagine the country turned against Christianity and any who practised it. Imagine that Christians had to declare their faith when going to a job interview, applying for a loan, or sitting a school exam.

Q – How would that make you feel? (Discuss)

Q – What would the dilemma be when being faced with a form to declare your religious beliefs? (If you don't put down that you are a Christian, you would feel like you are denying Jesus. But if you do put it down, you would be risking your results being prejudiced).

Q – What do you think God would do in such a situation? (God will find a way where there is none. He provides for us).

Back to Moses.

Q – Who came to the river and why? (The daughter of the king of Egypt came to have a bath).

Q – Do you think she did this regularly? Was this why Moses' mother chose this part of the river to put her baby in? (Discuss. Are we all creatures of habit and predictable?)

Q – What did she do when she saw the basket? And how did she react when she saw the baby and he was crying? (She was inquisitive when she saw the basket and send slave girl to fetch it and when she saw the baby growing it melted her heart ... all was going to plan!)

Q – Was that the end of it? Who suddenly appeared? And what was her suggestion? (No there was still more plan to unravel, the baby's sister suddenly appeared and offered to find a Hebrew woman to nurse the baby for her).

Q – The king's daughter agreed, little knowing that the woman who was fetched was actually the baby's mother. What did she

ask the woman to do? (To nurse her own baby and to be paid for it too).

Q – What happened when the child grew older? (His mother took him to the palace and the king's daughter adopted him as her own son).

Q – What did she called him and why? (Moses, because she had pulled him from the water).

Q – How do you think the mother felt? Do you think she ever thought that her son was going to be someone really special or was it just the natural instinct of a mother to look after her child that made her put him in the river? Was it a bonus that she got to bring him up anyway? (Often we will do things without knowing the outcome. But God has a way of making impossible things to happen; things beyond our wildest dreams).

Q - Do you think in our life time in this country we will ever be persecuted for our faith? (Discuss).

Round Up (5 Minutes)
Desperate times call for extraordinary steps of faith. Working within the laws of the land and honouring God in days of persecution can be a fine line to walk. It also calls for God's people to take a stand and not give up under the pressure. God is with us in the pressure, and will find a way.

It's in times like these when people really lean on God in desperation. God is able to make a way where there is none, and turn what some meant for evil into his good.

Prayer (As long as it takes!)

33) Moses murders someone

Icebreaker 1 – Who got shot? (5 minutes)
This game is one where the leader knows the secret and the rest have to guess what it is. The leader points at someone and says "bang you are dead." The leader then asks the whole group, "Who's going to get shot next?" People then get to guess. The more guesses people do the more likely they will figure it out. As the hands go up choose someone to guess. The secret is the first person you ask is the next victim.

Get everyone to put their hands down and then point at the person who guessed and say "bang you are dead," and ask "Who's going to get shot next?" Hopefully someone will eventually point at themselves!

Icebreaker 2 – Black Magic
For this game you will need one person to help you. Tell the youngsters that you have gained mind reading powers over the weekend and can now read their thoughts! Say that you will prove it by leaving the room, and they can select an object in the room and ask the leader to name the object when they return to the room. You will then go back in and name the object.

To do this you select your person as the spokesperson for the group to go through a list of items, by asking "Is it this chair?" or "Is it this clock?" or "Is it this bogey?" or whatever. For each item that it is not the leader will say "No it isn't that."

To guess the correct item, (say for example the item is a blue cup), your spokesperson would then indicate that is the item by pointing to a black item in the room first and asking "Is it...?" (Whatever item has black on it). The NEXT item named will be the item that the group have chosen. The group then has to guess how you are getting the answers correct.

Discussion (8 Minutes)
Show a clip from YouTube of a very old YELLOW PAGES advert: The party - French polishers.

Have you ever done something that you thought was really bad and you didn't know how on earth you were going sort the problem out? (eg. Accidentally knocked over a wedding cake during the speeches after the wedding, or gone up in the loft without permission and accidentally put your foot through the ceiling?)

Q - What did you do?

Q - How did you feel at the time?

Q - What were the consequences that you feared at the time?

Q - What actually happened? (Probably not as bad as you feared?)

Introduction (1 minute)
Last week saw Israelites under stress from the Egyptians. Joseph the guy with the technicoloured coat has died. Moses who was born as an Israelite was at risk when all Hebrew babies were threatened to be killed. Moses was rescued and was brought up in an Egyptian household. However Pharaoh's daughter asked a Hebrew woman to look after him... which turned out to be his mum! She would have taught him about God and Moses would have known who he really was. He was not an Egyptian, but rather a Hebrew!

So Moses would have been about 40 years old at this point in life. The Israelites' suffering would have gone on for over 40 years.

Teaching (30 Minutes)
READ Exodus 2:11-25

Q - What does verse 11 tell us about Moses' lifestyle? ("Visited his people" seemed like he didn't spend much time with Israelites. It almost seems to be a surprise to him "forced to work very hard").

Interestingly Moses would have seen both sides of the situation, being both an Egyptian and knowing his true identity as a Hebrew.

So Moses wanted to do something about the problem the Hebrews had. He had a degree of power since he was from Pharaoh's palace. So he thought he could do something to help, however when he went about things his way, it all went wrong.

Q - Have you ever tried to resolve a conflict between 2 people and ended up involved yourself? (Discuss)

Story of me (3 minutes)
Share a personal story or of one you have read of someone trying to resolve a conflict, but making things a whole lot worse. Sometimes situations like school bullies/gangs get to us, because of the injustice and arrogance of the people involved. But to sort it out on our own, we can end up getting into a mess.

Q - So what happened to Moses? (Pharaoh finds out and tries to kill him. So it's all got a lot worse and Moses gets out of the situation).

Q - What do you think helping his country meant to Moses? (His true identity was as a follower of God and part of God's chosen people).

Q - How does this failure affect Moses? Does he give up altogether? And say right, I don't care anymore. Or is he still determined to stand up for people who are oppressed? (See v17. It's in his blood. We can see something of Moses character and the way God made him. He isn't going to stand by and let people be pushed around).

Q - How easy is it to stand up for what is right in situations like this? (Discuss)

Scenario (5 minutes)
Imagine you are walking down the street with a friend, minding your own business. Then you notice on the other side of the street, five lads set upon this other lad and one is kicking him and pulling and stuff. So you say "Oi, stop that now" and go across the road. They all run off and you check to see if the guy was ok.

Afterwards you may think... "What on earth was I doing?? I could have been hurt." However you see that you have stood up for what is right and walking by just doesn't seem to be an option.

Q - Do you think God looks after those who stand up for justice? (Discuss)

Q - Have you ever prayed for God to protect you in a situation? (Discuss)

Maybe you have to walk places at night. Using common sense is our best defence when finding ourselves in a scary situation. Lifts home, walking with friends you trust, being sober, choosing the safe routes home. All of those are important as well as trusting God to keep us secure!

We see Moses' bravery pays off and he finds a wife. And it says in verse 23 "after a long time - Pharaoh dies. The people of Israel groaned, because they were forced to work very hard. They cried for help and God heard them. God heard their cries and he remembered the agreement he had made with Abraham etc..."

Q - So God remembered? Does God forget? What does this tell us about praying? (Prayer is the way of calling for God to change things. Sometimes God is waiting for our call!)

Q - What was it that God remembered? (His promise to Abraham was that he would be a Father to a nation and his wife would give birth to the nation of Israel).

Q - So do we need to remind God of his promises? (Sometimes we have to persist in prayer, maybe even until we are desperate).

James 5:16 (NIV) Therefore confess your sins to each other and pray for each other so that you may be healed. The prayer of a righteous man is powerful and effective.

Round up (1 minute)
Inside of Moses was this deep desire for justice. But unfortunately in his attempt to make things a lot better, they got a lot worse. And he was left running for his life. But God had put this desire in his heart and there was nothing that could stop it. Maybe Moses felt he had failed in his task.

But God had allowed him to fail. We learn a lot by our mistakes and failures; more than just knowing to not do it again, but also what it produces inside us is a determination, wisdom with the maturity to do things differently. God wasn't finished with Moses yet.

Failure isn't the end of things; it's just part of the journey. Romans 8:28 says "And we know that God causes all things to work together for good to those who love God, to those who are called according to his purpose." Although failure may sometimes seem to be the end of things, and that we've messed it all up. In the cold light of day, it will not stop us from reaching the destination God has for us. So never give up!

Pray

34) Moses the unsure leader

Icebreaker - Big Boss (10 minutes)
Each person is now an employee in a big business and been given a role within the company:

1 Toilet Cleaner
2 Tea Person
3 Post boy/girl
4 General Dogsbody
5 Enquiries Clerk
6 General Office Clerk
7 Team Supervisor
8 AMA (Assistant Manager's Assistant)
9 Assistant Manager
10 PR Consultant
11 General Manager
12 Manager
13 Managing Director
14 Area Director
15 Big Boss

The aim of the game is to obtain a promotion and work your way up in the company, to eventually become the Big Boss. If you are the Big Boss you will have to work hard to keep your job.

The game will depend on how many people you have in the group, so you may have to add or lose roles depending on the number of people. Make sure you have a toilet cleaner and a big boss, as businesses can't function without these two roles.

Make sure the youngsters are in a semi-circular arrangement. Give out a role to each person, starting at one end with the "toilet cleaner." The person next to them should get the "tea person," next the "post boy/girl" etc., until each person has a role better than the previous one and the last person (at the other end) gets the "Big Boss" role. Each person should make visible the piece of paper with their role on it for others to see.

The game starts with the toilet cleaner who will call out their role, "toilet cleaner," then they must call out another role, "general manager." The person with the general manager role must immediately call out their role, and then the role of another person, but not the person who just called them out (in this case not the toilet cleaner). The next person who is called out, must then call out their role and another. So it goes on.

The game stops when someone makes a mistake.
Mistakes are:
1) If someone calls out a role that has just been called out
2) Saying a role incorrectly
3) Pausing or hesitating
4) Taking too long or missing that they have just been called out.

When someone makes a mistake they must stand up, put their piece of paper down on the seat they were sitting on and sit on the seat of the toilet cleaner. That person has been demoted and become the toilet cleaner. The person who is the toilet cleaner is now promoted to become the tea person, they must then take the seat of the tea person. Depending on who has made the mistake, this trend of moving up a role happens until the empty seat of the person who made the mistake is filled.

The game will then continue, starting with the toilet cleaner who then says "toilet cleaner to..." Once you have played a number of rounds, whoever is Big Boss at the end is the winner.

Discussion Starter (10 minutes)
Imagine it is your first day of a new job working for your dad at a large company. Your dad, the Big Boss gets you on the phone for a meeting. In this meeting he tells you that you are very talented and have been promoted to Managing Director of the company. He tells you that the company is in big trouble and that you are to make sweeping changes in order to save the company. Your first job would be to tell the current Managing Director that he is fired. The Managing Director hasn't met you before.

Q – How confident would you feel about going to this man to tell him he's done a poor job and is fired? (Discuss)

Q - What do you say to him to get him to clear out his desk?
(The Big Boss has just given me a job and told me to fire you, so you're fired. By the way he's my dad).

Q – Why is it important to say that the Big Boss has given the order? (He has the authority to hire and fire, because of his position in the company).

Q – What does the Boss's backing give to the words you say?
(The boss will confirm his words. They have to act on the Boss's instructions).

Q – How does the fact that you are the Boss's son/daughter make a difference when you get things done in the company?
(You are the Boss's heir, your close relationship to the boss gives you a unique authority where what you direct in his name is done).

Q – What happens to our words when we follow God's orders?
(We have the backing of heaven, God's army of angels. God's power is with us. The enemy can't stand against our words).

Q - What is the main job or responsibility of the boss or leader?
(The leader sets the focus on what the aim of the company is and leads the people on how to accomplish it).

Teaching (10 minutes)
Exodus 3:1-22, 4:1-17
Q - So Moses was a Hebrew baby, then an Egyptian Prince. What is he now? (A shepherd for his wife's dad).

The period of time that has passed is nearly 80 years from when he was born. Moses was 40 when he ran away from Pharaoh (Acts 7:23) after killing an Egyptian, and now he has 40 more years in Midian.

Q – So God talks to Moses. Why is this incident remarkable?
(Not only does God give Moses a sign, but he also speaks audibly).

Q – This is probably the first time that Moses has heard God speak audibly. Moses is 80 and has been through some difficult times, what with killing the Egyptian and hoping to help the Israelite slaves only to harm their cause. Why do you think that God speaks to him now? (Some people have the idea that God was doing miracles every day in Bible times and that his people were amazing all the time. But this is a new experience for Moses. He needs God to do something memorable to cement his calling).

Q - What do you think the fire symbolised? (God's powerful consuming presence).

Q - Why do you think God told Moses to take off his shoes? (God was showing Moses he should respect God's presence, that God was different from humans. He was teaching him that to come close to God requires a respect for God's awesomeness, his purity, and his power).

Q - Why do you think God introduces himself to Moses as the God of Abraham, Isaac and Jacob? (God is reassuring Moses that he, the God of his ancestors is still living and active today. Just like the Big Boss scenario. He is not unknown. He has not been on holiday).

Q – When he killed the Egyptian, Moses was really keen to lead God's people. With this in mind read 3:10-11. How do you think Moses feels about it now? (He's not so keen).

Q – What does 3:7 encourage you about when you pray? (Not only does God hear, he is concerned and comes to our rescue).

Q – There are 2 sides to this conversation. What is God trying to tell Moses? And what is Moses trying to tell God? (God is giving Moses instructions for his mission "I want you to go do this and that...". Moses is trying to say "Woah, hang on a minute I'm not sure this is going to work... I think you are talking to the wrong person; you're looking for some amazing superhero."

Q – Which side do you relate to more, God or Moses'? Why? (Discuss)

Q – How can doubt about our own abilities stop us from doing the simple things God has asked us to do? (We can end up thinking we can't do it, think twice about it and miss the moment. The truth is we really can't do it and shouldn't even try. It's not up to us. God does the powerful bit, we just have to obey and do what he asks).

Q - So God calls us to do stuff for him when he's ready, rather than when we feel ready. Why does God do this? (It's important for us to go in God's strength and our weakness, rather than trying to rely on our own strength, because it just won't match up to the task).

Q – Do you think leaders are born or made? (Some people can try to be leaders, but just not have what it takes, either in character or in calling. However if God chooses a person, if they are teachable, he can make them into a great leader).

Q – Do you think a leader has an easy job? After all they get to decide what to do, how to do it and who does it? (Discuss).

Round up (5 minutes)
Here God is demonstrating that his presence would be with Moses and that he (The Almighty) has given Moses the message and his power to do miracles. Moses was going with God's full authority to pretty much

tell the Pharaoh that he was fired in his responsibility for the Hebrew people. Although Moses didn't think he could do it, all he had to do was to speak knowing that the rest was up to God. It's important as leaders and people on a mission for God, that we know who we are in God.

We aren't simply employees in a company we are sons and daughters in the business. With this in mind we can go confidently, knowing that we go with God given authority to cause events to happen through a power not our own. Galatians 4:4 tells us we have received the "full rights as sons," being both in God's family, but also as heirs with access to God's supernatural Kingdom resources.

However absent God seemed to be during the slavery of the Hebrews, God still called himself "I AM who I AM." This describes his "Is-ness" which is his presence. In the times when things aren't going so well, it's not a time to fall back from following God, he is still there. His timing is perfect. Why did God choose now and not 40 years before? Chapter 2:23 of Exodus tells us that this was at the time when the King of Egypt had died along with all the other men who wanted to kill Moses. Yahweh, God was going to show them that he is the God who is present.

When there is an increase of God's supernatural power, it is often because he is about to do something. He requires us to be ready whether we feel ready or not.

Pray for those called to be leaders (5 minutes)
Have everyone close their eyes. Then ask those who feel they may be called to become a leader to silently raise their hands. Then pray for them (obviously not making it known who you are praying for!).

35) Moses hits a brick wall

Icebreaker – Guess who?? (10 minutes)
Split the group into two teams. The teams then have to each think of a famous person. The teams have to guess who their opponent's famous person is by asking 20 questions. The first team asks a question and has one guess after that question. Then the second team asks a question with one guess. The winning team is the one that guesses the name of the famous person first.

Then think of another famous person and the second team gets to ask the questions first.

Discussion Starter (5 minutes)
Imagine the scenario. You have a friend who doesn't go to church and she has just found out that she has a serious illness. You tell her that you believe God can heal her and you tell her about other people you know who have been healed. You offer to pray with her (which she is happy to), but no healing takes place.

Q - What do you do? (Discuss)

Q - If you prayed for a person to be healed and they weren't, would that stop you from praying for someone else again? (Discuss)

Q – Would you find it more difficult praying for someone who had a broken leg or someone who was crippled and was permanently in a wheelchair? Or would you find praying for both people the same? (Discuss)

Q – Do we sometimes let our fears stop us from doing things for people? (Discuss)

Q – Would hearing reports about people being recently healed have an effect on whether you might feel confident to pray for people's healing more often? (Discuss)

Teaching (10 minutes)
(Exodus 5:1-23)
We saw in the last few weeks how Moses had this vision to save the slaves but then he went about it in the wrong way, accidentally killing an Egyptian. So he ran away, got married, and became a shepherd. Then God called him. And now he isn't so keen. The vision has faded and he doubts his ability to do anything. After way too much

persuasion, God has convinced Moses to go for it. God has promised to do miracles to back Moses and his message up. So Moses has left Midian and arrives in Egypt to kick some Pharaoh butt.

Q – How does the initial meeting with Pharaoh go? (It goes as expected, with Pharaoh refusing to let God's people go).

Q – Do Moses's actions have a direct effect on the welfare of the people? If so, how does it change things? (He makes things a whole lot worse. The Hebrews have to make bricks, but now they have to locate the straw before they can make the bricks. Also they have to produce the same amount of bricks daily).

Q – How do the Hebrews feel about their new situation? (They are now working in a lot worse conditions. They are upset and resort to blaming and cursing Moses. They accuse him of being deluded and working against God rather than for him).

Q – Verse 20 tells us that Moses and Aaron were waiting for the Israelite foremen after their meeting with Pharaoh. Unfortunately Moses and Aaron don't seem to get a chance to say anything to them before they get cursed by the foremen. What do you think Moses and Aaron were going to say? (They were probably there to find out what happened and to encourage the foremen with what God had told them).

Q – What do you think Moses expected the foremen to say? (He probably expected them to see the potential of what could take place and the important job that Moses and Aaron were doing).

Q - What effect did the words of the foremen have on Moses' outlook? (He has lost his focus on what God has told him would happen. He is discouraged).

Q – What effect can discouragement have on us if we're not careful? (It can make us anxious. It can get us down. It can negatively affect our trust and relationship with God).

Q – Take a look at verse 22-23. From Moses' prayer, what does this say about what Moses expected God to do next? (He expected that after Pharaoh's refusal, God would immediately come with plagues and pestilences).

Q – So Moses has gone for it and it's all gone pear-shaped and now he's in trouble. The Hebrews are upset with him, Pharaoh

is now his powerful enemy and God hasn't shown up. If you were Moses, bearing in mind that he didn't want to go in the first place and didn't know what was going to happen next, how would you be feeling at this point? (Your worst fears have been realised. Moses had been saying that he didn't want to go, not because he thought God would do something powerful, but rather that he feared that God wouldn't).

It's important to trust God even though we might not understand what is going on. Sometimes we hold onto our fears so much that we have to experience those fears before we can step into what God has for us. Sometimes we need to come to the realisation that *we* just can't do it.

Q - Why do you think God would do that? (Moses needed a complete dependence on God).

Q – What does Moses do after the Hebrew people curse him? (He goes back to God and honestly tells God how he feels. Moses is doing exactly what he needs to. We see him going back to God, reliant on him rather than being reliant on Aaron, or his staff that turns into a snake or anything else).

Q – What would Moses have missed out on if he had given up at this point? (God is about to unleash wave after wave of plagues upon Egypt and show many signs and wonders. Just not giving up is the way to getting a breakthrough).

Round up (1 minute)
When we step out in faith for God we are going to face resistance. Once your worst fears have been realised then there is nothing more to fear! You've been there and you survived! It's a very very hard place to be, but sometimes it is necessary to hit rock bottom. Once you face difficulties after that time there is a certain strength that has been added to your character, a trust in God that cannot be shaken. Persevere in what God is calling you to do. He will not fail you. He says do not fear. He knows the end of the story. To finish show some "testimonies" of people who have been physically healed.

Prayer (10 minutes)
Does anyone need healing? Pray and see what happens...

36) Moses experiences signs and wonders

Icebreaker 1 - Egyptian gods question sheet (15 minutes)
Today we're looking at a well-known part of the Bible; Moses Vs Pharaoh. Hand out the Egyptian gods question sheet. Say that today we are looking at a series of events that took place in ancient Egypt. Here are some pictures and carvings of Egyptian gods that went alongside some of their hieroglyphics. Can you fit the correct name and the description of the Egyptian god with the picture below?

Introduction
Last week Moses hit a bit of a brick wall situation. God had told him to request from Pharaoh that he let the people go for 3 days to worship God in the desert. He told Moses that Pharaoh's heart would be hard and that Pharaoh would refuse his request. Unfortunately Pharaoh became angry and forced the Hebrew workers to work much harder. The workers then blamed Moses for their woes. Moses expects God to immediately respond with a show of force. At that moment God is holding back and Moses realises that he has to depend on God more than ever...

Teaching
READ Exodus 7:1-7

Egyptian news reports coming in... (25 minutes)
Over the next 4 chapters something amazing is about to happen. (Rather than reading through the next 4 chapters we are going to split the youngsters into 5 groups to read about just two of the plagues). Have a read and note down anything interesting that you maybe haven't noticed before.

Then in your groups we would like you to compile a short 3 minute news story from BBC news 24 to perform to the rest of the group. Feel free to imagine and report the details... They have 10 minutes!

Team 1) 7:14-24 (Plague of blood) & 7:25 + 8:1-15 (Plague of frogs)

Team 2) 8:16-19 (Plague of gnats) & 8:20-32 (Plague of flies)

Team 3) 9:1-12 (Plague on livestock) & 9:8-12 (Plague of boils)

Team 4) 9:13-35 (Plague of hail) & 10:1-20 (Plague of locusts)

Team 5) 10:21-29 (Plague of darkness) & 11:4-9,12:1-30 (Plague on the firstborn)

Question and Answer sheet (15 minutes)
Referring to the pictures on the Egyptian gods question sheet (and the notes below). Begin to explain how each of the plagues that occurred demonstrated that God (Yahweh) was deliberately showing how the gods the Egyptians trusted in were nothing compared to him. See if the youngsters can pair up the gods on their sheet with the plagues that the Lord used to defeat them.

Blood and Frogs – Exodus 7:14-25 & 8:1-15
The *plague of blood* in the Nile was to show he was more powerful than Khnum the guardian of the Nile and Hapi the spirit of the Nile. They could not prevent God from making their own river stink.

The *plague of frogs* was aimed at Heket water goddess of fertility, who was depicted in the form of a frog. The Egyptians would have gone to this goddess expecting her to do something about this, since this was apparently what she was god over. However the fertility goddess of the frogs had no control to stop them multiplying.

Gnats or lice and flies - Exodus 8:16-32
God made the *plague of lice* come up from the ground, to show how powerless Geb the god of the earth was. He was also husband of the goddess Nut who was goddess of the sky. Thus God was showing he was more powerful than two gods of earth and sky.

It was The Lord God Almighty whom Moses worshipped who made the earth, sky and everything in it. So Khepri the god of creation (with a beetle head) had no power over the insects as God sent the *plague of flies*.

Livestock - Exodus 9:1-7
The *plague on the livestock* was an assault on Apis and Hathor, who took the likeness of a cow and was supposed to provide protection to the Egyptian livestock. However, no livestock belonging to the Hebrews were harmed, showing that the Lord God Almighty was at work. It was time for the Egyptians to stop believing a lie and see who really was God.

Boils – Exodus 9:8-12
The Egyptians depended on the goddess Isis for healing. However when the Egyptians including the magicians were covered in boils, but not the Hebrews, another god whom they looked to was shown to be powerless in comparison to God.

Hail - Exodus 9:13-35
When the hail came from the sky, the Egyptians would have looked to the goddess Nut to save them. But even Pharaoh and his officers would not escape this one. Those God-fearing Egyptians took precautions and saved their slaves and livestock. Those who still couldn't see the powerlessness of their gods suffered the consequences.

Locusts – Exodus 10:1-20
Next the Lord sends in a storm to bring a huge swarm of locusts. The people were powerless to stop such a disaster and so were the gods whom they worshipped to protect the Egyptian crops. Osiris was the god of the underworld and also strangely responsible for crops! And Seth the god of storms and disorder was not causing this and could not stop it from happening.

Darkness – Exodus 10:21-29
Ra the Egyptian Sun god was next being shown up! What good is a sun god if he can't protect his people from the darkness! The darkness remained for 3 days... yet the Hebrew Israelites had light in the places where they lived, showing that unlike Ra, the Lord God Almighty could take care of his own.

The Firstborn – Exodus 11:1-10
Lastly God had to challenge the Pharaoh himself. He was also worshipped by the Egyptians and they believed him to be the son of Ra. The Pharaoh had many opportunities to let the people go and didn't take any of them. However God had to keep proving that he was the Lord and that he would protect his people in a way that the Egyptian gods couldn't do v7 "Then you will know that the Lord makes a distinction between Israel and Egypt."

The Passover - Exodus 12:1-30
For the last plague, the Israelites would have to exercise faith. They were told to kill a lamb and to smear their doorposts with its blood to avoid their firstborn children being killed. The lamb had to be perfect. The life of the lamb would pay for the life of the firstborn child of that household.

God was providing a hint of something that he was prepared to do many years later. One day his own Son would be slaughtered like the lamb was. The blood that was produced when Jesus was killed would become a protection from judgment. Jesus was killed that we could be protected from perishing. To go on to have eternal life, we have to have our lives covered by Jesus' sacrifice. By believing that he bled and died for our protection and promising to follow him will bring us safety from death after judgement. We can be judged not guilty for all of our wrongs because of Jesus.

Round up
At the time of Moses, the Pharaoh of Eqyptians would go to a specific god for help for the provision of the people. He trusted the magicians and priests to communicate with these gods. Were they simply just ornate carvings? Or did they represent something more real in terms of demons and spirits?

It was clear that the magicians were used to supernatural powers that were not from God and they were oppressing the people of the Lord God Almighty. Therefore God acted in power to show the nation of Egypt that they were worshipping idols that could do nothing to stop his power. For every idol that the Egyptians had set up as a god, the Lord God Almighty showed that he was greater.

This would also show the Hebrews that the Lord Almighty was a saving God; that there was no-one greater. This would also give them a reference point to his even greater saving act that was to come.

Pray (3 minutes)
Give opportunity for people to pray this prayer in their hearts: "Father God I believe in you. I can see that there is no God more powerful than you. Thank you for sending your Son Jesus to live and to die and to rise again. I realise that he did this so that I can be rescued from death after judgement. I am sorry for all of the wrong things that I have done. Lord Jesus I give you my whole life. I choose to follow you for the rest of my life. Please put your Holy Spirit in me, so that I may know that you are with me. In Jesus' name amen."

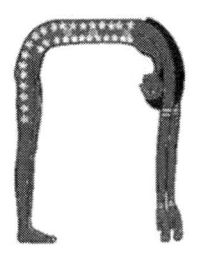

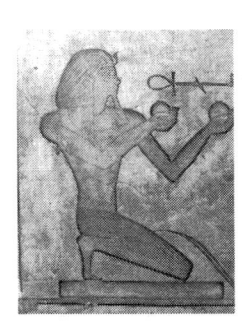

Egyptian gods question sheet

a) Hapi guardians and spirit of the Nile
b) Heket water goddess of fertility & frogs
c) Geb ground god of the earth
d) Khepri Beetle god of creation
e) Apis Moon god
f) Isis god of medicine and peace
g) Nut goddess of the sky
h) Osiris god of the underworld and crops
i) Seth god of storms and thunder
J) Rah the sun god
k) Anubis god of the dead
L) Pharaoh

Egyptian gods question sheet

a) Hapi guardians and spirit of the Nile
b) Heket water goddess of fertility & frogs
c) Geb ground god of the earth
d) Khepri Beetle god of creation
e) Apis Moon god
f) Isis god of medicine and peace
g) Nut goddess of the sky
h) Osiris god of the underworld and crops
i) Seth god of storms and thunder
J) Rah the sun god
k) Anubis god of the dead
L) Pharaoh

d)

e)

b)

a)

g)

f)

h)

i)

j)

c)

L)

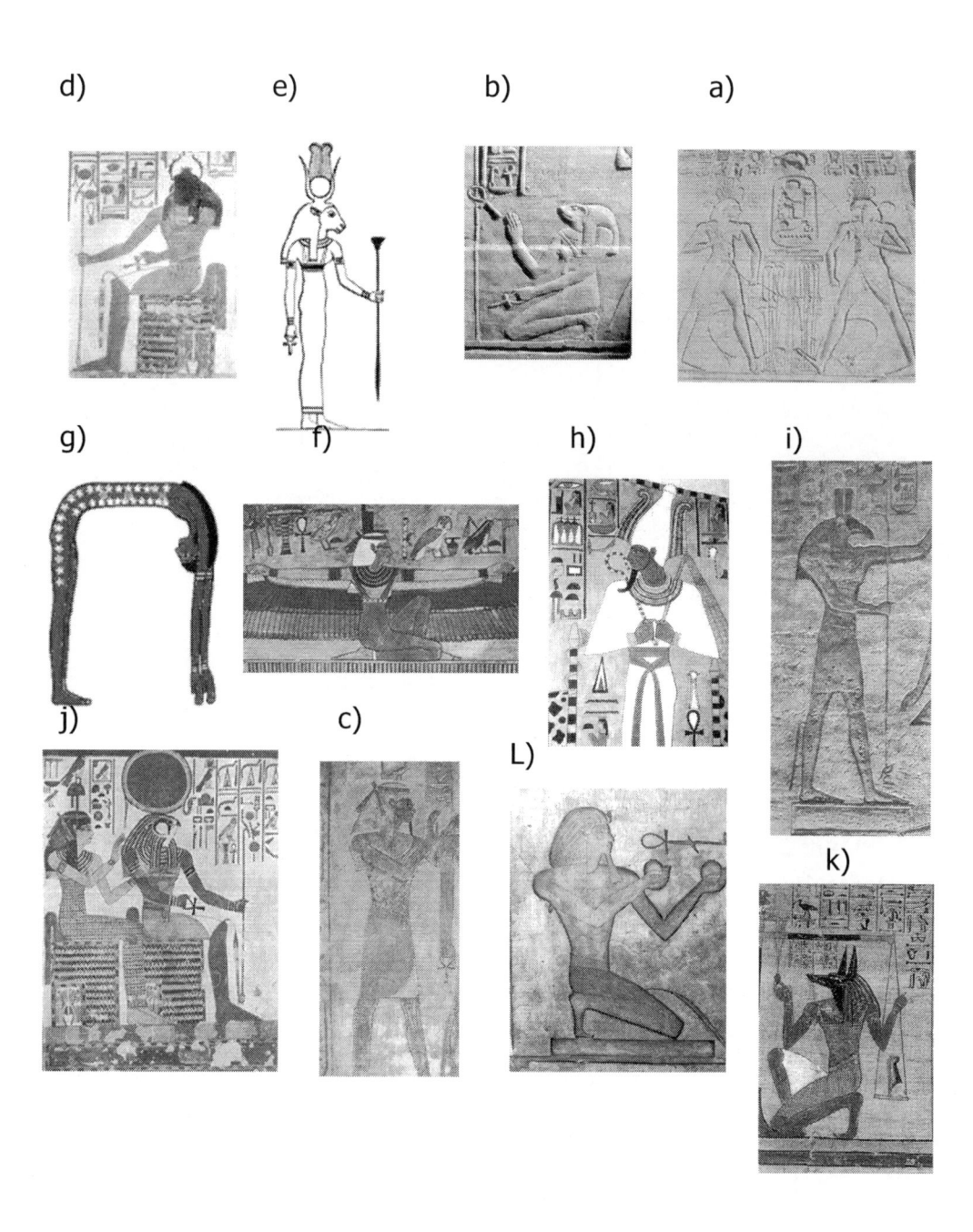

k)

37) Moses disobeys God

Icebreaker - Battleship (5 minutes)
Draw a 10 x 10 grid on a flip chart and also on a normal piece of paper. Write the letters A to J next to each row along the vertical axis and the numbers 1 to 10 next to each column on the horizontal axis. On your small piece of paper plot the places of 4 ships. One ship 2 squares long, one 3 squares, one 4 squares, one 5 squares long. Keep this hidden.

Tell the group the enemy navy are attacking your country, you each have a missile. They can go up to the flip chart and draw a circle in a square (to fire their missile). If it is the same grid reference as a ship on your sheet, you say hit and draw an X through the square. For successfully hitting the ship, that person then gets to fire another missile. The aim is to destroy all the enemy ships.

Discussion Starter (5 minutes)
Next is a test where instructions have to be followed. Give each person a sheet with this written on it: Please read all of the instructions before doing anything, you are allowed 10 minutes to complete this task.

1. Find a pen and paper.
2. Write your name at the top of the paper.
3. Write the numbers 1 to 5, one per line.
4. Draw five small circles beside 1.
5. Put an "X" in the second and fourth circles next to 1.
6. Write the word 'encyclopaedia' beside 3.
7. On the back of the paper multiply 7 x 9.
8. Put an X in the lower right-hand corner of the paper.
9. Draw a circle around the X you just made.
10. Underline your name.
11. Say your name out loud.
12. Draw a circle around 4.
13. Count the number of words in this sentence and write the answer beside 2 on your paper.
14. Put a square around 1 and 5.
15. Punch 3 small holes anywhere in the paper.
16. Write your first name beside 4.
17. Write today's date beside 5 on your paper.
18. Circle every letter 'E' you have written.
19. Stand up and say 'I HAVE FINISHED FIRST' if you were first, else say 'I HAVE FINISHED' out loud, then sit down.
20. Now that you read all of the instructions, skip all of them except the first two! If you have followed the instructions correctly, you should only have your name on the paper!

Comment on how people feel during an exam when it looks like someone has finished the test super-early, has turned the page, when you haven't even finished reading it or other exam experiences.

Q – Why do you think we do the wrong thing even though the instructions tell us plainly what to do? (Discuss. Maybe feeling rushed or nervous causes us to miss things).

Q - When you are familiar with a particular test, why might you not pay so much attention to the instructions? (Discuss. Maybe when you have done it before you think you know what to do without the need to refer to the instructions).

Q – What pitfalls are there with this approach? (You can end up making silly mistakes).

Q – How do you feel when a teacher tells you to do some work that you don't want to do? (Discuss)

Introduction (1 minute)
The bit we are about to read is 40 years after the Hebrews had been miraculously rescued from Egypt and the Pharaoh. They have reached another desert, but will soon discover that they have made it to the Promised Land.

However before this happens, the Israelites begin to voice their doubts and oppose Moses and Aaron their leaders. This is not the first time the people of Israel rebel against Moses. Miriam, Moses sister is now about to die. She was a Prophetess; however she was one who disobeyed God by opposing Moses sometime earlier.

Teaching (15 minutes)
READ Numbers 20:1-13

Q – What problem has suddenly come upon the Israelites? (There is a lack of water).

Q – Who do they immediately look to as the cause of the problem? (The leaders).

Q – Do you think this is a fair approach? (Discuss)

Q – Do you think the lack of water came as a surprise to the leaders? (Probably not, since as leaders their responsibility would be to provide for the needs of the group).

Q – Do you think that there is a culture of criticising our leaders in this country? If so how do you think this has come about? (Discuss)

Q – Take a quick look at Numbers 12:3. What does it say about Moses' character? (He was the most humble man in all the earth).

Q – Whose fault was it that there was no water? Was it the leaders' fault or the peoples'? (Discuss the previous actions of the Israelites and whether if they had obeyed, they would be in the Promised Land by now anyway).

Q – Does it matter whose fault it was? Does it help to say whose mistake it was? (Discuss).

Q - Why do we feel the need to apportion blame? (Sometimes people use things like these to remove leaders from their roles in the hope of a more successful outcome).

Q – The Israelites complained that the fruit and vegetation that Moses had promised was nowhere to be seen. What do you think they were saying? (They were saying that they had been led up the garden path – to somewhere worse than Egypt).

Sometimes when a leader has a vision, it takes time for that to come to fruition. The in-between stage when it hasn't all happened yet, and maybe things aren't looking that good can be a vulnerable time for a leader.

Q – How do you think Moses and Aaron felt about what was being said? (We can see in verse 10 that Moses is feeling angry. It is probably a result of feeling discouraged by the treatment of the people he was serving as a leader).

Q – So what is the best response that a leader can do in this sort of situation? (Go away and pray!)

Q – What was the best thing that the people of Israel could have done for themselves? (They could have brought to the leaders the problem, but also spoken encouraging words and tried to support and build up their leaders).

Q – What should we do if we believe the leaders are getting it wrong? (Discuss)

Q – In answer to prayer, Moses and Aaron receive a set of instructions from God of what to do. What are those instructions? (1. Take the staff 2. Moses and Aaron gather the people 3. Speak to the rock, and it will pour out water immediately).

Q – So they do the first thing right, to get the staff. Why do you think they had to get the staff, if they weren't going to use it? (The staff was a symbol of the leaders' authority. Many miracles had taken place by God in partnership with Moses and Aaron using the staff. It was to remind the people whom God had chosen to lead them).

They do the next thing, get the people together, but then Moses is so mad with the people and their treatment of him that he lets loose some abuse, and strikes the rock. But this is not way God wanted it to happen. God had a more gracious way in mind. Moses had deviated from the clear instructions God had given him.

Q – Bible test! Do you know of anything similar to this happening in the Bible? (READ Exodus 17:1-7)

Sometimes when something familiar comes up we can revert back to the way we did it last time. Like some advice we gave someone, or how God answered a prayer, so we use the same way next time. God is not into formulas or always doing things in the same way. Some principles remain the same but his methods of doing things may vary.

Q – Have a read of the instructions God gave Moses v8. Moses has used the staff and also stretched out his hand for miracles to happen, but Moses had never spoken to something to happen. Imagine you are God and you aren't thinking ahead, you are just giving Moses these instructions. Can you guess how God is feeling? (It's like God is letting Moses into a secret. You have my words in you and by my power all you need to do is speak them and right before their very eyes, they will see that I am God and that you are my servant. It's almost like God is a little excited about what is going to happen).

Q – Unfortunately Moses wrecks it big time. And God is not happy with Moses. Why do you think God is not happy with Moses? (God has promised to do this miracle. Whatever happens, it will take place. Unfortunately Moses has said things with the wrong attitude and God's miracle has taken place. God's holy miracle and Moses' unholy words have become one and the same incident).

Q – Because of Moses' disobedience, Moses would not now be able to enter the Promised Land. Do you think God normally treats people like this who mess up? (It's important that we honour God in the supernatural. Moses was a leader, and leaders are judged more harshly, since they are called to represent God. Moses had misrepresented God during a key moment. When it comes to stepping out in the supernatural gifts of God, we must honour him, but if we make mistakes, it's okay, it's all part of learning. We won't be punished for mistakes – though we may need to clean up our mess and apologise when we get it wrong).

Round up (2 minutes)
So today we have seen the challenge and responsibilities of leadership. We have also seen that those who are following their leaders can actually make things worse for themselves when they resort to fear or blame. Moses has just lost his sister Miriam. During this time of grieving the people turn on him instead of supporting him. Moses does the right thing in bringing it all to God, but dishonours God in his anger. The bible tells us that in our anger we should hold back from doing wrong. It's not easy, when all we want is to defend ourselves, hit back and apportion blame.

The people of Israel had a problem with submitting to the authority that Moses had as a leader. This had an effect on the timescale for them entering into what God had promised.

The best outcome in life always comes when we follow the maker's instructions. Like when you buy a new piece of tech you need to follow the instructions, so God our Maker has good instructions that he wants us to follow. If we deviate from what he has instructed us to do, we can risk a malfunction. If we view the malfunction as punishment from God we would be wrong. The malfunction comes because we stepped in a different direction to God's wise words, contrary to the way he made us.

The Bible tells us that leaders are judged more harshly. Moses was a great leader who represented God, but it was time for him to step aside for Joshua to lead. As we lead it is important that our attitudes represent God well. There may be times that are not so enjoyable when God has to teach us and develop character in us; but through those times God will shape us and make us more like him.

38) Moses gets moaned at
Icebreaker - Spot the ball (5 minutes)
Find a few pictures of sporting moments with a ball in. Using Microsoft Publisher or picture editing software and 3 add circles to the picture (one covering the ball). Then get the youngsters to get into teams and guess where they think the ball is.

Discussion Starter - David Nalbandian disqualified (5 minutes)
The Argentine 10th seed had won the first set on a tie-break 7-6, but after his serve being broken by the Croatian sixth seed midway through the second set to (putting him behind) Nalbandian kicked out in frustration at an advertising hoarding.

Unfortunately, the hoarding was right at the feet of line judge Andre McDougall, who caught the full force of Nalbandian's kick on his legs and eventually limped off court for treatment with his left shin bleeding.

After prolonged discussions between a number of tournament and ATP officials, umpire Fergus Murphy handed a code violation for unsportsmanlike behaviour to Nalbandian and awarded his opponent Cilic the match and his first title of 2012.

The relevant ATP code states: "Players shall not at any time physically abuse any official, opponent, spectator or other person within the precincts of the tournament site. For purposes of this rule, physical abuse is the unauthorized touching of an official, opponent, and spectator or other person."

As a result, Nalbandian not only lost his right to play for the trophy, but also his prize money (around £36,000) and his ATP ranking points for reaching the final.

Q – Do you want to see the incident?? (Show clip from YouTube).

Q – Have a think... Can you pinpoint what the root of Nalbandian's problem was? (Was it his inability to control his temper? Or was it something deeper than that?

Q – Allowing yourself to express your anger in a violent way can store up problems. What can happen when we leave our anger unchecked? (We can take it out physically on those around us).

Q – Sportsmen are very self-disciplined in what they eat, drink, the time they spend practising and exercising. However this

kind of problem is not related to Nalbandian's ability, but rather his lack of self-discipline in his character. How can we best find an outlet for our anger? (1. Controlling angry thoughts. Not simply counting to 10, but rather putting the negative thoughts into the context of the good things going on and being thankful to God for those good things. 2. Breathe, and pray and ask God to bring calm to your heart. 3. Go do some exercise. Use the energy in a positive way to kick a ball or go boxing!).

Introduction (2 minutes)
So the part we are reading is now into the 40th anniversary (40 years) since they left Egypt. Nearly forty years since Moses had stretched out his hand over the Red Sea which immediately parted so that the people of Israel could escape the pursuing Egyptians. They were travelling to the Promised Land, a walk which was not a forty year walk. A more realistic estimate of how long it could take would be about 2 or 3 months. However, the people of Israel did not always trust. They criticised, grumbled and argued with Moses and Aaron who were leading them.

They are now nearing the Promised Land, but the Edomites (supposedly friends of the Israelites) won't let them travel through their land, causing the route to be extended still further.

Teaching (15 minutes)
READ Numbers 21:4-9

Q – Take a look at verse 4. Are there any landmarks mentioned here that you recognise? (The Red Sea).

Q – Does this surprise you to see that they are travelling by the Red Sea? (Yes?).

Q – Why might it be surprising to read that the people of Israel have just travelled to the Red Sea? (The surprising thing is that they went through the Red Sea at the beginning of their journey. At first glance it appears that they are back near where they started).

Before jumping to any conclusions on this, we probably ought to check a map to see... If you were to look for a map (online or elsewhere) you would find a few differences of opinion in the exact route they took, however there is a general consensus as to their rough journey.

Q –The journey is detailed in Numbers 33, with the names of the places the people of Israel passed by. So why do you think

people might have cause to disagree on the route? (Some of these ancient places have been renamed, which has made it difficult to place some settlements).

So is this the same part of the Red Sea? Maybe the Red Sea is big and this is the other side? The answer to those questions is that the Red Sea is big and that it has two Gulfs which were also referred to as the Red Sea. It is definitely a different part to the Red Sea that the Israelites passed through.

Having said this, they have been to this exact place before. So the people are obviously upset at being stuck back here again with no water. Echoes of last week's problems!

Q – What do the people do next? (They grumble to the leaders).

Q – What did they say they didn't have? (Bread or water. They did actually have food. It was called Manna which God had been miraculously providing for them, by making it fall out of the sky fresh every day).

Q – Where did grumbling get the people last time? (They got their water, but they made Moses react in a bad way and will soon be losing him as their leader as a result).

Q – This time God sent snakes among them, instead of providing water. What do you think was different this time to last time? (They hadn't changed their attitude, but also they had also insulted God by calling the food that he miraculously provided for them as "miserable food").

Q – Why is grumbling such a serious thing? (We ought to be careful when we complain when God's provision is so obvious. Thankfulness brings us close to God; the opposite may cause the opposite effect).

Q – So poisonous snakes invade the camp. Do you think there is any symbolism here? (Grumbling in a community is like a poison that gets into the system of an organisation. It can lead to distrust and lack of faith in the motives of the leaders. This in turn can make people feel not so supportive of their community and thus weaken the whole group; it's like poison).

Q – Do you think they would have realised their wrongdoing if the snakes hadn't appeared? (No. It caused them to seek God and when they did they realised).

Q - Do you think some innocent people died? (Yes I expect the snakes weren't limited to just biting those who had grumbled).

Q – The people see the effects of what they have done, on both the innocent and the guilty. So what do they do? (They say sorry and ask for forgiveness).

Q – What does Moses have to do? (Forgive them and pray for them).

Q – What happens next? (Moses has to make a snake and put it on a pole, so that the people, who get bitten by a snake, can go to the snake thing, look at it and live).

Q – Why doesn't God just take the snakes away?
Two reasons:
1. This would be an effective reminder to the people who keep forgetting about how bad grumbling is!

2. This would cause the Israelites to learn a dependence on God. Now any time in the future they come across a snake that bites them during their journey, they know they will be okay.

So God has turned this bad situation into something that will bring future good. The sin of the Israelites was having a devastating effect on their estimated time of arrival into the Promised Land. However, God was still looking after them and still patiently teaching them about having an attitude that depended on him for the answers, rather than freaking out.

Q – What did they have to do to get healed? (Just go find the snake on the pole, look at it).

Q – What would happen if they didn't go and look at the snake? (They would die).

Q – What does this tell us about faith? (Faith is putting into practice the words of God).

Q – Do we have to be sure that a healing will take place to pray for it? (No. The first step to faith is obedience. We don't have to worry about whether our mind is certain on the outcome. As we obey faith begins to happen. We mustn't let a lack of certainty stop us from stepping out in faith. After all faith is the belief in something we cannot see!).

Q – What is the other thing mentioned that the Israelites had to do to get healed? (They looked to the snake)

We're obviously not advocating that you look to snakes to be healed! But it is the turning your attention to God as the healer. Jesus said this in John 3:14-15 "Just as Moses lifted up the snake in the wilderness, so the Son of Man must be lifted up, that everyone who believes may have eternal life in him."

Q – How was Jesus lifted up? (He was nailed to a cross as a form of Roman execution).

So just as God provided a way of taking the punishment for the sins of the people of Israel including making them better, so God came as Jesus as the ultimate way of taking the punishment of our wrongdoings. Looking to him brings a rescue from perishing (everlasting life) and healing from the things we suffer from in life. READ Isaiah 53:5.

Round up (2 minutes)
Although at first this appears like a very negative turn of events, we are left with a valuable connection to the heart of God. It's really important to see how poisonous and destructive grumbling can be. This incident led to the heart of God which is forgiveness for our wrongs and his supernatural provision for healing us. The need for forgiveness is a need we all have, as is the need for healing. God will provide both to those who look to him.

Pray for healing time! (As long as you have!)
Take time to thank God that he heals and ask for healing. No need for long prayers. Check anyone that you have prayed for to see what is going on.

39) Joshua is called to lead

Icebreaker – Scategories (10 minutes)
5 columns, categories: Bible names, sweet or choc bar, car make, name of shop and Total.

Someone calls out a letter of the alphabet. The first person to write down a word beginning with that letter in each category says "STOP." Everyone must then stop writing. The person who called stop must then go through their answers for each category. If no-one has that word they get 5 points, but only 2 points if someone else has it. If you have nothing down you get 0 points.

Add up your scores as you go along!

Discussion - I believe in you (10 minutes)
Playing the game of golf better than it has ever been played; Tiger Woods won the Open Championship at St. Andrews, to become the youngest man ever to win all four of golf's grand slam tournaments.

The 24 year-old won the US Open, by a record margin, leaving his opponents bewildered by his skill. Since turning professional as of June 2008 he had won a total of $81,004,376 on the PGA tour. This is only tournament proceeds and does not include any endorsements. In 2007 he made $100 million dollars just from endorsing products including sportswear, credit cards, watches, breakfast cereals etc.

Since becoming a professional golfer Tiger Woods (up to June 2008) has won 64 PGA Tournaments. His father, Earl Woods, was accused of going ridiculously over the top when he spoke of how good he thought his son, then a teenager, could be. However, following his US Open victory a journalist asked if Tiger's father had maybe underestimated his ability! "Dad always had a big belief in my abilities," said Tiger... "I will probably do the same when I'm a proud dad."

Tiger Woods is the first black golfer to break through into the big time. Historically many golf clubs have been racist. One American golfer even resigned in protest at racist attitudes he came across whilst playing golf professionally.

Q - How important was it that his dad believed in his ability? How much do you think it had to do with Tiger Wood's success?
(Discuss)

Q - Do you think we all need someone to believe in us to achieve well? (Why/why not?)

Teaching 1 (10 minutes)
READ Numbers 28:12-22 & Joshua 1:1-10
Q - So what do we know of Moses? (He was a great leader. God used him to rescue the Israelites from Egypt and lead them to the border of the Promised Land.)

Q - Moses dies. Kind of a massive statement, "Moses is dead." So what is the big question that they have to deal with? (Who is going to lead now?)

Moses had been a brilliant leader. It's a bit like being a singer at a music festival concert and having to go on stage after Leona Lewis; it's a difficult job. Everyone is comparing you to the previous person.

In Numbers 26:51 it says that there were 601,730 Israelite men. If you double that number to include women 1,203,460 and then add children, it could possibly be 2 million people? To give you an idea of what that is like, according to a 2006 census, there were around 1.6 million people living in Kent. That's a lot of people to feed.

Q - What is the task Joshua has been given? (To lead the people into the promised land and the army to take cities by force)

Q - So this is a massive task read verse 2. This is Joshua's first instruction. Imagine it was you having to sort it out. Can you think of any difficulties with what he is being asked to do? (Ok. You want 2 million of us to cross the Jordan river? How exactly are we going to do that? In boats? Or a bridge?)

So Joshua faces a mixed bag of emotions; excited that he has been promoted to leader, but possibly freaked out by the enormity of the task. It's at this point that God says some things that are reassuring... What are they??

"I will give you every place you go in the land."
The actual Hebrew reads "I have given," past tense. Although they weren't there, the land was actually their possession. God had given it to them as theirs to have. It's like being told all the sweets in the Tesco are yours, with no issue of having to pay you just have to go in and get them. This was reassuring because... he didn't need to worry about whether they would succeed, whether they would win the battles. God had promised victory.

"No one will be able to defeat you all your life."
Amazing, to know whatever battle you fight, can't lose! God had already planned the victory. No matter how powerful the opposing army looked or what the odds were.

"Just as I was with Moses so I will be with you. I will not leave you or forsake you."
Just because Moses was dead, God wasn't going away. He was going to be with Joshua in the same way. He could expect the same help and closeness that Moses had with God.

Much like Tiger Wood's dad, God says "I believe in you Joshua". God had chosen Joshua as the leader and told him "I have chosen you to do this; all you need to do was to be strong and brave." It's like "you can do it, I believe in you, just boldly step out and you will be successful in whatever you do."

Q - What does this encourage you about doing things God has called you to do? (The very reason God chooses us to do things is that he believes in us to do it, and he will cause what we do to be worthwhile if we are doing what he asks us to).

Sometimes we may doubt our ability to do things. Knowing God is with us gives us more courage to be braver for God. We don't mind being brave if we are assured that the outcome is going to be worth it. But this is the very nature of faith; the "before the event" scenario where we can't say exactly what is going to happen. However, we can be assured that if we have that inner conviction that God is wanting us to do something and we boldly do it, God will step in and do it (in his way).

So we don't need to worry about the end result, because God has that sorted. He doesn't run a second rate outfit where things go wrong, so we don't need to doubt.

Q - Have you ever had an inner conviction that God wanted you to do something? What did you do? (Discuss. Have a personal testimony available in case the youngsters are not very forthcoming!).

Q - Did you have any doubts along the way? (Probably when things were not going as expected!).

Q - What did you do to get through the doubts? (Remind yourself of God's promises).

Summary (1 minute)
So when God wants us to do something, we are ready and we have all we need to do it, all he encourages us to do is to be strong and brave. This is a key part of being a Christian. Yes it can be a bit scary, but it turns out that when we step out it's the most exciting thing about being a Christian; stepping out in faith and seeing God do something amazing.

Pray (5 minutes)
Get the youngsters to write down the biggest challenges that they have ahead of them that are a concern to them (whether in the immediate future or longer-term).

Thank God that he gives us bravery that is equal (or greater) than even the biggest challenges that we face. With that in mind, ask for bravery and vision for the challenges ahead.

40) Rahab Protects the Spies

Star Trader Icebreaker (15 minutes)
We are going to do a brief trading game. Each player has 6 chips (pieces of card). You must trade your chips to get the best final scores. You do this by obtaining the chips that will win you the most points.

The Rules (These may need to be printed out).

- All chips must be hidden.
- Trading will last 5 minutes.
- You cannot trade 2 chips for 1.
- Only equal amounts can be traded: Eg. 1 for 1, 2 for 2 etc.
- Chips of the same colour cannot be traded (red for red).
- Only chips of different colours can be traded (blue for green).
- To begin a trade with someone you must first shake hands with them.
- You must not talk unless you have entered a trade by shaking hands.
- Once you have shaken hands with someone, you must do a deal.
- People with folded arms do not want to trade with other traders.

At the end of the game:

5 chips of the same colour = 25 extra bonus points

4 chips of the same colour = 15 extra bonus points

3 chips of the same colour = 10 extra bonus points

2 chips of the same colour = 0 extra bonus points

Discussion (8 minutes)
Q- Think about the phrase "going against the crowd..." What does it mean? (Explain the picture language)

I found this on the internet entitled "Going against the crowd"

The other day in Religion our teacher was having a rant about how our generation never wants to stand up for what they believe in and they are always moving with the crowd. She said "No one anymore ever wants to stand up and say 'I'm a Christian'" so I just said "I do!" really loud and nearly everyone laughed at me, but it felt really good!

I know this may not really seem like much but it did take a lot of courage and I think it might be a small step to something big!

Q - What do you think about this story?

Q - Why do you think the people laughed? (Was it more to do with the way it was said rather than what was said?)

Q - Ok so it's good to take a stand for what you believe in, but is there a way of going against the crowd that works?

People who are Christians have something different from those who aren't. There's spiritual depth, we have the powerful Holy Spirit within us, as we follow God's ways we deepen in character and have a trustworthiness and integrity. As young people mature they begin to realise that these characteristics are valuable in friendship.

If we follow God our lifestyles will inevitably go against what the crowd does. Yet in times of need people know who they can go to and trust.

Teaching 1 (15 minutes)
Where we're at in the story so far is that God's people, the Hebrews were slaves in Egypt. But God had promised them a land of their own. Now possibly around 2 million people, they had to find the place God had given them to settle in. Those who were currently in the land would not be able to live peacefully with the Israelites. Those who were already in the land were described as a disobedient people. This was a time when different kings would attack each other. Thus settlements often had walls around their cities to prevent the threat of attack.

READ Joshua 2:1-24
Q – So summarise for us... why is Joshua sending out spies to the city of Jericho? (He believed this was the place God wanted them to attack next and that they needed some inside knowledge).

Q - Ok so these were God's people on a mission. Why do you think they went to a prostitute's house? (Well it's a bit like Spooks, MI5 agents on a mission. If the spies were discovered they would certainly have been harmed/tortured/killed).

So it's a scary situation, and it turns out that these guys aren't the best spies in the world; they certainly weren't masters of disguise. They did well to get through the city gates, but it didn't take them long before they were spotted.
Q - Have you ever been faced with a scary situation where you had to go and do something bold or risky for God? How did that turn out? (Discuss)

Q – Can you remember the promise God gave Joshua last week? See Joshua 1:3. (I will give you or "have given you" every place where you set your foot).

Q – How do you think this is an encouragement to the spies? (They see the success ahead and have bravery to take risks in order for it to happen. See Joshua 2:24).

Q - So Rahab finds herself face to face with enemy spies, and ultimately with a choice: Do I help these people or not? But faith rises in her heart and she decides to help the spies. Why was that? (Because she had heard of the way God had taken these people out of Egypt; she knew nothing and no-one could stop them).

Q - This is an unlikely person to find in the Bible, that someone who trusts in God is a prostitute. What is the natural reaction to seeing someone like this who believes in God? (Discuss. Maybe because of their lifestyle we think there's no way they can believe in God. Many people believe in God with lifestyle choices that we might not agree with, alcoholics, homosexuals, prostitutes. When Jesus was on earth these are the people he would be found eating dinner with. His words were "it's not the healthy who need a doctor, but the sick." It's not for us to judge another person's lifestyle. We might think we know what's right and wrong, but it's God's part to judge).

Q - The fact that Rahab was prepared to help the spies is interesting. What does this tell us about God? (That when he wants us to do something, he will prepare the way so that we can succeed in the task, when on our own we would fail).

Round up (1 minute)
This is an encouraging thought that we can know God is with us when we try new things for him, things that we wouldn't normally do, or tasks that seem really daunting, we go with the help and strength of God.

Hebrews 11:31 "By faith the prostitute Rahab, because she welcomed the spies, was not killed with those who we disobedient/unbelieving."

Just like the trading game at the beginning, sometimes we are required to take risks in order for something great to happen.

Prayer (2 minutes)
Lord, help me to take risks for you!

41) Joshua is successful

Icebreaker - Geiger Counter (5 minutes)
This is a simple game where one member of the group leaves the room whilst the group decide to hide an item. This item then becomes a highly radioactive bomb. Once the item is hidden the person who left the room, re-enters and the rest of the group become the "Geiger counters."

So the group will indicate by the use of "tick tick" noises to show how close the player is in relation to the radioactive item. If the player is far away, the group must make their "tick tick" noises slow. However when the player is close to the radioactive item the "tick tick" noises must be fast.

The player has one minute to find the item before it explodes.

Discussion (10 minutes)
In 2002 Brazil won the football world cup... again. During the on pitch celebrations after their 2-0 win over Germany, several members of the Brazilian World Cup winning team openly witnessed to their faith. At the final whistle Marcos stayed in his goalmouth on his knees praying, while another trio of players, Lucio, Edmilson and Kaka huddled together in a prayer triplet. Then the whole squad knelt in a heart-shape to pray and give thanks.

Defender Lucio repeated his witness from the European Champions League, when, playing for Bayer Leverkusen, he pulled his team shirt off to reveal a T-shirt with the message "Jesus loves you." Kaka used a similar method to communicate his Christian faith at the World Cup final. His T-shirt had the message "I belong to Jesus."

Even Neymar when he and his team won gold at the Rio 2016 Olympics wore a bandana saying "I love Jesus."

An estimated 1.5 billion people worldwide saw the Brazilians celebrating their win in Japan.

Q – What do you think about this? Is this a good way to tell people about Jesus? (Discuss. Often fans of the players want to know more about them and this could be a good way to introduce them to Jesus).

Q - What might stop teenage Christians from witnessing to their friends? (Fear of being insulted or having discussions that turn aggressive).

Q - In your opinion what is the most cringe-worthy way to witness and what is the best way to witness? (Discuss).

Q - What is stopping you from telling your mates about the Christian faith? (Discuss).

Q - Do you think the Brazilian team had a helping hand from God to win the match? (Discuss why you think he might have?)

Q - How would it feel to play in an important game like that and know you were going to win even before kick-off had started?

Q - So if God wanted us to do something for him, how would *knowing the end result* help us in achieving the task? (If you knew it would be a success you might have more confidence to go for it).

Q – Here's a question to think about rather than to answer... Would you go for it even if it meant taking a stand for God by doing something you felt embarrassed or shy about doing?

Teaching (15 minutes)
READ Joshua 6:1-27
Q - So where have the Israelites come from? Who can give us a bit of background of events leading up to this? (Slavery in Egypt, Moses tries to do his bit, but ends up killing an Egyptian and running away. God calls him to lead the slaves out, it takes a while, he dies and Joshua is chosen to take the lead, spies go in to check out the land, nearly get caught, but are protected by Rahab in exchange for the lives of her and her family).

Q - So how were the inhabitants of Jericho feeling? (Very afraid).

Q – Why were they feeling afraid? (They had heard of Israel's exit from Egypt and how God was powerfully with Israel. They also knew that they had been infiltrated by spies).

Q – Why does this help the Israelites? (If an army is afraid before it even fights, it is already at a disadvantage).

So the inhabitants of Jericho were feeling extremely afraid. Rahab had already told the spies that everyone had heard about the crossing of the Red sea and the defeat of 2 Kings (Sihon and Og). They were not only determined to keep the advancing army out, they were also keen not be infiltrated by any more spies.

Q - And how do you think the Israelites were feeling? (To give you a bit of context, they may have been a bit unsure. They have seen victories happen, but there is still the issue with the first group of spies giving a scary report about there being giants in the land: Numbers 13:26-32).

And God tells Joshua that Jericho has already been given to them. This is a little bit like going to play in the World Cup Final and knowing what the end score would be! This may sound easy if the team looks easy to beat, but if it's against some massive odds (a world class team or city with walls as thick as a house), especially if you know you can't do it with your own ability. This is when we have to rely on God.

Q – Take a look at all that the Lord asked them to do in verses 3-5. What do you think was the most important of all of those things that God asked them to do? Eg. To march around the walls? The time they should do it? Having the priests in position? Blowing the trumpets? Carrying the Ark of the Covenant? Or was it the shout? (Obviously all of them were important, as they had to obey all of God's instructions; but taking the Ark of the Covenant was really important. This represented God's presence. If God did not go with them, there would be no success).

Q - Who had given them this victory? How did this change things for the Israelites? (God had given them the victory, and this indicated how he would help in the future. It also meant they had to follow and obey his directions and put their trust that God would do things his way).

The battle and the victory would be God's responsibility. They didn't have to plan out the strategy. They didn't have to know how the victory was going to come about. They only knew that if they did what God told them, the victory would be theirs. This would be a key moment in the history of the people of Israel. It would give them great confidence to go on, and would frighten the living daylights out of those living in God's land.

It's the same for us today. In our lives, we often think we have to think of the plans we have for our future. It might be that we fret about exams that we haven't done as well in as we think we ought, or the choosing of what to study, or looking ahead to Uni. It might be in the moment, in wanting a romantic relationship, or some big project that you have taken on.

God wants to be honoured in what we do. So as we give him these "battles," he will help direct us, inspire us and lead us to success. So we need not fret for the victory is his.

First of all, for the Israelites the first thing they had to obey God in was in getting up early in the morning, something we all find difficult to do.

Q - Would you get up earlier in the morning if you thought God had something he wanted you to do? Have you ever tried this? (General thoughts: getting up is a challenge, but with our days being so busy and full of things is there any other time? It's easy for God's plans to be squeezed out, even before the day starts. When the battle to get out of bed is lost, the rest of the day can become an uphill struggle).

Q - What effect do you think they had by doing the marching early in the morning? (Discuss)

Maybe those inside were beginning to wonder what was going on. Why aren't they attacking?? Have they actually got an army or just a group of musicians? Are they going to break into song?? Or maybe they were trembling in their boots thinking "God is really with these people." The same can be said for us. When we step out for God we really can't tell what's going on inside people's minds and hearts.

Faith only comes about when we do something that God wants, when the outcome is uncertain and unknown.

Q - Think for a moment (maybe in small groups) of some possible scenarios of what could have gone wrong for the Israelites... they can be amusing!

Faith is relying on God, when there is the potential for things to go really pear-shaped. When we face the big challenges in our lives sometimes knowing what to do is not the problem. Actually doing it is the scary thing, when our heart knows it, but doesn't make a lot of sense to our minds.

Round up (1 minute)
We asked the question at the beginning: Would you do something for God even if it meant taking a stand for him by doing something you felt

embarrassed or shy about doing? And we discussed cringe-worthy ways of telling people about God that maybe don't work.

Maybe wearing a t-shirt saying Jesus loves you doesn't work for you, maybe a youth group hoodie is a good starting point? Maybe inviting your friends to an event gives you more opportunity for conversation about God at a later date?

Just remember whatever God tells you to do, do it, and he will give you the victory in it.

Prayer

42) Achan makes God well angry

Icebreaker 1 – Memory madness (5 minutes)
Think of things you may be likely to take to for camping at Summer Camp… "In my bag to Summer Camp I packed…" and get each youngster to say what the previous people have mentioned and add their own. Go round til someone fails.

Icebreaker 2 – Forfeits (8 minutes)
You will need sweets as an incentive to get people to play this game. Have a list of simple forfeits (like try to sell someone in the room an invisible TV, or sing a Christmas song). Use a dice where if they roll an even number they get a sweet. If they roll an odd number, they have to do a forfeit.

Forfeits:
- They must pinch their nose and say the alphabet
- Get someone to laugh without tickling them
- Do 5 press-ups
- Teach everyone a dance move (everyone must copy it)
- Sell someone and imaginary vacuum cleaner
- Tell a "knock, knock" joke
- Sing a Christmas song
- Perform a DVD workout routine (everyone must copy it)
- Smell someone's foot
- Pretend to be a waiter and take a food order of the person next to you
- Pretend to lay an egg like a chicken

Introduction (1 minute)
Tell me about last week. What was that all about? We talked about doing something for God. The Brazilian football team celebrated winning the world cup by acknowledging Jesus as their Saviour. Joshua went into a battle that God told him he had already won. We thought about getting up early for God, doing things to tell about Jesus. So they had an amazing victory with the walls of Jericho falling down. This demonstrated that when God was with them they were pretty unbeatable. This week however, we're going to find out that when he wasn't with them, they were a pretty mediocre army and they find out what it is to lose.

Discussion - Doing the right thing (5 minutes)
Imagine you have got a weekend job working at McDonalds and you are fairly new. Your work colleagues excitedly show you the new toy for the Happy Meal and you know someone whose birthday is tomorrow who would really, really like it. You haven't got any money with you, but

later a friend of yours (who has been very kind to you) comes up to you and stuffs the toy in your pocket. He tells you that you can have it as others have had one too. You know he hasn't paid for it.

Q - You don't want to insult your friend, but you don't want to steal either. What do you do? (Discuss).

It's a massive challenge to do the right thing, as we'll see today...

Teaching (15 minutes)
READ Joshua 7:1-26

Q - Tell us what goes wrong here...

Q - What's the problem with them losing? (The other nations will find out and they'll all attack).

Q - So Joshua prays to God when do you think they attacked? (What time? Probably another dawn raid)

Q - When does God answer Joshua's praying? (In the evening)

Q - What does this tell us about praying? (1. That God does answer 2. They probably did another dawn raid and came back with the news. Joshua went to pray to God and "stayed there till early evening" then God spoke. There are times when we need to wait for God to speak. He does it in his own time).

Q - Do you think it was God's fault that they lost, since God had given them the previous victory? (No. God had told them he would give the victory if they obeyed him Joshua 1:16)

Q - So how does God deal with the person who did this?

Q - How do you think they found out it was Achan? (Urim and Thummim. Like yes/no dice)

Q - Why is God so angry with Achan? (He becomes well angry with Achan, because he had to take away his protection and innocent people died. He also wanted the whole camp to be pure and his people to be righteous (unlike the other nations) He wants his people to be holy. However, just one person caused them all to lose).

Q - So is it better to confess you've done something wrong before being found out or after? Why? (It's better before, as it shows you have a conscience and can be trusted to figure out what is right and wrong).

Q - God had told them specifically that they were to leave any of the shiny things alone. They weren't to be taken. What sort of things today do we know God doesn't want us to do? (Getting drunk, sex before marriage, telling lies, stealing etc. We know them all)

Q - So this was the Old Testament. Now that we have Jesus, do you think God is any less angry when we do this stuff? (Sin still has a price, which Jesus suffered and died to pay for. So it is still a big deal. He didn't die so we could sin all we wanted, he died so that we could escape God's anger against sin. Sin hurts others and destroys our lives and that's why God hates it).

Q - So Achan's sin affected the outcome of the battle. They lost. In what way do you think our sin might hold back God's plan for us? (Think of a scenario: Sin can hold back our prayers from being answered (James 5:15-16) Say for eg. you are asking God for something eg. money so you can go to Summer Camp, but you are going out getting drunk at clubs, then that answer may be delayed 'til you work out why God isn't answering! Sin must be confessed to God and dealt with. God wants his people to be holy. This is important to him).

Round up (1 minute)
No matter how hard we try, we can't hide our actions from God. And sometimes God needs to highlight to us what we have done. Often this comes in the form of our conscience, or when we are reading the Bible and we realise our actions.

Occasionally God may try to get our attention by causing things to not go as well for us, so that we find ourselves returning back to him to supply our needs again. Sin will form a barrier between us and God. This barrier can easily be broken through prayer, when we confess our wrong deeds to God, and ask for his help to live differently.

Prayer (3 minutes)
The Bible tells us that we should confess our sins to God and that he will forgive us. In the quiet of your heart we'll take a few minutes to do that. (It might be worth playing an appropriate song whilst they silently interact with God).

43) Joshua Forgets to Pray

Icebreaker – Team building (10 minutes)
You need to prepare a pre-made structure using building blocks (such as Lego). The aim of this exercise is for the teams to build an exact copy of your structure. Make sure you have the correct building blocks for 3 teams. Distribute the same blocks to each team.

Then one member from each team will have 2 minutes to examine the structure you have made. They must then return to their team and instruct the team how to build it. The person who has seen the structure cannot build it. After a few minutes another team member can return to examine the structure, they also cannot then touch their team's Lego bricks. The team that builds the structure that most resembles your one is the winning team.

Discussion (8 minutes)
In those same teams we now want them to discuss the following scenarios (one per team):

Two people having an argument at school. You can see who's right and who's wrong. So you put in your two-penny's worth to help end the argument. However you end up making an enemy who decides to target you because of what you did.

You've got to work in twos at school and you go with someone who is your friend, however, they turn out to be lazy and you end up having to do the bulk of the work to maintain a good grade.

You're on the internet. And a naked picture comes up that you didn't expect. You exit the site immediately. But as you continue using the internet you can't stop feeling curious about clicking on links that might show you more of that stuff.

Q - So what could you do to help you have a better outcome? (Get the youngsters to report back).

Sometimes we find ourselves suddenly in a set of uncertain circumstances that just end up going wrong. Maybe there's times when we wished we'd prayed about it first to so that God would lead us in the right decision. God is intensely practical. You wouldn't need to go "Hang on I'll be back in a minute" and pray for 20 minutes and come back "now where were we." The idea is that we have our prayer time with him at other times, but then fire up a quick prayer thought for guidance at the time and his wisdom comes to us.

Introduction (1 minute)
A while ago we saw how Achan messed up big time and got found out. When the army went to attack Ai and were beaten by the opposing army. We asked the question is God any less angry with disobedience now that Jesus has come? And we realised that God doesn't change. He is still a holy God; yet we can now recognise his amazing love in that because of Jesus. He doesn't treat us as our sins deserve. We are his and he gives us his grace by forgiving us.

So the Lord's army go up to take Ai again. Now the size of the army is ten times what it was before (30,000). They set an ambush for the opposing army and attacked early in the morning. The men of Ai came running out to fight, but Joshua had some of his army go in the back door. So during the battle the men of Ai turned round and saw their city on fire. They ran back to save the city, but got sandwiched between the armies of Joshua. So it was curtains for the city of Ai and Bethel too.

Teaching (10 minutes)
READ Joshua 9:1-27

Q - See verse 2. What were the Nations that lived around the Jordan area planning to do? (They heard of all Israel's battles and they were preparing to go up and fight them).

Q - So with all these armies joining together, why did the Gibeonites feel the need to get together some old stuff to make it look like they had come a great distance? (They knew the Israelites were unstoppable because they were God's army. They knew they would all be killed when this army reached their land, so they hatched a plan to save their own lives using trickery).

Q - Why were the Israelites so keen to check that the Gibeonites weren't from a place nearby? (If the Israelites made an agreement with the Gibeonites, that would mean that they couldn't fully destroy that part of the Land God had promised them. The problem was that the Gibeonites would be used to other gods and this may tempt some of the Israelites to adopt their gods. God wanted to eliminate the use of other gods by other generations to come).

Q - So what checks did they make to see if the Gibeonite story was true, and what did they not do? (v 14. I think the comment "typical blokes" comes to mind... They tasted the manky bread, surely if it's green and dry that's all the indication you need, however they didn't ask God).

Joshua decides it is okay. The bread is definitely wrong and swears an oath of agreement. He makes a deal with them as friends as they aren't going to take up the same space; maybe they could form trade links in the future.

Q - Why could Joshua not have gone back on his agreement? After all the Gibeonites had told *them* lies? (Joshua had made a promise in front of God. He had to keep his word. Also, his promise may have included a curse on him if he broke it v20).

Q - So Joshua now has a bit of trouble on his hands. This is his first mistake as leader, and now the people are grumbling against him. How should the Israelites have responded? (Forgiven him and realised that he has a difficult job).

Q - Is it a mistake to think that leaders are perfect and will never make any wrong decisions? (Yes. Leaders are the same as anyone else. They have a lot of things and people to consider when making decisions and are only human).

Q - How do you think Israel's grumbling affected Joshua? (It gave him another thing to deal with, made his job harder and probably discouraged him a bit).

Round up (2 minutes)
We see here one thing has led to another, and now Joshua has several issues to deal with:

- There is now land that he has to share with people of other nations
- This is not what God wanted
- The people have started grumbling against Joshua
- The potential for the Israelites to marry non Israelites and follow their gods is now a real possibility.

One decision has now had a knock on effect and caused some lasting problems. And the thought is... if only he had prayed! He wouldn't be in any of this bother! Sometimes we think we know best, and it's when we take the lead in our lives instead of giving God the opportunity to lead us, is normally when we end up going into some bother or another. Self-sufficiency leads us to errors, mistakes and failure which God can help us to avoid.

Sometimes we might think that we are too busy to pray, when in fact in those times that we are rushed off our feet with tasks, we are too busy NOT to pray!!

Pray (5 minutes)
Take time to talk to God about something that you need his help with. Ask him to fill in the gaps in the things that you just can't do. He will provide for you.

44) Deborah Leads

Icebreaker 1 - Would you rather?? (4 minutes)
Choices stand either side of the room...

M&Ms or Revels?
Look bad or smell bad?
Locked out or locked in?
Bitten by a shark or spider?
Star Wars or Star Trek?
Watch telly or be on telly?
Hungry or thirsty?
Write or draw?
Burp or fart?
Coke or Pepsi?
Maths or Languages?
Arsenal or Man U?
Long hair or short hair?
Choc or sweets?
Holiday in South Africa or Norway?
Lead or follow?

Icebreaker 2 – Scissors clap (4 minutes)
You are to take on the role of a pair of scissors. Tell the group that every time your hands meet they have to clap. You right hand will start above your head, and your left hand will start next to your leg. As you bring your left hand up in front of you and your right hand down they will cross (like scissors!). When that happens they must clap. If someone claps when they don't cross that person is out. See if you can get a winner.

Discussion Starter (10 minutes)
Q - Do you think God can help you pass your exams? (Discuss).

Q - If so, in what way do you think God might be able to help you? (Discuss).

Q - What if God gave you the answers to the exam before you got in the exam room? (Discuss).

Q - Do you think God helping is cheating? (Discuss).

Real life story – help with exams
When I was at College I had the option to study Ancient Hebrew. This was a tricky decision as language was not one of my strong points. I

decided to choose Ancient Hebrew as I knew it would be a big help when interacting with Hebrew words as part of my future job.

So we had been studying the text of Joshua and it really hurt my brain. It was not easy to learn ancient Hebrew with new letters, tiny "pointings," words and their pronunciations, grammar, tenses and reading from right to left; but I kept going with it. One day, my Hebrew teacher told us our translation exam would be coming up. We'd be given several verses of a part of the Old Testament in Hebrew. Our task would be to translate it to English and make comments on it. Sound difficult? It really was.

The only thing the class had to go on was that it would be a similar text to that which we had studied. For me that didn't narrow it down, as the book of Joshua is a fair sized book. The text could be anywhere in the Old Testament.

Then one day when I was in church, someone read from the book of Judges, chapter 1. At that moment a lightbulb switched on in my head! I realised this text was very similar to the first chapter of Joshua! I felt this was God's way of showing me that I needed to focus my studies on this text for the exam.

There was a lot of work to be done. I wasn't as good as others in my Hebrew class. So I researched the text, going through all the Hebrew words, writing them out, sticking them all round my wall. I looked at them every day. By the time the exam came round I was fairly prepared.

In the exam room I realised that I had put all my eggs in one basket. What would happen if I had researched the wrong text?? I sat down, nervous, knowing that I would either get a great result or have a challenging couple of hours ahead of me.

I turned the page over to read "After the death of Joshua..." To my relief it was the text that was stuck all-round the wall in my room!! I wanted to jump around and punch the air, but instead I got my head down and had a little chuckle with God.

Needless to say, that without God's help I would not have passed this exam. But with his help, mine was one of the best in the class.

Q - Was I a special case? What do you think the circumstances might be for receiving God's help in an exam situation? (Discuss)

Anyway, today we start the book of Judges...

Introduction (2 minutes)
To bring us up-to-date a lot has happened. Adam and Eve were made, their son Cain killed his brother Abel, God flooded the Earth, but saved Noah and his family. Somewhere after Job was a prosperous man, until he faced a lot of troubles, given him, and God pulled him through. Abraham was called by God and left his family. He couldn't have children, but God promised him that he would be the Father of a great Nation. Jacob his grandson had many sons; one was Joseph who became a great leader in Egypt. The Hebrews settled there till they were made slaves by the Egyptians after and that they cried out to God.

Along came Moses, killed an Egyptian, ran away; God spoke to him from a bush that was on fire. Using Moses, God took the Hebrews out of Egypt and promised them a new land. Led by Joshua they battled the inhabitants and took the land. Read Joshua's final speech, very interesting Joshua 23.

So now Joshua is dead. Chapter 2:10 of Judges says "After those people had died, their children grew up and did not know the Lord or what he had done for Israel." It goes on to say that they began to worship other gods and the Lord wasn't happy, so he let their enemies around them defeat them. When the Israelites went out to fight they always lost.

So God chose Judges to lead the people. They were warriors and leaders of all of Israel. However the Israelites didn't listen to them. The fourth judge was a woman, Deborah.

Teaching (15 minutes)
READ Judges 4:1-24
Q - So Israel is in a lot of trouble, what has caused all this? (They had forgotten God).

Q - What things could they have done to not forget God? (They should have taught their children about God).

Q - So comparing this with being a Christian today. Could this happen to you or me? What is it that might cause us to forget God? (We need church more than we think. People say you can be a Christian and not go to church. And yes this is technically possible. However, more often than not we will find our lives sliding away from God. We need Bible teachers to encourage us with God's word. He gives them things to say that are meant for us, to help us not forget who God is).

Q – Who was Deborah? (A Prophetess).

Q – What was her job? (Leading Israel and being a judge. Just like Moses' job used to be).

Q - So we have a woman leader here. What do you think these verses tell us about women in leadership roles? (God calls people to lead and to fulfil roles in the church. There are a lot of male leaders, but don't let this put your off from wanting to serve God up front).

Q - So again the odds are against Israel. What is the problem this time? (Chariots. They would be quick, provide protection and imagine getting to the battle line being faced with 900 chariots. It's like standing in front of a toll gate as the cars come racing out).

Q - How does Israel face this new challenge? (God speaks to Deborah and gives her word that they ought to fight, as he would give the victory).

Q - Tell us about the man Deborah calls to lead the army? (His name was Barak. And he refused to go if Deborah didn't hold his hand).

Q - Why did he want Deborah to go with him? (He didn't want to lead the army. We see in verse 14 that he waits for Deborah to give the order to go. It can be a daunting thing to lead. To do something up front where people are going to see you. He seemed to not want the responsibility – choosing the easier option of letting someone else lead).

Q - What things does Deborah say that Barak would miss out on by not leading the battle alone? (He lost the recognition and possible promotion).

Q – Sometimes it's a lot easier to follow rather than to lead. There was an obvious struggle ahead of Barak. What things can we miss out on when we go for the easy option? (We miss out on the character forming that happens during the battle, the experience of learning to trust God in the hard times, the joy of the victory and the capacity to take on greater things).

Q - Can you name 2 leadership characteristics that Deborah shows? (She heard from God and she mobilised people to carry it out. She also got involved in the battle part - she was right in there).

Round up (1 minute)
Leaders need to be able to see ahead. To see what the needs of the people are. Through their connection with God they can bring the group to where it needs to be. Leaders have to see the potential of those involved and encourage people to see and use their gifts.

So the fortunes of Israel were turned around! Peace again! But it took the strong leadership of a woman who heard from God and took responsibility to make it happen. She may well have felt inadequate for the task, but she saw what needed to be done and was available to God to do it. Often great leaders don't feel able to take on the responsibility that they face. However in God we can do all things. He is able to grant us the wisdom and the strength to lead when no-one else will.

Prayer (5 minutes)
Pray for all the girls in the group who sense a calling to lead.

45) Gideon chosen for mighty works

Icebreaker (5 minutes)
Find 5 volunteers. Choose one to stand at the front not facing the rest of the group and to close their eyes. Then get the rest of the group to move around. Choose one person to say "Greetings mighty warrior" in their most angelic voice. The person with their eyes closed must guess who spoke. Those of the 5 who get it right first time go through to the next round. Continue until you find a winner.

Introduction (1 minute)
The people of Israel needed good leaders to help them live well and to make the right decisions as a nation. Following the leadership of Moses and Joshua they had Judges, people who would uphold justice and make wise decisions for the nation. Deborah was a great leader who stood up to the attacking enemies, and as a result brought about 40 years of peace.

Unfortunately the people of Israel did not honour God or follow his ways... let's read.

Teaching (15 minutes)
READ Judges 6:1-24
Q – What do you think it means that God "gave them in to the hands of the Midianites"? (He allowed the Midianites to beat Israel in battle and to have power over them).

God had temporarily removed his covering of protection over the people of Israel.

Q – How would you feel if you were constantly being attacked by armies and even after you were rebuilding from the last attack, another attack would follow? (Discuss)

Q – What were the Israelites doing to solve the problem? (They were providing protection for themselves).

Q – What did the Israelites come to realise? (That they needed God's protection. They depended on his protection to make it, rather than their self-sufficiency).

Q – What did God say to the people? (That he was their rescuing God, but that they had not listened to his words. God wanted the people to be free from oppression).

Q – Are we in danger of stepping out from under God's protection if we don't listen to his words? (Yes to protect and provide for us).

Q – What if we read something in the Bible that we don't agree with. Some people think that this gives us reason not to follow it. Is there ever a time when we no longer have to do some of the things it says? (We no longer have to sacrifice animals. This was part of the Old Covenant the old agreement with God. Since that point in time Jesus gave his life as a sacrifice for many. This is part of the New Covenant with God).

Q – Does this mean that we don't have to obey stuff in the Old Testament now, like the 10 commandments? (Absolutely not! The same moral code applies in the whole Bible! However the rituals that they did in the Old Testament have been done away with. Jesus said that the two most important commandments were to love God with all your heart, mind and strength and to love your neighbour as yourself. Can you love your neighbour whilst stealing from them?? Can you love God whilst worshipping another?).

So things are going badly for Israel. But God had a plan and he sends an angel to speak to Gideon.

Q – What does the angel call Gideon? (Mighty warrior).

Q – Was Gideon a mighty warrior at the time? (No, a farmer).

Q – What do you think the angel meant then? (He was speaking of the potential there was inside him and of God's purposes for his life).

Q – Gideon asks the angel a question. What is the question? (Gideon asks "If God is with us, why is this happening? In days gone by God did mighty things to rescue his people? Why not now?)

Q –What is the angel's answer? (He doesn't answer the question).

Q – Why do you think he doesn't answer the question? (Because in verse 8 it says that he sent a prophet who said why).

Q – So if we ask God a question and don't get an answer, what might be the reason why? (He's already given the answer; you just have to listen to what he's been saying).

This is so huge. We really need to understand this. When things are going pear-shaped or not the way we hoped and things just seem so confused, we need to go back to the last point we heard from God and re-examine what he said. Maybe we weren't listening, or maybe we didn't take him seriously or didn't understand. Take it back to God. If he was speaking he will make it clear!

However at this point there's no need for context. The angel has a message for Gideon. Go in the strength of the Lord mighty warrior!

Q – So if you were met by an angel and told you are a mighty warrior and to go in God's strength, do you think that would be enough to send you on your way? (Discuss)

Q – What doubts does Gideon have? (He thinks that because he doesn't come from a warrior clan that he can't have what it takes to be a warrior).

Gideon seems to have bad hearing. He seems to think God said "Go in the strength that you already have." However, the angel standing in front of him says "Go in God's strength."

Q – How do you suppose Gideon is going to do that? (Discuss)

This is what Gideon does: **READ Judges 6:25-32**

Scenario
Imagine you have just been visited by an angel and he has told you that you are a brave person who will heal lots of people and to go in God's strength.

Q – How would you feel about that? (Discuss in 3s)

Q – What would you do next? (Discuss in 3s)

Q – What does Gideon do? (He worships God and then goes about his business as normal. Then God speaks to him and says what to do next).

Round up (2 minutes)
So Gideon doesn't come up with the plan, because it's God's plan. He just keeps an ear out for God and does what he says, even though it is pretty scary! This is what we mean when we say someone has a "calling." That God is saying to someone that he has a plan for their life, a purpose that needs to be completed.

If you ever feel God is calling you to do something but you don't know what to do, see what comes to mind. If you've got nothing else, it may well be God telling you what you need to do next...

Prayer (5 minutes)
Is there something that God is calling you to do that you are struggling with because it seems too difficult? Write it down on a piece of paper and pop it in your pocket. Then sometime today when you talk to God, ask him about it and open up the Bible in Psalms and think on God. It is likely you may be encouraged in your struggles.

46) Gideon is it okay to test God?

Icebreaker - Toilet roll mummies (6 minutes)
Split the group into two teams giving them both a couple of rolls of toilet roll. Get them to wrap a volunteer with the toilet roll, like a mummy. The first team wins. Allow both teams to complete their mummies.

The team who completed their mummy first gets an arm's length head start. Find a space to walk race them, (maybe only 5 metres, as their legs will be tied). Be safe, have someone available to catch them!

Introduction - Read the following story (5 minutes)
Imagine one of you wins the lottery... obviously you have to be over 16 to do this... and you win the jackpot. You decide to buy out the building next door and make it into an amazing youth space. You've got a proper pool table, huge TV to play games and watch films, taps that pour out sweets when you turn them... a pizza oven, with all the ingredients...

Then whoever won the lottery tells you all, "Because you are a part of this youth group, you can each have a key to my place and hang out whenever you like." (Imagine the excitement!!). The only other thing she tells you is that you have to keep the place tidy and cut the grass sometime.... "Otherwise I will have to release the hounds" (you hear the distant sound of dogs barking).

So you all say "yes of course we can do that... gimme the key..." It would be amazing. So the day comes, there's pool (and a swimming pool), chill-out areas, a place for 5-a-side footy. Thereafter you are always round there having a great time.

However, after a month the owner comes back. No one has emptied the rubbish; in fact rubbish has been left on the floor, down the back of the sofa. One of the toilets is clogged, the grass is long and there are black marks on the wall. Immediately your friend is shocked and says "What have you been doing? I told you that you could enjoy my place, not mess it up. With the privilege that I gave you, came responsibility to respect me by looking after my stuff. Okay! Release the hounds!"

You get chased by snarling dogs and run off into the woods. For a time you have to live in tree houses, and only play footy when the dogs are asleep. You long to be back with your friend and regret abusing her house. Then all of a sudden you call out to her from the trees, "Please come and help us, we've done wrong and we're so sorry!"

Q – For those of you who were here last week, does this sound familiar to you? (See what they come up with!)

Q – Last week we heard the people of Israel crying out to God. Where had they been forced to live? (In caves).

Q – Can you remember why? (They had disrespected God by worshipping other gods whilst living in the land that God had given them).

But God still had a good plan for his people and he spoke to Gideon about it, although Gideon didn't feel able to do what God was asking him to do. So Gideon realised that he didn't need to be able, but that God would give him the directions as well as the ability.

Teaching (15 minutes)
READ Judges 6:33-40

Q – Imagine for a moment that you are at the top of a hill looking down to a valley. Picture a valley that stretches almost as far as the eye can see in all directions. It's a big valley. And imagine that you could see an army approaching that numbers in excess of 132,000 (Judges 8:10). What do you think would happen if the army was allowed to succeed? (The people of Israel would be injured, killed and captured and lose their land).

So this is a serious problem for the Israelites. They face the threat of a heavy defeat that could take years to recover from. If you were to look on to the next chapter you would see that many of them were trembling with fear.

Q – What does Gideon then say to God v36? (He asks if God is going to save them and if God can give him a sign, so that Gideon would be sure).

Q – So is it okay to test God? (If they say "no" ask them if they know of somewhere in the Bible that confirms their opinion, and do the same if they say "yes").

Three parts of the Bible immediately come to mind on this issue.

The first text is in **Deuteronomy 6:16** where one of the commands is "Do not follow other gods... Do not test the Lord your God as you did in

Massah." This relates to an incident in Exodus where the Israelites grumbled against God.

In **Matthew 4:1-13** there is the incident where Satan tempts Jesus to jump off a high place, saying that God's angels will catch him. Jesus replies "you shall not put the Lord your God to the test."

In **Matthew 12:38-39** where the Pharisees and Teachers of the law say to Jesus that they want to see him do a miraculous sign. Jesus says "A wicked and adulterous generation asks for a miraculous sign! But none will be given to it."

Split into groups (8 minutes)
Get them to split into three groups and to briefly look at one of the texts mentioned, reading the bits before and after them. Get them to explain what is taking place and to tell the reason why testing the Lord is wrong in those situations.

Feedback (10 minutes)
Deuteronomy 6:16 (also Exodus 17:7): The meaning of testing the Lord here is to do with testing his patience. Like a young child might test the boundaries (how far they can get away with something before being punished). God was saying to the people of Israel not test him by having no faith and grumbling against him when there was no water.

Q - Is this the same as what Gideon was doing? (No)

Matthew 4:1-13. The meaning of testing here is of deliberately putting yourself in unnecessary danger, on the presumption that because God has said he will protect and that he will miraculously swoop in. Again this is carelessly testing God's boundaries.

Q – Is this the same as what Gideon was doing? (No).

Matthew 12:38-39. These people had already seen him do lots of signs and miracles. They were looking for Jesus to prove he was the Messiah. They were not looking for someone in need to be helped, they were looking for him to do something they could scrutinize and analyse. They were looking for a magical solution.

Q – Was Gideon looking for God to prove he was God? (No).

Q – What were Gideon's reasons for doing this? (He was looking for God to confirm his guidance).

Many times before battle, kings have enquired of the Lord. King David would often ask "Shall we go up and fight?" There is a wrong way to test God and a right way.

Q – Does Gideon say "If you won't give me a sign, I won't go?" (No, he was ready to go either way).

The wrong way
The wrong way to test God is to demand that he produces a magical solution to a problem, with no interest in trusting him. An example of this could be to demand that Jesus make an appearance during the national anthem of a football game. To test God is to believe he doesn't have the answer. To test God is also to see what the limits are to how much we can get away with disobeying him.

The right way
Gideon was testing God's leading. He was committed to following what God was telling him to do, he just wanted God to confirm the right course of action and he would follow. Asking God for a sign to help direct us means that whether God gives a sign or not, we will still follow him. God does speak today and still gives signs today. They are for us to take note of, but are always for his purposes.

Right or Wrong (2 minutes)
Read out the following scenarios. Are the following ways of testing God right or wrong? Remain seated if you think it is okay to test God in this way, or stand up if you think it is a wrong way of testing God (or they can put hands up or down).

Choosing whether or not to give God 10% of your weekly money, so that he can bless your life. (It is a right way of testing God, see Malachi 3:10).

Asking God if a person is someone that God wants you to date. (It is a right way. Genesis 24:12 – though you must listen carefully and obey if he says no!).

Asking God to show your non-Christian mates he's alive by healing them. (Yes it is right. Romans 15:18-19).

Asking God to show you the lottery numbers to win next week's lottery. (Neither right nor wrong. However, God wants us to depend on him for what we need).

Asking God to give you a sign as to whether you should help an old lady across the road. (Come on! Really? No I don't think so. The Bible tells us we are called to good deeds).

Round up (2 minutes)
God wants us to partner with him in supernatural ways. Therefore asking for God to do miraculous things in order to help others is part of what it means to be in the Kingdom of heaven. Sometimes he will give us clues which mean we have to step out in faith. We may not ever get a fleece experience, but we can learn to hear his whispers, see his pictures in our mind's eyes and go with the thoughts he gives us.

We have to depend on him according to the level of gifts he has given us and step out in that, rather than waiting for something more before we go for it.

God also wants to talk to us in ways that will guide us. If we want God to speak to us in supernatural ways, we need to read our Bibles! We can end up missing a lot of what God wants to say to us, just because we aren't taking the time to read his words. There are times when we really need to know his guidance. If we pray and ask and find no real leading, and are acting according to his word, then we are free to just choose one! God also leads us through our circumstances.

Pray (5 minutes)
Is anyone in need of God's guidance? We can pray!

47) Gideon overcomes fear

Icebreaker 1 – Heads down thumbs up (5 minutes)
Have the group sit in a circle. Depending on your numbers, select a quarter of the group to stand up. They will be the thumb pressers. Then when the leader says "heads down thumbs up," everyone else (sitting down), must close their eyes, put their heads down and their thumbs up.

The pressers must find a person with their thumbs up and press their thumbs. Once they have pressed a person's thumbs they must go and stand at the front. The person whose thumbs have been pressed must then put their thumbs down.

Once all the pressers have pressed and are standing at the front, the leader can say, "Everyone open their eyes." Then those who have had their thumbs pressed, must stand in front of the person they think has pressed their thumbs. More than one person can stand in front of the same one if necessary.

Then those who guessed correctly can now become the pressers and those who were guessed can sit down and join in the game as pressees.

Icebreaker 2 – Phobias (8 minutes)
Here is a list of phobias with their meanings. Mix them up and get the youngsters into groups of 3 to see if they can match the phobias with their meanings.

Arachnophobia	- Fear of spiders
Chronophobia	- Fear of time
Dutchphobia	- Fear of the Dutch
Glossophobia	- Fear of speaking in public
Hippophobia	- Fear of horses
Insectophobia	- Fear of insects
Kleptophobia	- Fear of stealing
Linonophobia	- Fear of string
Ophthalmophobia	- Fear of being stared at
Phobophobia	- Fear of phobias

Introduction (1 minute)
Last week we asked if it was okay to test God. Thoughts of verses in the Bible that say it is not okay to test God came to mind. Yet, as we looked at those verses we could see that the word for "test" in OT times meant different things in different situations. It isn't okay to test God's patience by complaining, or to test God's boundaries to see what we can

get away with, or to test God's miracles by foolishly putting ourselves in danger.

However, we can test God's guidance for our lives when big decisions come our way, as long as we are prepared to trust God whether he miraculously shows us or not.

This week is crunch time. Gideon has received God's guidance in a very clear way, but he still has a scary task ahead. He knows what to do. He just has to do it trusting that God will fight for him.

Teaching (15 minutes)
READ Judges 7:1-25

Q – Take a look at verse 12 to picture the size of the opposing army. Describe what you imagine it to be. (Like a swarm of insects, or that's what they looked like from a distance, but they were the opposing army of 132,000 people).

Q – How do you think Gideon is now doing with regards to hearing from God? (He now seems confident that he is able to clearly hear from God).

Q – How do you think we can become more confident in being able to hear from God? (The more we do it the easier it gets. Asking God for opportunities and speaking what you get).

So this young man who said "who am I? I'm not from a clan of warriors," is about to lead an army to battle against a swarm of soldiers.

Q – If you were Gideon what would be your worries at having to tell your army to reduce in size? (He might be concerned that those who are left would not have faith in him to lead them).

Q – How many left after the first announcement? (22,000).

Q – How do you think those twenty thousand felt, not having to fight? (They seemed very relieved v3. Probably just as well they went. You don't want fear spreading through the camp).

Q – Did they miss out on anything? (Yes, being part of an amazing victory).

Q – Do you think it's possible for fear to actually prevent us from fulfilling our future destiny? (Yes. To overcome fear we have to have a trust in God. Our trust has to outweigh our fear enough for us to make the right decision. God is bigger than our fear, but in our minds we must prioritise whether we want to win enough to take a step in the right direction. God tells us "Don't be afraid.").

So it's God's turn to test Gideon! He's testing Gideon's faith in God's ability to win this battle to its limits.

Q – How many men has Gideon got left? (10,000).

If you have ever played team games in the playground and there's one team who has all the best players, you know the result is going to be a one sided victory for the better team. Well God says that the sides still aren't fair and wants to reduce his team even more.

Q - What is the test God gives to Gideon's men? (God wants to see how they drink water from the spring. Those who lapped like dogs would be chosen and those who drank using their hands could go home).

Visual Illustration
Why do you think God chose those who lapped? What do you think he was looking for? To figure out why God chose some and not others, why not get a couple of youngsters to act out this part. Get some youngsters to drink using their tongues and others to use their hands. Now that they can see what is going on, can they draw any conclusions as to why God chose those who lapped, not those who didn't?

Q – If you were an army who could be subject to a surprise attack at any moment, which do you think would be the wiser way of drinking the water? (Discuss. To crouch and use your hands, also gives you the ability to keep a look out for attackers. Someone who is on all fours facing the water is less likely to be ready for an attack).

Q – Why then do you think that God chose those who weren't so battle ready to be in his 300 dream team? (He was choosing those who were less likely to succeed, so that they couldn't say that they had won the battle by their own abilities).

So the more alert ones were allowed to go home! It is interesting. In verse 8 it says that Gideon sent the rest of the Israelites to their tents, but kept the 300. The Hebrew word for "kept" takes the idea of detaining people against their will.

Q – How would feel being part of an army of 300 (or more of a regiment really) of people going up against one of 132,000? (Discuss. It probably felt like a suicide mission).

Q – Take a look at verse 10. How does God help Gideon to overcome his fears? (He uses some of his bravery, by suggesting he goes in disguise to listen in to a conversation that gives Gideon the answer he is looking for).

Q – Difficult question... What made the Midianite believe that the Barley bread represented Gideon and his army? (Barley was a crop grown by the Israelites, something the Midianites would know well since they would often steal the Israelites' crops. Also it would have been flat bread since the Israelites ate unleavened bread).

Q – Take a look at Gideon's tactics. Why does Gideon make his army even smaller? (Since it is dark, no-one can see his army. He separates the army so that when they reveal their torches the enemy will assume that the gap in between is vastly populated by an attacking army).

That is exactly what happens. The Midianites think that the opposing army is upon them. They start attacking whoever is around and in the confusion start killing each other. That's one way to significantly reduce the size of your army!

Q – What does this text tell us about our weaknesses? (They shouldn't hold us back from doing something for God).

Q – What does this text tell us about our trust in God? (The size of the opposition that we face is no match for people who trust that God is what he promises to be).

Round up (2 minutes)
There's a lot of fear going around. Gideon's men are afraid to fight. Given the choice, they don't stick around. The opposing army of Midianites are fearful too. The joy of success comes after a struggle of faith. It's never the other way around! We can't expect the miraculous success without stepping out in the presence of fear and doubt.

It takes courage to step out when you feel that God is speaking. But after you have spoken out the joy of knowing that God used you is awesome! What will you do when you feel God pressing your thumbs and saying, "Know that it is me who is speaking. Do you want to go on an adventure?? Follow me!"

48) Samson is born

Icebreaker 1 – Paper towers (8 minutes)
In teams of 2 or 3 try to make the tallest structure, using just paper and nothing else! If people are struggling, an idea is to get them to fold a piece of paper in half and then wrap it around a pen and then open it out a bit to form a pillar. If they are into origami, they'll have no trouble!

Discussion Starter (8 minutes)
Read the following story, "A long time ago when I was younger and rebellious I ended up downtown in Santa Monica, California at about 1:00 AM. It was my birthday I just hopped on a bus from LA to the beach not knowing where I was going to end up. I was dressed in a mini skirt and a halter top. I was ready to go home when I realized I had no idea how to get back. This was my first time in this city and I had only been in California for about a month.

I was 20 years old, had 1 bus token and was sitting on a bus stop bench freezing. I remember closing my eyes and asking God to please help me get back home, which was a Motel I was staying at for 35 dollars a night. The next thing I can remember was a man that came up to me. It started to get warm. He looked like a normal man wearing blue jeans and a navy blue hood shirt. He asked if I was going home and I said yes. He then began to tell me to take the next bus that comes to the last stop. The bus driver will give me a transfer and take that bus to Vine St. Then he walked away. I would have seen where he went but the bus came right then I hopped on the driver gave me a transfer when I didn't even ask for one.

The next turn of events happened just like the man told me. I ended up at the Motel. I realized I have no idea where this man came from. I was not scared when he approached me in the middle of nowhere and I never told him where I was going. All I can think of is he was an angel."

Q – Do you think this was an angel? Why? Why not? (Discuss).

Q – Have you ever had help from an angel? (Discuss)

Q – Why do you think angels don't stick around to answer questions? (Their purpose is to be messengers and not to draw attention to themselves).

Introduction (1 minute)

Last week we saw the Israelites under attack from the Midianites. This week it is the turn of the Philistines! I expect Gideon wondered, "What can one man do against an army?" He was soon to find out that with 300 soldiers he could beat 132,000. Again the Lord moves to find someone who can defeat the enemy controlling them. What can one man do? The baby to be born is well.... you'll find out.

Teaching (20 minutes)

READ Judges 13:1-25

Q – Take a look at verse 1. Does any of this sentence this sound familiar from last time? (In Judges 6:1 it says that the Israelites again did evil in the eyes of the Lord and that God gave them in to the hands of the Midianites for 7 years. They've done the same thing again, but now it is 40 years).

It would be easy to think from reading this that it is saying that 40 years of Philistine rule has passed. What it's actually saying is that during the 40 years of Philistine rule, Samson was born... probably 5 years into their rule.

Q – Can anyone summarise what took place? (An angel appears to a lady called Hazelelponi, but we can call her Hazel. She tells her husband Manoah. Manoah then wants to speak to the angel to ask how to bring up the boy. The angel returns. Manoah asks some questions and sorts out an offering, not realising the man is actually an angel. There is a sign and a while later Hazel gives birth to Samson).

Q – As soon as Manoah hears about it there seems to be some confusion... almost a comedy of errors. What problems does Manoah have?

He doesn't get from Hazel's description that she has spoken to an angel. He thinks a prophet has spoken to her. Manoah also wants more information from the messenger and asks God to make him to return.

Q - Does he get any more information? (Not really, but the angel returns and says that the boy should have no grapes either!)

So Manoah tries to offer a sacrifice to the angel.

Q – Do people worship angels today? (Yes they do. Often people have ornaments and believe it brings them a connection with angels. This is a bad idea!).

Q – Why is worshipping an angel a bad idea? (Worship is reserved for God, angels are created beings. God will send them when we need them, so we shouldn't contact them directly. That can risk communicating with a wrong spirit).

He freaks out thinking they are going to die when God lights up the sacrifice.

Q – Why is it silly to think that God is going to kill them? (The angel has just told them that they are going to be part of God's plan. God is hardly going to kill them!)

Q – Look carefully at what Manoah's wife tells him. Is there anything she doesn't tell him what the angel said? (That Samson would begin the defeat of the Philistines).

Q – Why do you think she didn't tell him? (Interestingly the angel says in verse 13 "Your wife must do all that I have told her." Maybe he hadn't appeared to both of them for a reason. Perhaps Hazel picked up on this and didn't think Manoah had the level of faith to see Samson doing such a thing. Maybe she was concerned that he might negatively influence Samson away from this calling).

Perhaps Hazel would probably be better at bringing the boy up!

Q – Remind us what a Nazirite should do? (Drink no alcohol, not eat anything not permitted by Jewish law and not cut his hair).

Q – The angel obviously appeared because he had an important message. What was so important about the need for him to be a Nazirite? (Samson would be given a significant ability. This ability would be one which no-one has ever had before or would ever have since).

Q - Why do you think Samson had to observe these Nazirite laws? (God knew that Samson would need to keep his feet on the ground and be reminded that this power was from God for God's purposes and not for his own purposes).

This was something he would constantly need reminding of.

Q – If Samson decided to do his own thing and not obey these instructions, what do you think might happen? (He wouldn't have his super strength).

So keeping close to God was the most important thing that Samson could do. If he had a relationship with God he would rely on God to live and doing those things required of him would come naturally. However if Samson did not regularly spend time with God, he would take his eyes off God and live his own way. Inevitably there would come a time when what he wanted to do would conflict with what God required of him. Then Samson would begin to resent doing what was required of him. He would see it as a ritual, and annoyance rather than devotion to his Lord.

Q – So in our lives, what can take over and get in between us and God? (Lots of things can take up the key times that we need to be setting apart for him. Computer games and social media sites can cause our time to disappear very quickly, leaving nothing for us and God).

Q – Would you ever give up a computer game or social networking site, if it meant you would discover a closer relationship with God? (Discuss)

This can happen to all of us, when we forget to spend time with Jesus. We can forget that he is truly with us and our hearts can become misdirected by things that are meaningless. It is really important to guard that which is valuable in our lives as we can all too easily get into bad habits.

Round up (1 minute)
So the Lord has something incredible lined up for Samson's life. He had his whole life ahead of him. However before any of the incredible things could happen, God wanted to do some very important things in Samson's life. He was looking to build both character and a dependence on God rather than a self-dependence.

Samson would face some things in his future that he simply couldn't overcome unless he received that inner strength that comes from God. If Samson could learn to value his relationship with God above everything else, then he would succeed in everything he would do.

For us it is the same. If we will appreciate the value of knowing God and getting to know him more and more, we will become strong and be able to face the challenges that will come our way. There will be some big, big, challenges that we will only be able to succeed in if we can find a place of trust with our heavenly Father. This comes through relationship; an investment of time that will reap big rewards.

Pray (5 minutes)
Take time to talk to God and ask if there is something you need to give up, in order to know him more. Make a promise today to make that sacrifice and not go back to it.

49) Samson grows up

Icebreaker 1 – Paper ball throw challenge
Ask for 3 volunteers. You are going to test their skills at throwing whilst laying down. Get them to lay on the floor facing upwards with a bin 1 metre away from their feet. Give them 5 chances

Icebreaker 2 – What superhuman abilities do you have?
Find out from the youngsters if they have any unusual party tricks. Can you break bricks with your hands? Sit in a bath of ice? Can you raise one eyebrow and not the other? Lick your elbow? Wiggle your ears? Make bubbles with your mouth?

Q - If you had a superpower what would it be? (Discuss).

Introduction (1 minute)
Last week we read about an angel appearing and announcing the birth of a baby boy called Samson. This is an important birth.

Q – Some of you might already know something about the story of Samson. What do you remember of Samson, was the Samson of the Bible a good man or a bad man? (They might be on their guard knowing that because you have asked the question might mean that there is an unusual answer... Discuss).

Teaching (15 minutes)
READ Judges 14:1-20

Q – Having read this. Can any of you describe what you think Samson might look like? Height? Build? etc. (It's easy to imagine he was built like a superhero. Did he have big muscles or was he huge like Goliath? But actually his size isn't mentioned in the Bible. In fact later on the Philistines would get Delilah to nag him to find out the *secret* of his strength. So maybe it wasn't as obvious as having big muscles).

Q – How would you describe Samson's character by his actions?
(He seems to be a bit of a renegade. A bit naughty, hardly the man of God we would expect him to be. Maybe you can't see it yet, but keep listening!).

Q – Take a look at verse 5. Where was Samson? (At the vineyards of Timnah).

Q – Can you remember what the angel said that Samson was not allowed to eat? (Grapes).

Q – Imagine you were told not to eat chocolate; can you name some places where it would be inappropriate for you to visit? (Cadbury world, the Lindt shop etc.)

Q – So Samson sees a Philistine woman and tells his folks about her. How would you feel about telling your folks that you fancy someone? (Discuss)

Q - What did his parents say? (They gave him some advice... go for an Israelite woman).

Q - Why did they advise that? (That's what God had said that his people should do).

Q – Why did God say that? (Discuss)

Q – Why was it more important for Samson to marry an Israelite woman? (Because sleeping with someone from the enemy side could make him vulnerable. Plus he was a leader and needed to set a good example for God's people).

Q – What should Samson do then? (Listen to his parents).

Q – How would you feel if you fancied someone who was not a Christian and your folks advised you to not pursue it? (Discuss what you might do).

Q – Take a look at verse 4. "But his father and mother didn't know it was of the Lord." What do you think that means? (That God had a plan to annoy the Philistines, and it involved Samson having a Philistine wife).

Q – Does this mean that the Bible says it's okay to date people who aren't Christians? (Well if you continue reading you'll find out how that one turns out!).

Q – Take a look at verse 9. Something is going on there. Can any of you say what that is? (Take a look at the previous Chapter 13 verse 4. He has violated his Nazirite vow by eating something that is unclean).

Q – Do you think Samson knew that he shouldn't do this? (Yes. His parents would have told him about the angel visit).

Q – So Samson is quite a strong guy. But can you tell me what you think his weaknesses are? (He is easily persuaded by women. He didn't seem to care about God's laws. He didn't want to listen to his parents).

Q – What do you think will happen if Samson gives into his weaknesses? (He's going find his life will become more and more of a mess, and he will be risking his future happiness).

Q – When we are weak in an area, what can we do to be protected from failing in that area? (Go to people we trust for help, support and advice).

Samson's weaknesses are becoming quite clear, and his future wife also seems to be a weakness that the Philistines are also targeting in order to hurt Samson. If only he had taken his parent's advice! Rather than telling Samson about the threats, she acts against their best interests. This makes Samson very vulnerable. Here is an important lesson that Samson has to get. Or will it be something we'll look back at and say "Why didn't he learn??"

Q – Samson has allowed this situation to come about. He has allowed what he wants to get in the way of what he needs. What does Samson need right now? (Loyalty and someone he can trust).

Round up (2 minutes)
It sounds strange to be talking about weakness today, when Samson was known only for his strength. Our weaknesses can be our undoing if we aren't teachable and allow our characters to be shaped. When God requires our obedience it is for our protection and our good. Sometimes our folks might say to us "It's for your own good." We know that they are saying that although we might not agree with their decision, that they are making the decision with our long term interests in mind.

Although Samson had great physical strength, he had great character weaknesses too. With such weakness, Samson needed good friends around him and he needed to lean wholeheartedly on God. When we are weak it is not a time to become depressed or self-destructive, but take it as an opportunity to know God and let him make us strong.

Pray (8 minutes)
Take time to think where you are weak and hand that weakness over to God. Ask him to replace your weakness with his strength. Remember his strength often flows through worship. Take time to thank him for all he is doing in your life.

50) Samson doesn't learn his lesson

Icebreaker 1 – Hum that tune (10 minutes)
Split the group into teams. Each team must select a player to hum a tune (you can also use a kazoo if you want for extra fun!). That player is then given a piece of paper with a tune to hum or play for their team. If they get it right they get a point. Play then moves to the next team.

For added fun you can get two people from different teams to hum their tunes at the same time! Here is a random selection of some tune examples you might like to use:

Old MacDonald had a farm	Rocking around the Christmas tree
The wheels on the bus	My Lighthouse
Humpty Dumpty	Happy Day
Johnny B Goode	You don't know you're beautiful
Somewhere over the rainbow	I believe in angels
I'm a believer	Rule the world
Fly me to the moon	Thriller
I will survive	God save the Queen

Introduction (1 minute)
This morning we're going to be looking at an unusual turn of events involving a man of God. It's unusual because this man shows that God is with him, but he doesn't seem to be that godly. And figuring out what good to copy and what mistakes to learn from is a bit tricky.

Samson is our guy. He has this maverick attitude that has both good and bad points. Good in that he is fearless in the face of evil, he will stand and fight when others settle thinking that things can't be changed. He is not so good in that he forgets his promises to God, he only prays in an emergency, he doesn't think about his mistakes and he doesn't seem to care what happens as a result of what he does.

That said, he is a great guy to have on your side, but an unconventional man of God. Samson lived near the border between the Israelites and the Philistines. The Philistines were trying to rule the Israelites, but there was no Israelite army at this time trying to stop them.

Teaching 1 (15 minutes)
READ Judges 15:1-13 (don't let them read on yet!...)

Q – Who can tell me what is the first thing to get Samson angry? (His wife had been given to someone else).

This might throw up a couple of questions. How could Samson have a wife and then someone else marry her? Where was Samson in all this? Why did this make him go attack the Philistine field? If you remember, he made a bet with the Philistines that they wouldn't guess the answer to his riddle. Well those whom Samson bet with made his wife give them the answer. So Samson lost the bet and went off in a rage to find the 30 linen jackets that he bet. He took them off people whilst they were wearing them.

It seems he was away for a while, and his wife was given by her dad to marry someone else.

Q – How many of you girls would be happy for your dad to choose who you should marry? (Discuss. Your dad would probably make a good decision, but you would rather marry whom you loved?).

Q – So why do you think this made Samson go off and attack the Philistine field? (It was at Samson's wedding, whilst he was off that his wife was married to someone else. It was her Philistine dad who made the decision and she was probably married to a Philistine man).

Q – So Samson uses this as an excuse to go annoy the Philistines. What did he destroy? Tell me exactly. (Fields where grain was growing, stacks of cereal grain that had been harvested, as well as vineyards for wine, and olive trees).

Q – How serious do you think this was? Explain. (Very serious. It would have been a criminal offence. If there was no grain it would be difficult to make bread, no grapes mean no wine, and the markets would soon run out of food).

Q - On a scale of 1 to 10 (1 being lowest), how cross would you be if you were about to make some toast for lunch and you were out of bread, so you had to go to Tescos and they were out of bread too? (Discuss).

You probably wouldn't be angry enough to kill someone, but Samson's wife who wasn't his wife was killed in revenge for the field burning.

Q – Take a look at verses 9-11. How has this changed from a small family dispute? (It says that the Philistines camped in Judah, which was Israelite territory. They would have done that in a large number. This is reflected by the number of Israelite men who then go to talk to Samson).

So this has turned from a local dispute with a few fights to the national army of the Philistines being mobilised.

Q – So the 3000 Israelite men, do they go up to fight the Philistines? (No).

Q – Why don't they go up to fight the Philistines? (They don't want any trouble. Instead they go to hand Samson over to the Philistines).

Q – So the Philistines are forcibly controlling Israel. Samson tries to pick a fight with them all on his own and his fellow Israelite men don't want to join him in battle. What do you think about this? (This probably reflects something of how they view Samson, as a bit of a Lunatic, but more importantly rather than fighting the Philistines, they have already accepted defeat, see verse 11).

Our actions often reflect whether we have faith or not. They had given up on trusting God for a solution to the Philistine problem. God seems to be far from their minds.

Maybe this helps us to understand a bit more why God made Samson such a lary character. If no-one else was going to get up and fight, Samson had to be a bit "unusual." Unfortunately the Israelites seem prepared to hand over their only hope of victory to be killed by the enemy. As Samson is brought over to the army of Philistines they intimidate him by approaching him with a loud battle cry.

Q – How would you feel, as one person being brought to a group of men numbering about 1000, who all hate you and want you dead? (Discuss).

But something is about to happen. How on earth can Samson get out of this? Maybe this is how...

[Optional] Fight scene clip – Jackie Chan "First Strike" (5minutes)
(Just to get people ready to picture the scene that they are about to read next, why not play the ladder fight scene from the Jackie Chan movie "First Strike.")

Teaching 2 (10 minutes)
READ Judges 15:11-20

So maybe like Jackie Chan, Samson grabs an object nearby and takes on a large group of enemy attackers. It's difficult to picture the scene of 1 verses 1000. Maybe the one at the front got hit and the others were like "let's get 'im." People are flying left right and centre, bodies piling up, some trying to have a go and getting clonked on the head. Others go charging in and getting the same treatment. And those at the back have realised they are just going to be part of the destruction so they quickly turn and run. And Samson is like "Oi, come back you yella bellies!! I haven't finished yet!"

Q – This is an impossible story. So how did Samson win? (God gave him supernatural strength and power to attack and do what the Israelite army wouldn't).

Q – Take a look at verse 16. God has just given Samson this great victory. Is there anything Samson has forgotten to do? (By saying "I have made donkeys of them... I have killed a thousand men," he is forgetting to give God the credit for the victory. It was God's Spirit working on him that gave him the physical strength, not his own abilities).

Q – Is there anything that then reminds Samson to thank God? (Yes. When he realises he is so thirsty, with no water around he realises he needs God! So he admits that God has given him the victory and says he needs water).

The place Samson had this victory was called "Lehi" (means Jawbone). What would have happened if all Samson could find was a toilet brush! God provided the ability for Samson, but also the equipment to win!

Q - One last question... Can any of you figure this out: It says in verse 20 "Samson led Israel for twenty years in the days of the Philistines." Normally a comment like this is put at the end of a person's story, but we still have the story of Samson and Delilah to go. Can you guess why it is put here? (It is probably because Samson's contribution as a leader ended at this point, no longer effective for the cause, though his biggest victory was yet to come).

Round up (2 minutes)
Samson has the most amazing victory. He seems invincible! He's a super hero! But unfortunately he doesn't have a super attitude. We've seen this is his weak spot. He's got some serious character flaws which will cost him if he's not careful. He's starting to show that he is relying on the strength of his hair, rather than on God.

If you've ever watched Captain America, he is hero who leads an army from the front. Samson is confident in his independence and can't even lead himself! He only thinks of God in an emergency, which will be a problem as there will be times when he needs wisdom before an event happens. He's not that hot on obeying God either. So with an independent attitude a failure to obey God and a vengeful heart, he's in for a whole lot of trouble...

We can be the cleverest or most gifted individual. However that will only get us so far in life. We need someone by our side who has great wisdom to lead us and guide us. Someone who can see the troubles that are ahead and prepare us for them. When we invite God into our lives, he isn't just an emergency service to get us into heaven. He wants a relationship with us, where he can shape our characters to make it through the toughest of challenges.

Next week we're going to see how things end for Samson...

Pray (As long as it takes!)

51) Samson rejects God's warnings

Icebreaker 1 – Human Bop it (5 minutes)
If you can get the Bop it music, it will help with this game. Otherwise the backing track from Britney Spears' "Toxic" will work! Instead of using the "Bop it" game, allocate a hand sign for each of these actions:

BOP IT, PULL IT, TWIST IT, FLICK IT, SPIN IT, PASS IT.

Start the music and the first person to start will have to immediately respond with the sign that you call out. Do a number of calls before saying "pass it" and moving on to the next person.

When enough people are out, maybe have a head to head battle with two of the best players.

Introduction (1 minute)
Last week we read of the amazing story of how Samson defeated 1000 Philistine men all by himself, but it was actually God who gave him the victory. Samson sort of forgot that, until he realised he was about to die of thirst and that he needed God to provide some water for him.

Before Samson was born, an angel appeared to Samson's mother and told her that she would have a son who would lead Israel. The angel also had some instructions to be passed on to the boy, "He mustn't have any wine, or eat any grapes or anything unclean. He must also not shave his head and to live according to Nazirite laws." The angel didn't say this to Samson's mother, but he would have great strength too.

So far Samson has had trouble keeping to these instructions, yet he has benefitted from the supernatural power given him by God.

Teaching 1 (10 minutes)
READ Judges 16:1-22 (don't let them read on yet!...)

Q – In the first verse of chapter 16 we read about Samson sleeping with a woman who isn't his wife, who isn't an Israelite and who has a questionable work situation. How do you think this describes where he is at with his relationship with God?
(Distant. He seems to have very little self-control, or care about what God wants for him).

Q – Remind us about what is so special about Samson? (God has given him the role of leading Israel and with that super strength to fight them).

Q – Samson isn't representing God very well. Does anyone know why God hasn't just taken away Samson's super strength ability or caused the ground to open up and eat him? (God had promised his gift to Samson. It says in Romans 11:29 "God's gifts and his call are irrevocable." Irreversible, he won't take them back).

Q – How does it make you feel that the gifts God gives you, he won't take back? (Reassured that when we make mistakes, we are given second chances?).

Q – The Philistines who lived in Gaza find out that Samson is in their territory and they surround the place where he is opting to wait til dawn to get him. Why do you think they were going to wait until dawn? (So they could see as it was dark and Samson was very dangerous).

Q – Can you describe the size of the gates that Samson picked up? (They were not just a front garden gate to a house, they were the city gates. They had to keep out an army, so they were large and very sturdy. To read that he also carried them up a hill tells a lot about his great strength).

Q - Why do you think it says Samson picked up the gates? (The Philistines must have locked the gates, thinking they could keep Samson within the city and have him cornered).

Q – Samson falls in love with another woman. This woman, Delilah is located in the Valley of Sorek in Philistine territory near Israel. "Sorek" means redness as in the redness of grapes in a lush vineyard. How do you think this might tie in with what the angel said? (The angel said he was to keep away from grapes. The Valley of Sorek would have been a fertile area, perfect for vineyards to grow. Alarm bells should be ringing in Samson's head).

Q – Why do you think Samson hasn't been paying attention to the way God said he should live? (Because he is distant from God, he's going his own way to get what he wants).

Q – Do you think Samson should have to choose between God and the woman he loves? (God has a better plan for Samson. One that involves living! His plan was also one that involved a woman who will be loyal to Samson).

Scenario (8 minutes) Online chat
Imagine the scene: You are at school. The boy or girl whom you have admired from afar for some time notices you and get chatting with him/her. You can't believe it, but he/she gives you their phone number and says they would like to chat online later. They ask if you can be online at 7pm and you say yes, however when you walk away you realise you don't have access to chat online.

Your folks have already said that you aren't old enough to chat online. You feel you are old enough and that lots of your friends chat online. You know that if you don't chat online with this person, they may not be nice to you the next day. You are torn between obeying what your parents have said, and chatting with this person you have a crush on.

Q – How would you deal with this issue? (Discuss)

Q - What would you say to a friend who might suggest you go online at their house? After all it is just chatting? (Honouring your folks keeps you protected).

Q – Imagine that this person you had a crush on began pestering you to go online with you. You really like them and feel so happy with them. How would you deal with that? (It's important to know that sometimes people have hidden motivations for why they want you to do something. They may want to draw you out from your parent's protection to take advantage of you).

Teaching 2 (10 minutes)
So Delilah is offered money to discover the secret of Samson's great strength, a lot of money. She is offered 1,100 shekels of silver. A shekel was a weight. In 17:10 we see that 10 shekels of silver is suggested as a yearly wage (be it a low wage).

Q – As Delilah pesters Samson, how does he treat her questions about his strength? (He treats it as a bit of a joke).

Q – When Delilah first called out "Samson the Philistines are upon you!" I always thought that he beat them all up each time. What does the Bible actually tell us? (It says they were hidden, but it says nothing about him discovering them).

Q – Take a look at verse 15. What word does Delilah use which contributes to Samson giving up the secret? (She says "How can you say 'I love you' when you won't confide in me. In other words, "If you love me you will do what I want").

This is a phrase that should always make alarm bells sound in your head. If someone has to test your love for them by making you do something you don't feel is right, you can tell that they don't love you back. Samson couldn't tell that Delilah had riches as her hidden motivation for pestering him.

Q – How could Samson save himself? (To run away from Delilah was his best chance of safety).

Q – At last Samson gives in, and it is too late to change his mind. What does it say he expected to happen, even though his hair was gone? (He still expected to have his strength).

Samson had given up the last of the commands that the Lord had told him to keep. There was nothing left. Though God still didn't take away his gift). READ Judges 16:23-31

Round up (2 minutes)
God still used Samson against the Philistine army, but Samson's attitude made the whole situation very messy. Samson lacked two key things: a relationship dependent on God and self-discipline to keep him protected.

It has to be said that Samson tested God and not in a good way! He's often found in vineyards when he needs to steer clear of them. He touches dead stuff and even eats from it; he's often with women of other nations. But the last thing to go is his hair, which he's told not to cut. Even then, his attitude was "I'll still be okay."

However it turned out that it wasn't going to be okay. Though we might not want to hear it, sometimes what we want for ourselves can actually do us more harm than good. It takes trust in God to give up something or someone that we really want in the interests of being loyal to God.

When it comes to love we can be in too close and need a friend to help us make the right decisions. Samson had become a lone ranger. He was separated from those he had known when he was young and now was making friends with people who didn't have his best interests at heart.

Pray (As long as it takes!)

52) Naomi blames God

Icebreaker 1 - Sweet Russian Roulette (5 minutes)
Have a bag of sweet and sour sweets (eg. Skittles). Pass the bag round for each person to take one (without looking) and eat it. If it is sweet, they are through to the next round. If it is sour, they are out. The winner gets a pack of sweets.

Icebreaker 2 – Friends questionnaire (5 minutes)
Get each youngster to write down the following 3 questions:

    1) Tell us something interesting that you were born with.
    2) Tell us something interesting that you have learned.
    3) Tell us of any interesting experiences you have had.

Then get the youngsters to spend 5 minutes mingling asking each other those questions and writing down the answers. They are not allowed to give the same answer twice.

The person with the most interesting answer is the winner.

Discussion - Steve Johnson blames God for his overtime drop (8 minutes)
Read the following report on an American football game:

"It wasn't his own hands or the wind or the pitch that made American Footballer Steve Johnson drop the ball, in what should have been a game-winning Touchdown catch in the end zone. It was God. Johnson had a perfect pass in his hands that would have given his team an overtime victory over the heavily favoured Steelers. Instead of walking off the field the hero, however, he dropped a crucial pass.
The 24-year-old then wrote this on Twitter:

"I PRAISE YOU 24/7!!!!!!" "AND THIS HOW YOU DO ME!!!!! YOU EXPECT ME TO LEARN FROM THIS???
HOW???!!! ILL NEVER FORGET THIS!! EVER!!! THX THO..."

Players always thank God after a victory, so it's sort of refreshing to see one blame him after a loss. Not that I think the Almighty is overly concerned with sporting events or played any role in Johnson taking his eyes off the ball, but I'm glad Steve Johnson does."

Q - Do you think it is right to blame God when things don't go the way we expect them? (Discuss).

Q - Do you think Christian sports people get special treatment from God? (Discuss).

Q - What other reasons could there have been for dropping the ball? (He hadn't trained well enough, or that he was just rubbish on that day).

Q - What do you think Steve Johnson can learn from this? (Like Batman, sometimes a hero needs to be tested!)

Q - If God was testing Steve do you think he passed or failed? (Even when we fail a test there's still a lot we benefit from through the experience).

Today we're going to talk about when times go wrong and we feel like blaming God. Before we read from the book of Ruth, it's important to picture where these events took place in history.

Q - If I was to ask you, could you tell me what sort of things took place in the mid-1800s (140 years ago) what would you say? (Maybe the first ever international football match? The first underground railway under the Thames? An industrial revolution and a public health act? Horses and carts were being used for transport rather than cars? Ruth lived about 140 years after Joshua and the walls of Jericho).

The Old Testament so far
So Abraham had left Hur to go to land God promised and God gave a son. Abraham nearly sacrificed his son Isaac, but God provided a Ram. Issac's son Jacob (stole his brother Esau's birth right), Jacob's son Joseph (with his coat of many colours) ended up in Egypt with a famine. Moses led the Hebrews out of Egypt back to Promised Land. After the death of Moses, Joshua leads the attack and the walls of Jericho fall down. We now pick up about 140 years after the Jericho incident.

Time of uncertainty
There has been war and conflict between Moabites and Israelites and famine in Bethlehem. Bethlehem is a key place in history, where King David would be born, of whom one of his descendants would be Jesus. This was not only a key place in history, this story is a key event in history and if this doesn't happen there will be no king David. This is the story of King David's great grandmother Ruth.

The whole book of Ruth takes place over a course of 6 weeks.

Teaching 1 – (20 minutes)
READ Ruth 1:1-22
Q - Why do you think God went all the way out to Moab to choose Ruth to be King David's great grandmother? (Destiny!)

DNA? There is character in the genes! Not only can we inherit certain characteristics from parents, like a sense of humour and tendency to be athletic or arty, in Ruth's case we can see she has determination. She is a risk taker, with faithfulness and has integrity of heart.

But also we receive the benefit of parents and grandparents where we receive their influence, teaching, discipline and ethics as well as their prayers their love, support etc. So parents and grandparents etc., have a massive influence over us. They have a tough job, helping to shape us to turn out, with the ability to make the right decisions and be loving people.

Q - So they're settled in Moab. What two things happen to make Naomi want to go back home to Bethlehem? (Her sons die and the famine had ended in Judah).

Q - Why does Naomi tell Ruth and Orpah to return to their parent's home? (Because she is going back to her home, and doesn't feel she is any use to them).

Q - What on earth is Naomi going on about having a new husband and having more sons so that Ruth and Orpah could marry them? (In Jewish tradition if a woman marries and her husband dies before they have any children, she can then marry his brother to carry on the family name).

Q - What would they have had to do in order to leave and move back to Bethlehem? (They would have had to sell up their stuff that they had accumulated over 10 years. There were no removals companies in those days, so they would only be able to take belongings that you could carry or put on a donkey, and exchange the rest for silver or gold or something).

Q - These are sad times and Naomi doesn't have much to show for her life, and no family to cherish. So who does Naomi blame for her sad times? (v13 "the Lord's has been against me!" and also v20 "the Almighty has made my life very bitter")

Pleasant to Bitter

We see here two times that Naomi says that God is to blame for her sadness, which she calls bitterness. Her name "Naomi" means pleasant or sweet. But people are shocked to see how this pleasant lady who has only been away 10 years looks so different. Perhaps her changed look is because of her sadness, it can add years to your face!). (A bit like our sweet and sour test)

She explains how her life has changed to bitterness and as a result has changed her. And she places the responsibility with God. She uses the word for God "El Shaddai" which means Almighty, the ruler of creation, but also God our provider. Like she is saying that she believes that the all powerful God has provided her with a bitter life.

Q - Did God provide her with a bitter life? (Discuss)

Q - Do you think there is a danger in blaming God? (The danger is that we could be wrong and bitterness towards God can result which can steal the joy that God wants us to have).

Q - Can you think of anyone else who blamed God in the Bible? How did it turn out for them? (Job. God gave him and his friends a telling off, and reminded them that as the Almighty, he can do what he wants).

Q - Do you think God can allow our lives to become bitter for a good reason? And what reason do you think that might be? (There may be times when God will allow this for a season, a period of time that is appropriate for God to work in us. The reasons are always appropriate to the person, but in Naomi's case God was working though she could not see it). Naomi's name was "pleasant" but her expectation that her life would be pleasant had not turned out that way. She wanted to change her name to reflect her present experience.

Q - So what does she do about it? (She changes her name to "Mara")

Q - What does "Mara" describe? (It reflects a disappointment with her circumstances)

Q – We all have certain expectations for our lives. How they might go, what we might do. Humanly speaking, how do we respond when we become disappointed? (We might get grumpy, maybe not pray, or not attend church or react in a different way and turn to comfort ourselves in our disappointment with alcohol or food).

Q – Do you think actions like these make our situation better or worse? (Worse).

Q – Is there another way, a better way of dealing with our disappointments? (Talking it through helps a lot. Talk to others, talk to God. Sometimes we won't gain an understanding of all that is going on straight away).

Q - Should we expect God to only bless us? (Sometimes God allows harsher circumstances to happen in our lives with an end goal that helps us. Sometimes God has to take what the enemy meant for evil and turn it for our good).

Q - So Naomi is disappointed. What does she do about it? (She accepts it, and carries on still respecting God).

Q – Maybe Naomi asked God why all this was happening. Do you think we are always going to know why? (Sometimes it's better to ask God "who are you for me in this time"? to get a reassurance of how God is working things out for us).

Round up (1 minute)
During his lengthy discussions in the book of Job, Job asks the question, should we expect only good things from God and not hardships too? The American footballer was under the assumption that if he gave God the glory for everything (making it known that he was a Christian) God would in turn bless his game and cause him to win.

But actually it isn't so much about our story, as about God's story. God doesn't revolve around us, but the other way around. Naomi returns from Moab feeling empty and disappointed. Unbeknown to her, Naomi's situation is full with potential as she returns home with Ruth: person of great importance.

At times when life for us is bitter, we can look for answers and come up with nothing but negativity. Importantly the story isn't over yet. Oftentimes we can't see the good things that God has prepared for us; sometimes they are just around the corner!

Pray (5 minutes)
Take time for people to consider disappointments they have experienced, to write them down anonymously and post them in a box to hand back to God.

53) Ruth finds favour

Icebreaker 1 (5 minutes)
Get the youngsters to stand in a circle and look to the floor. Tell them to look up at someone. If two people are looking at each other, they are eliminated. The winning person or pair are those who last to the end.

Discussion starter - Woman's blind date with long lost brother (10 minutes)
Sarah Kemp, 42, from Edinburgh met London-based George Bentley, 47 on a dating website. After swapping photos and emails the pair met up at a pub near George's home in East Ham.

After talking for an hour about shared childhood experiences, she realised he was her brother. It was the first time they had seen each other in 35 years. According to bookies William Hill the odds of such a meeting are 500million-to-one.

Cleaner Sarah (speaking to The Daily Record) said: "We had so much in common and we really enjoyed each other's company. It was as if we'd known each other all our lives. "To meet your long-lost brother, in a bar, after over 30 years would be something by itself.

"But to meet him in those circumstances, on a date, for crying out loud, really is something else." George and Sarah were born in Ashford, Kent but were separated in 1975 when their parents, David and Felicity divorced.

Six-year old Sarah joined her mum in Edinburgh, while David, nine, joined his dad in London. From then on, the families stopped speaking.

When they grew up the pair did try and make contact, but without success. The search was made more difficult after Sarah got married in 1989. She got divorced years later but kept the name 'Kemp'.

George, a builder, said: "After a while, I think both Sarah and I gave up looking."

When the pair made the discovery they felt embarrassed, but were soon celebrating the happy news by drinking champagne all evening. They have since met up several times and George said: "This was the meeting of a lifetime and we are now planning to see each other as often as possible to catch up on the time spent apart."

Q - Do you think God has an influence over the people we meet?

Q - Do you think that we are "meant" to bump into some people?

Q - Is it possible that just by having a brief meeting with one person that our lives can be changed forever?

Introduction (1 minute)
Last week we looked at how we deal with disappointments, and asked "Is it ok to blame God when things seem to go wrong?" And we realised that actually life isn't so much about our story, but rather it is about our story with God. He doesn't revolve around us it's the other way around. We know that he has the very best of plans for us. Today we're going to discover a way in which God might lead you to meet someone, just by going about your business…

Teaching (15 minutes)
READ Ruth 2:1-23
Story so far Naomi is from Bethlehem. She got married, but there was a famine, so they moved to the land of Moab. Naomi's husband Elimelech dies and her two sons die having no children to pass on the family name or land to. Ruth, the Moabite wife of one of Naomi's sons refuses to return home. Instead she promises to stay with Naomi and go with her back to Bethlehem.

Q - How are Naomi & Ruth doing financially? (Really bad. They are very poor and will have to sell their land).

Q - What job is Ruth doing? (It's harvest time. Ruth is gleaning. She is picking up any grain that may have been dropped by those collecting the harvest).

Q - Do you think she is stealing? (Gleaning was allowed in the O.T. for those who were poor. Things like not harvesting the corners of your field to allow poor people to collect were also done, although not all land owners did this).

Q - Have a look at the first few verses. Sometimes when something is important it is repeated. It's like someone holding up a big sign saying "golf sale" with massive arrow. Can you find what's being repeated? ("Boaz from Elimelech's family")

Q - Why is this so important? (For Hebrew people the land and the family name were tied together. Those who were "wider family" had the first opportunity to buy it. Not only was it important to keep the family land it was also the family name. Boaz was from the same family as Naomi's dead husband which would enable them to keep the family name).

Kinsman Redeemer
Ruth and Naomi needed to sell Elimelech's land. However, legally this would also make Ruth a slave to whoever bought the land. Slaves often remained slaves, never being able to buy their own freedom. Therefore in law there was the role of a person called a Kinsman-Redeemer. Youth bible "close relative." Kinsman (relative), redeemer means to "buy back" something, like someone's freedom.

Act it out (5 minutes)
Q - Anyone ever been to a Pawnbroker's? How does it work? (You will need someone to be the shopkeeper and someone else to be the person trying to get as much money as they can for the item).

It's the idea of buying something back. Say you need some money. You take in an item of value (eg. Jewellery). The pawnbroker then lends you a certain amount of money (eg. £200). You then have the choice to either repay the loan to "buy back" your jewellery within a certain time period or you can keep the money, but you'll never see the jewellery again.

So a Kinsman-Redeemer is someone who takes on the role of buying back freedom for someone who was in slavery. And the way it works is that the closest living relative gets first choice for buying someone and allowing them to have their freedom again.

Why is this important? Well in the first few verses we've got this big "GOLF SALE" arrow, pointing at Boaz. God has brought Ruth into place from Moab to be King David's great grandmother. But for that to happen, she needs to meet someone from Elimelech's clan who can buy her land and marry her.

So I've already said that we're going to discover another way in which God might lead you to find a girlfriend or boyfriend, by just going about your business.

Q - Read verse 3. What do you think the Bible is trying to get across by the words "It just so happened"? (That Ruth didn't go looking for Boaz. They hadn't met. However the place that she unknowingly chose to glean for wheat was in Boaz's field).

Q - Do you think there is a deeper meaning to it? (Yes. That God just "so happened" it! God ordained it).

Q - Some people think they need to know their futures. Who they are going to meet and when they are going to meet them. What do the words "It just so happened" tell us about the way God works sometimes? (God will put us in the right place at the right time and he knows the plans he has for us. Sometimes for us to know it all would take some of the fun out of it.).

Q - Take a look at verse 6. The man in charge of the field gives a report to Boaz about Ruth. What does he say? Do you think he is giving a good report or a bad one? (This is a good report. We read in Ch1 about how the whole town was stirred because of Naomi's story and Ruth having left her home to support Naomi. The foreman says "this is that woman." She was respectful to ask to glean, when by law it is her right to do it. And she was very hard working).

Q - A lot of people are afraid of hard work. What does this tell us about the benefits of being used to hard work and not being lazy? (People notice those who work hard, as it is a rare quality. A lot of people don't seem to show stamina when it comes to a bit of hard work. Some go missing when there's a job to be done, or just don't volunteer for things, others give up before the job is finished. So when someone steps up and is ready for some hard work and see it through to the end, people notice it. Proverbs 14:23, "All hard work brings a profit, but mere talk leads only to poverty.")

Round up (2 minutes)
Today we've seen things take an upturn for a lady whose mother-in-law Naomi was disappointed with life. With chance meetings (God-incidences!), hard work and God given favour, she has been able to bring home a great deal of food for Naomi. Here we see the way God often provides for us. Where we do what we can and leave the rest up to God, particularly the things that we can't do. So there is hope for Naomi and Ruth, news of hope that they won't be sold into slavery.

We see the benefits of hard work first hand. Have you ever wanted to be noticed at school? Then live out these character traits that Ruth shows: being faithful to Naomi, being respectful and honest, working hard where the opportunity presents itself and you will reap a reward. Yet in all this, God is responsible for the outcome, not us.

Pray (As long as it takes)

54) Ruth makes her move

Icebreaker 1 – Ninja (10 minutes)
This is a cool Karate game. Everyone forms a circle and holds out one hand pointing into the middle of the circle. With everyone's hands touching people must jump backwards taking a Karate pose (like a statue). One person starts by moving to strike someone else's hand nearby. That person also may take one move to avoid getting struck. If they get struck on the hand by the attacker, the person being attacked loses an arm (which must then be lowered to the person's side). If they move it away in time (without getting hit), play then moves to that player. (Please make sure no-one hits hard!)

Introduction (2 Minutes)
Last week we discovered God-incidences! Where God orders our circumstances and makes things happen in a way that initially seems random and just normal life decisions, but God has something and someone planned for us. He has opportunities that we know nothing about, things that we would love.

The story began in a place called Moab, near Israel around the life of a woman called Naomi. Possibly due to war or disease her husband and two sons die. She is left with two daughters-in-law as family. She decides it is time to return to her homeland, to Bethlehem. But this is where things get interesting. Ruth the wife of one of Naomi's sons refuses to let Naomi go without her. Ruth commits herself to Naomi and at the same time commits herself to follow God.

As they return to Bethlehem, their circumstances are desperate. They are poor and Ruth goes out to find food by picking up bits left behind by the harvesters. Little does Ruth know, but in doing this mundane thing she has stepped into God's plan for her life. She is about to meet someone. She hasn't had to work out this meeting, this is not her plans that have got her here, it is all God.

Since Naomi is so poor she had to sell her land. However according to Jewish customs, Ruth would have to marry whoever bought the land. The first person in line to have the offer of buying the land was a "Kinsman Redeemer" the closest relative to Naomi who would be able to keep the family name going and marry Ruth.

Well as things develop, Ruth coincidentally meets such a person. He is called Boaz. Ruth has unknowingly ended up in his field! Boaz is kind and looks after Ruth's safety and it just happens that she really likes him!

If you're ever concerned about whether you will meet the right person to marry, just read the book of Ruth and see how God will order your steps! So there is hope for Naomi, that the family name will continue...

Paper
Before you read Ruth get 2 small pieces of paper and stick them together in front of everyone with glue UHU or Pritt stick will do (as long as it will dry in the next 20 minutes or so!).

Teaching (10 Minutes)
READ Ruth 3:1-18

Q - What does Naomi hint to Ruth? (That Boaz might make good husband material and that Ruth should go and see him).

Q – How does she suggest that Ruth approaches Boaz? (She suggests Ruth visit him, when he's alone at night).

Q – Why do you think she advises Ruth goes to him at night time? (With customs such as they were in those days, Ruth couldn't just approach him whilst others were around and ask on a date).

Q - Do you think that our parents are good at suggesting suitable boyfriends/girlfriends for us? (Actually sometimes they are better than us. They have experience of people, they notice things that we don't, and they have known you for a long time too. Sometimes someone from the outside can have a better perspective on things.)

Q - So how has Boaz impressed Naomi so far (see ch. 2)? What character traits have we seen in him? (He is very kind, protective, and able to provide for Naomi's future).

Do you think this is a bit like a Jane Austen novel where she is looking to marry well so that she can be well looked after? (There's nothing wrong with choosing someone who is good with money, as choosing someone who is the opposite can be a recipe for disaster. However Ruth's report does show an appreciation that she has for his character and personality).

Have you ever seen Judge Judy? Play a clip from Judge Judy where she asks questions and finds out who is really telling the truth.

SHOW a Judge Judy Clip*

Judge Judy (5 minutes)
Every day Judge Judy makes judgements on the evidence and by asking the right questions she finds out a lot. But also her experience enables her to see a person's character. It is vital that we look for good character when we're interested in dating someone. Looks can be a factor too, but if the person is shallow, selfish or unkind you will end up being miserable and heart-broken! A person with good character can be trusted and will see you through hard times. A shallow person will be out for themselves and gone when the going gets tough.

Parental role
Although we might not want to hear this, sometimes listening to our parents is the best thing we can do. You might occasionally think they are killjoys, but most parents want the very best for you and instinctively they act to protect you. No parent is perfect, they aren't all-knowing and possibly will all do things they regret. But their advice is priceless. They know the power of influence and what can result by getting mixed up with the wrong people. A parent's help comes with the desire to protect us from years of hurt and regret, and their experience counts for an awful lot.

READ Proverbs 15:22 "plans fail for lack of counsel," and Proverbs 19:20, "Listen to advice and accept discipline, and at the end you will be counted among the wise."

Q - What and where is the threshing floor? (It was the place where you thrash the wheat and separate the outer shell of the wheat to get the grain - a dry place probably in the barn).

Q - So what do you think Naomi is suggesting that Ruth do? (Boaz is going to be working late to get the harvest threshed. He is expected to be sleeping in the barn. He would make you a good hubby).

Q – So is Naomi suggesting that Ruth sleep with Boaz? (Yes probably).

Q – Why do you think it might be okay in their situation, but not okay today? (Discuss)

Marriage
This was very early in O.T. and marriage happened basically by an agreement made with the bride's father (and obviously the bride). A

date was set to marry and there would then be a party and a procession of the bride from the parent's house to the husband's house, at which point they would be married.

Ruth's situation is slightly different, since Naomi has become her parent and given her the instruction to go get married! So Ruth has made herself look nice etc., sees where Boaz is sleeping. She uncovers his feet from the blanket, which would have woken Boaz up. She then offers to share his bed ie. to marry him.

Q - What is Boaz's response? (He says "Hang on a second, there's another guy with legally more right to marry you, so we'd better wait before getting too cosy.").

Q – Does he like Ruth? (Yes. And he was fairly advanced in years and Ruth was still young).

Q - What does this tell us about Boaz's character? (He had this young lady willing to sleep with him, but he had in mind her wellbeing too. He thought ahead about the consequences of what would happen if they did sleep together, and showed self-control in being patient.)

Q – You might say "Hang on a second." Boaz says to Ruth "Lie here until morning," it looks like they did sleep together. Why do you think Boaz said this and what do you think it means? (He said it as it was late and if she travelled back at that time, it might not be safe. Also it appears that Boaz slept in his blanket and she slept outside at his feet. Don't try this at home though! Not everyone has the same self-control that Boaz showed!).

The problem is many young people (often it's the boys) have the opposite attitude to Boaz in mind. They don't care who you are destined to marry and a lifetime commitment is not something they are willing or ready to give (although they may well say something different). The only way to know if someone is committed enough is to wait until you are both married!

Q – What were the consequences that could have gone wrong? (If the other man who had the first right to marry her had wanted to, Boaz would have been guilty of sleeping with another man's wife. The act of sex is a deep commitment by two people to each other, so to have done it without knowing they were going to be together for the long term would have been dishonest).

Paper (3 minutes)
Remember those two pieces of paper. Tell the group that when two people have sex it's a bit like these two pieces of paper. There's a physical attachment, but also an emotional and spiritual attachment too. Try to pull the two pieces of paper apart. (Hopefully they will not separate easily, but just pull them apart). Say that just as these pieces of paper have bits of the other, so if two people who aren't committed to each other do it, they take with them emotional attachments of previous relationships. It's like they are carrying round with them emotional pieces of another person.

Q - How does her mum's advice now benefit Ruth? (She saw that Ruth was safe with Boaz and that he would do the right thing by her and not take her for granted).

Q - Why is it that people don't want to wait when it comes to sleeping together? (Sometimes people don't want to face up to the longer-term consequences that sleeping with someone brings, compared to the excitement of the moment).

Q – What do you think the longer-term consequences are for two people who slept together, but no longer want to be in a relationship? (Babies! But also there can be regret or feel used because they are no longer with that person, it hurts a lot more! They may feel guilt and all sorts of negative feelings that taking the right decision doesn't have).

Round up (1 minute)
So we have one more chapter to go to find out what happens to Ruth. Will this other guy want to buy the land and have Ruth as his wife? Or will Boaz get the chance? When we do things right according to God, he honours our faithfulness. You can never go wrong when you obey God!

Sometimes we can be tempted to do things our way, because we want something straight away. When it comes to sex, waiting is the most important thing we can do. Discipline is really important and doesn't just end when you get married. Love is patient and kind. It isn't selfish or rude or evil. It is always interested in protecting the one it loves, it is pure and perseveres through sacrifice.

Pray (As long as it takes)

55) Ruth – Is God going to give me what I want?

Icebreaker 1 – Snowball fight (6 minutes)
Hand out a piece of paper and a pen to each person playing. They then need to write down one unusual fact about themselves. It obviously has to be true and hopefully something people may not know about them! Once they have finished writing down their fact, get the youngsters to scrunch up the piece of paper into a "snowball".

The next stage of the game is the snowball fight. Kids can throw the paper balls at each other from across the room. This can go on for as long or as short as you'd like.

Once you're ready, call out "stop" and get each youngster to pick up the nearest piece of paper to them. They then need to un-scrunch it and read aloud the fact, before guessing who they think it belongs to. Check if the youngster chose correctly and find out more if you like!

Icebreaker 2 – Prize draw extravaganza (10 Minutes)
If you have the money for this icebreaker it is a good one for getting people to connect with feelings of really wanting something and hoping that someone else doesn't get it. Have a good number of small random prizes, whether chocolate, sweet or something else. Place them into three different bags with different colours on them.

Have 2 different dice. On one dice have the words "take prize," "no prize," "give away." The other dice should have three different colours each on two sides.

Players will then roll the first dice to see if they get to take a prize, they get no prize, or they give away a prize to someone else. Then they must throw the coloured dice to see which bag they can take a prize from. They can either take a prize from a bag or from a person. If they get "give away" they must give a prize they currently have to someone else. If they don't have a prize they can take from the bag and give it to someone.

At the end youngsters get to keep their prizes.

Introduction (2 minutes)
We've been on a journey which began with bitterness and blaming God for things that had gone wrong. Naomi and her daughter-in-law returned to Bethlehem in poverty and having to sell their land. The situation looked bad. They were two widows who faced hardship and no home to go to.

But then God changes everything by leading Ruth unknowingly to a field to scavenge grain, the field of a man who can rescue them from their difficulties and bring joy to their lives again. Now all that Ruth wants is to marry this man Boaz.

However there is a big spanner in the works, something that could derail all of this potential happiness. Naomi has to sell her land, but in selling the land Ruth must then marry the purchaser of the land. According to Israelite law the land must first be offered to the closest relative to Naomi's dead husband. This man is not Boaz. If the man gets the land, he gets Ruth as well.

Will this man want to buy the land? Or will Boaz get the chance to buy the land?

When you really want something, the question is this: Is God going to let me have what I want?

Teaching 1 (20 minutes)
READ Ruth 4:1-22, Deuteronomy 25:5-10

Q – The very next day after Ruth has met with Boaz and shown that she wants to marry him, what does Boaz do? (He is out looking for the man with the first choice to buy the land).

Q – What does this communicate to us about what Boaz wants? (He is very keen to get this sorted as soon as possible).

Q - You know when you want something so badly? What might some people be tempted to do in order to get what they want? (They might cheat, steal or deceive).

Q - Some people are ready to scheme and lie in order to get what they want. This might be our way of doing things (trying to make our own way). How does Boaz give the situation over to God? (He deals with people honestly. He figures if "I do things God's way, then he will provide the answer." He obeys the laws given in the Old Testament that relate specifically to this issue, see Deuteronomy 25:5-10).

Q – So there is this tension between what we really want and then letting go to let God lead the course of our life. Doubts may come in... What if God does nothing? Should I make it happen? What if God says "no" to it? Suddenly our minds are filled with worry and anxiety of what to do next.

What would you say to a person in this situation? (There is a verse in the Bible which covers it really well: Proverbs 3:5-6).

> "Trust in the Lord with all your heart
> and lean not on your own understanding;
> in all your ways submit to him,
> and he will make your paths straight."

Q – How do you think Boaz feels when the man says that he will buy the land? (Discuss).

It's easy to fall apart when our worst fears are realised. Suddenly our hopes for the future are dashed. Yet there is an element of faith that is required. To trust God when the situation looks like it is going to plan and to trust God when the situation looks like it isn't going to plan.

We sing Matt Redman's songs a lot. And they might be easy to sing when there's nothing much to be concerned with. But the challenge is to sing it in the times when things are not going as we planned. This is to express faith and trust in God even when we don't get what's going on.

> Blessed be your name
> When the sun's shining down on me
> When the world's 'all as it should be'
> Blessed be Your name
>
> Blessed be your name
> On the road marked with suffering
> Though there's pain in the offering
> Blessed be Your name
> Every blessing you pour out I'll turn back to praise
> When the darkness closes in, Lord still I will say
> Blessed be the name of the Lord

Q – Although the man says he will buy the land, Boaz proceeds to point out the outcome of this man's purchase of the land which includes marrying Ruth and providing for Naomi. Why do you think the man changes his mind? (Suddenly the deal doesn't look so good for him. The proceeds of the land would have to be divided with Naomi and Ruth. It may also compromise the other land assets having to share the profits of those with the women too).

Q – So when it looked least likely, suddenly everything has fallen into place and Boaz gets the opportunity to buy the land

and marry Ruth. And the question we ask ourselves afterwards is "why did I worry?" Why do you think we often find it so hard to trust God and not lean on our own understanding? (Discuss)

Jesus said this in Matthew 18:3 "Truly I tell you, unless you change and become like little children you will never enter the kingdom of heaven." A little child has the greatest trust in his or her parents. They rely on them and trust that everything is taken care of by their parents. Although human parents are imperfect, God reveals himself as the most trustworthy of parents who gives good gifts to his children. We can always trust that God will provide for us his children. We just need to obey even in the face of things that suggest otherwise.

So the elders speak a blessing over Ruth and Boaz, confirming their marriage. God's best comes through our obedience.

Q – Take a look at verses 21-22. What's the significance of the list of names at the end? (The names at the end tell us the reason why this romance story has been included in the Bible. Ruth turns out to be King David's Great Grandmother! The child that they have is part of the family line of David which will lead to Jesus!).

Round up (5 minutes)
So here we have a Moabite woman, and non-Israelite being directed by God to be an ancestor of his own Son Jesus. Although she was a non-Israelite she was a follower of God. God had rejected those who followed other gods (including his own people who did the same), but he welcomes any who will follow him.

In this story we see the hand of God guiding Ruth's circumstances, guiding her decisions, guiding her footsteps. There was no way Ruth could make this happen. She literally didn't know what she was walking into. Yet Father God had it all in hand. And when it looked like there was an impossible barrier placed in the way of Ruth's happiness, God had that covered too. Sometimes we think we need to make our own way, when actually the pressure is off.

We do what we can, but we must leave the rest up to God. He says to us "Be still and know that I am God." Literally "cease striving." He says "Stop trying to make your own way without me. I am the one who directs your paths."

Prayer (As long as it takes!)

56) God becomes real to Samuel

Icebreaker 1 – Red or Black (8 minutes)
Give each person 2 small coloured cards, one red card and one black card. Tell them that they will be given the opportunity to win a prize, by guessing the outcome of a set of random tasks by answering the simple question "red or black?" Each person will make their decision by holding up either a red card or a black card before a task is started. Each task will end with a result of either red or black.

Those who guess correctly will go through to the next round. Those who don't guess correctly will be eliminated. When there is just one player left, they win the prize.

Task 1
Blindfold a player. Using a deck of playing cards, get everyone to guess whether the player will pick out a red card or a black card.

Task 2
Coin flip. Heads or tails? Heads is reds, tails is black.

Task 3
Give someone (who is out of the game) five red balls and five of another colour. Have a basket to aim at. Get those still left to guess which coloured balls will have the most ending up in the bin, red or black.

Task 4
Using the blindfold. Put the red balls and other colour balls on the floor. Mix them up and get someone to pick up 7 balls. Did they pick up more red balls or the other colour?

Introduction (2 minutes)
What we are about to read can only be understood properly by taking a look at the background to the story...

In Old Testament times, the people of Israel would bring sacrifices to be offered to God (usually once a year). The priests in the temple were trained according to the instructions of how to do that sacrifice.

Eli was a priest in God's temple. His role in the temple was to offer the sacrifices that people would bring to the temple to honour God. As Eli got older his two sons took on the same role of offering sacrifices for the people. Unfortunately, there was a problem with Eli's sons... They were greedy and God is about to get very annoyed.

It appears that Eli is also to blame. So if Israel's top priests were dodgy, then it made the whole sacrificial system look like a complete farce. Let's take a look...

Teaching 1 (8 minutes)
READ 1 Samuel 2:12-26

Q – Can anyone summarise what is going on with the sacrifice here? (According to Leviticus 7:31-35, once a sacrifice of meat was offered to God and boiled in a pot, certain people could stick a fork in and eat certain bits that were offered. It was a special privilege for the priests).

Q – What were Eli's sons doing that was evil? (They were taking the food even as it was being offered, rather than after).

Illustration - A chocolate box gift (3 minutes)
Let's put this more simply. Imagine you buy your folks a box of chocolates for Mother's or Father's day or something. You know that it is fairly likely they will offer you at least one chocolate at some point. Now imagine how they would feel if before giving them the box, you opened it and ate the best choc, and then after that you wrapped it up and gave them the box of chocolates.

Q – How do you think your folks would feel? (It would be a bit of an insult and not much of a thank you gift. The reason why the priests were there was to make sure that the offerings were according to the instructions and to be an acceptable offering to the Lord).

Q – Obviously we don't offer animals to God now, because Jesus offered his life in our place. What things can we offer to God nowadays?

- Money. The Bible talks about giving 10% of our income to God.
- Time. Time is like a currency that we spend on things.
- Worship. Worship in the form of heart adoration, in using our creativity to praise him.
- Obedience. Reading his word and doing what it says.

Q – So with these things in mind, how can we make sure that we aren't taking away from God by what we offer to him? (We saw that Eli's sons took away what belonged to God and that was dishonouring to him. In the same way we honour God by not taking away what he deserves).

Q – What was special about the Tent of meeting? (It was the place where the powerful presence of God was. This was a holy place where the Ark of the Covenant was kept. The place where less than 500 years before where God met so powerfully with Moses that people said his face shone when he left the tent).

Q – Do you think Eli's sons actually believed in God? Why? (They were playing with fire! Acting like God wouldn't do anything about their behaviour).

Icebreaker 2 – Speedy Consequences (5 minutes)
If you feel time is on your side, do a super-quick game of consequences. Using the attached template, get people to write in the space provided. Once they have written one thing, they need to fold it over so the next person can't see it and hand it to the person on their left. They then write in the next space, fold it over etc. Then read out some of the funny ones...

Teaching 2 (10 minutes)
There are some serious consequences coming up for Eli and his sons, but before that all goes downhill, God is going to put a new guy in play to prepare for better days than this. READ 1 Samuel 3:1-21

Q – What does it mean… "In those days… there were not many visions"? (God often spoke through his prophets, but no prophets were speaking, so no visions were being communicated to the people).

Q – Why do you think there were not many visions? (See what they say).

Q – Do you think it had something to do with Eli the priest and his poor leadership? Why? (A faithful leader can help fire people up and lead them to God. God always answers in response to prayer).

Q – So where were Samuel's parents in all this? (They lived elsewhere. They dedicated Samuel to God as a thank you, since Samuel's mother couldn't have children. Samuel lived near the Tent of Meeting. They returned yearly to make a sacrifice to God and to give Samuel a new outfit).

Q – What role was Eli in Samuel's life? (Eli was a father figure to Samuel).

Q – How do you think Samuel must have felt to tell Eli that he had done wrong and that God was going to punish his family? (Awkward. He had been brought up by Eli).

Q – So Eli says "Tell me what God said and don't hide anything from me!" What do you think Eli was expecting Samuel to say? (He was expecting bad news).

So Samuel, a really devoted man of God is going to be used in a really difficult situation. Some people have the idea that if God is blessing someone's life, their work will all be brilliant and successful. Samuel is going to be put into a situation where everything is going pear-shaped. However, Samuel's faithfulness is going to shine out regardless of what others do along the way.

Q - So God speaks to Samuel audibly, something that hasn't happened for some time. Do you think there are times that God speaks more obviously than others? Why/why not? (There are times when God speaks very clearly about a calling, a role that he has for someone's life. He wants to set that person on a course and remember the time God spoke about it so that they won't give up in the tough times).

Q – So here God is using a boy to speak to someone who is leading in Israel. Does this thing happen straight away? (No. See verse 19).

Q – How would you feel as a prophet if you had spoken a word and for years nothing happened? (Maybe you would have doubts about if it was God or not).

Q - Why is this a good test for Samuel? (He's going to be a prophet of God and he needs to learn to trust what God has given him "We live by faith and not by sight").

Round up (2 minutes)
These happenings are so encouraging for us, because it tells us that God speaks to young people. He uses you for his purposes! You are never too young to hear God. And God has an important plan for Samuel. If there was no Samuel there would be no hope in the near future. So don't give up! Go against the flow.

Samuel was an ordinary chap, but faithful to God. Sometimes people think you need to be an amazing personality to do great things for God.

But actually just getting it right by honouring him and living according to his standards, even if there are Christians around you who aren't.

Don't give up on expecting God to speak to you. Don't write yourself off. God has a calling on your life too.

Pray – Quick prophecy activation (8 minutes)
Get the youngsters to place a random object in on the table. Then tell them that you are going to ask God to speak through the youngsters. If they are drawn to any object or an inspired thought comes, get them to share it. But first invite the Holy Spirit to inspire people's thoughts and to speak. Then ask them what just popped randomly into their minds about what God might be saying to an individual or the group.

Encourage risk taking and reassure them that it is a safe place, so they won't be judged by what they say. Affirm the good, and praise risk taking if anything said doesn't quite hit the mark.

Name (A)

Met (name) (B)

On a (mode of transport):   on their way to (place)

A said:

B said:

(What they did next)

How it all ended

57) Hophni and Phineas dishonour God

Icebreaker 1 – 1, 2, 3 or 4? (5 minutes)
Give each person a sheet of paper. Get them to fold it in half and then in half again. Open it out and it will have 4 equal quarters, then tear along the lines to make 4 pieces of paper of roughly equal size. Then get them to write 1 on one piece, 2 on the next, 3 on the next and 4 on the other (nice and clearly).

Tell them that you will count down to 1, and when you do, you want them to all hold up one piece of paper (number facing outwards, so people can see it). If they are holding up a number that no-one else is holding up, that person will get the same amount of points as is on the piece of paper (Eg. number 4 they get 4 points). The winner is the one with the most points... the first to 10?

Introduction (2 minutes)
Last week we saw the nightmare that was Eli's two corrupt sons being responsible for the sacrifices in God's holy Tent of Meeting. With the nation of Israel being led badly, things are about to go badly for the people too. The words that came from God were "Those who honour me I will honour, but those who despise me will be disdained."

But there is hope. A boy called Samuel, who is honest and can speak God's words. Even if it was an inconvenient truth, Samuel will not bite his tongue, but will tell it as it is.

Actually Samuel isn't in this bit we're going to read, except to say that the words he spoke some years ago are about to come to pass.

Teaching 1 (10 minutes)
READ 1 Samuel 4:1-1-9 (Don't read any further! You'll spoil the surprise!)

Q – The Israelite army goes out to fight with the Philistines. Why do you think they went to fight? (Maybe they got word that the Philistines were marching towards their territory. Verse 9 gives us a clue... The Philistines were still ruling over the Israelites).

Q – And how does the battle turn out? (Badly for the Israelites).

Q – So the soldiers return from the battle defeated. What question do the elders have when the soldiers return? (Why did the Lord bring defeat upon us today before the Philistines?)

So things have not gone well, and they do a post-battle debrief. Imagine they're on the TV and it's Match of the day. Following the game, the presenter discusses the reasons for a team's poor performance with ex-players, showing action replays and analysing the footage. But the elders aren't thinking about whether or not their strategy was right. To them, there is just one key reason why they didn't do so well.

Q- What was that reason? (God was not with them. The Israelites lived by the premise that an army doesn't win by the number of horses or soldiers, but by God's power. They'd have won battles against the odds before and seen God at work with them).

Q - Well if the reason for defeat was that God allowed it, what was their answer to this problem? (They said "go get the Ark of the Covenant." Not to be confused with Noah's ark, the boat).

Q – What two things were they hoping to happen by getting the Ark of the Covenant? (That God would go with them and that they would win).

Q – Why would carrying the Ark of the Covenant help them to win? (Because powerful things happened when it was carried. For example the waters parted when crossing the Jordan, and when it was carried the walls of Jericho fell down).

Q – Why was there an almighty shout when the Ark of the Covenant reached the camp? (The Israelites saw it coming and thought that meant certain victory).

Q – Who brings out the Ark? (Eli's sons)

Imagine this bizarre situation: the actions of Eli's corrupt sons have shown that they despised God and didn't believe he existed. They had taken bits from people's sacrifices even before offering it to God, and they had slept with the women who were from outside the Tent of Meeting. These two sons Hophni and Phinehas seem to be the cause of what is wrong, yet they come out representing God with all the honour that goes with carrying the holy and precious Ark of the Covenant, to a shout from the army of Israelites that shakes the ground.

Something seems off about it all. Shall we read on?...

Teaching 2 (8 minutes)
READ 1 Samuel 4:10-22

Q – Hophni and Phinehas are killed. Can any of you describe how they would have died, and what they were doing when they died? (They were most probably carrying the Ark of the Covenant, thinking they were invincible. However some crazed Philistine without a care for his life must have charged at them and cut them down with his sword).

Q – It seems like they are presuming God is going to help them, despite their obvious disobedience. Does this remind you of anyone we have read bout recently? (Samson was the same. After he had given away the secret of his hair being cut, he still thought he would defeat the Philistines as before).

Q – What does this tell you about God? (The words from God spoken by the prophet 2 chapters ago (1 Samuel 2:30) echo again "Those who honour me I will honour, those who despise me will be disdained").

Q - What had the Israelites mistakenly put their trust in? (In things, rather than in God).

Q – So as we read on about what took place, the Ark of the Covenant was not the reason why things went wrong. Do you think that God allowed things to go wrong for his nation, because they have lost their way? Why? (He is doing it to bring them back, but also it is the time for justice to come to Eli and his sons).

Q - Do you think that today God might allow trouble to come to a Christian who has lost their way, in order to bring them back to him? (God's love is sometimes a tough love that does what is right for the person in the long run. God was being despised by those who were supposed to be serving him. It was time for that to end).

However, this doesn't mean that we have to be perfect. It doesn't mean that when we fail that God will bring us to ruin. It is not that at all. There are a lot of people who claim to be a follower of Jesus, but choose to live in direct contradiction to what God wants for their lives. Living this way is risky, and unwise. Put simply following Jesus comes from relationship. You love, respect and obey because you are his and you want to. Anything outside of that is dead religion and is a waste of time.

Q – How do things end for Eli? (The last words he hears before his death are the worst news he'll ever get – his sons are dead and God's precious Ark has be taken. Both of these things he was responsible for as well as for leading the nation).

Q – Lastly which famous Philistine is about to arrive on the scene? (Goliath is due to be born in the next 30 to 50 years).

Round up (2 minutes)
To trace back to how on earth this disaster happened we have to take a look at Eli's leadership of which there were good bits and terrible bits. Of course he can't be responsible for everything his sons did, but importantly he seems to turn a blind eye to his son's activities and is weak when strong leadership is required. Maybe food was Eli's weakness! Sometimes Eli does do the right thing, mentoring Samuel for example.

God doesn't expect perfection from us, but if we are to follow him we must honour him by being honest about our mistakes and weaknesses and act accordingly. Maybe Eli's sons thought they could just give a sacrifice and everything would be ok. That is dead religion. It is not faith. It is not a relationship with God. Saying sorry is not enough if it isn't backed up by the will and the drive to change. To make right what was wrong and to live differently, this is honouring God.

Well the story gets even more interesting next week, as the Philistines realise that the Ark of the Covenant is not something they have been prepared to handle. God is still working, in the confusion, in the mess, there is hope.

Final Summary (4 Minutes)
The story gets even more interesting as things go on. Your group may want to know what happens to the Ark of the Covenant??? It's probably too much to read the next two chapters, but it might be worth summarising Chapters 5 and 6 of 1 Samuel.

Pray (As long as it takes!)

58) Samuel gives Israel a King

Icebreaker 1 - Hot Potato
Have a small bean bag or soft ball and some music ready to play. Explain that the ball is a potato that is too hot to hold. So if they get it, they must pass or throw it to someone else. The potato is so hot that it will explode when the music stops (in which case the player is out).

Icebreaker 2 – Best word (5 minutes)
Split the youngsters into 3 or 4 teams. Give each team a random share of some scrabble letters. Then ask them (using the letters they have been given), to come up with the most Biblical words they can think of. So we're not looking particularly for the longest word, but the ones they feel are the most Biblical ones.

Good, better, best
(If you have a whiteboard or flip chart, draw a medal podium like one you would see at the Olympics, with different levels for gold silver and bronze. In the bronze place, write the word "Good" in the silver place write the word "Better" and in the gold place write the word "Best").

Introduction (1 minute)
Last week we saw the disaster that came to the people of Israel because of the lack of honour that its leaders gave to God. Several years have passed since the day the Philistines captured the Ark of the Covenant.

Samuel has been a prophet for the nation, speaking the words God gave him to guide them. He has been doing a fantastic job travelling around Israel and visiting the people locally and leading nationally.

Teaching 1 (8 minutes)
READ 1 Samuel 7:13- 17 & 8:1-22

Q – Some great things had been taking place during Samuel's leadership. What significant things happened? (Israel took back some key towns from the Philistines. They started winning again!)

Q – What does verse 16 of Chapter 7 tell us about Samuel's leadership? (That he travelled to the people to oversee how things were going. He was a good leader, involved with the people and making sure he got round to everyone).

Q - Was there anything Samuel neglected in his life? (His sons didn't seem to turn out with a very good character).

Q – Does this remind you of anyone? (Eli put his sons in charge at the Tent of Meeting, but they did not honour God).

Q – Bearing in mind what happened to Eli's two sons; do you think Samuel should have done something to make his sons turn out better? (Parents can influence their children, but ultimately we each have to decide whether or not to follow God. It might be with Samuel's travelling that he didn't see his sons that often. Maybe being there they could have learned the importance of honesty and integrity).

Q – There is definitely one thing that Samuel could have done differently from Eli. What do you think it was? (Eli put his sons in charge in the Tent of Meeting, and Samuel put his sons in charge of judging Israel. He should have chosen someone else. Also the judges were meant to be chosen by God rather than the sons of the Judge).

Q – Do you think that God uses people's lives to warn us to avoid making the same mistakes? (Yes. God speaks to us in lots of different ways. We can't just restrict his warnings to us through dreams, words and visions. He definitely uses those, but sometimes he uses life experiences to warn us. Samuel was a prophet, but he missed the warning from Eli's life).

Q – Why do you think we go and do the same mistakes that others make anyway? (Discuss).

Scenario (5 minutes)
Picture the scene. One or two of your older Christian friends from your youth group have left to go to University. You keep in touch with them over social media and you keep up with pictures and posts they write. It's great to see them settling in well and making friends with their flatmates. However, after not very long you notice their friends tagging your friends in on photos of them at clubs a lot. They are often drunk and begin to share things that are inappropriate. It makes you wonder if they have an "alive" faith anymore.

Q – How do you think this happens? (To make friends in a new place you naturally socialise. Often this is by going to pubs and clubs to meet people or because that is the place that your flatmates are going. Its's easy to want to blend in by doing the things they are doing and not care about drink too much).

Q - What could you do to avoid making the same mistakes as your friends? (First of all talking it through seriously with God. You could make a promise to God or carry around a wristband as a reminder. Also thinking through how this came about for your friends and intentionally choosing to do things differently).

Q – Why is it important to connect with a church whilst you are away from home? (Because we all need support from people who will care for us and help our faith to grow).

Teaching 2 (10 minutes)
Q – What is the outcome of Samuel's mistake? (The Israelites ask for Samuel to appoint a king and not his sons to lead them).

Q – Who thinks this is a bad idea? (God).

Q – Why does God think it is a bad idea? (He says that the king will use his power to take from the people what belongs to them, their freedom).

They would experience forced labour, their sons wouldn't have a choice whether or not to join the army, and many others (both men and women) would be forced to work for the war efforts to come. They would become servants and slaves to the king. This wouldn't be so bad if all the kings that were to follow would be good kings, but many of the kings were not good kings and the people would suffer.

Q – So God says "This is going to be bad for you" and the people say "No. We want a king over us." How do we feel when God wants something for us, but we really want something else? (Maybe we might feel that he is being unfair, or controlling, or react like our freedom is being taken away from us).

Q – What might we do if we feel we are living in a way that is not honouring to God? (We might stop going to church, feeling people are judging us).

Q – How does God respond when the people of Israel insist on having a king? (He says listen to them and give them a king).

Q – Does this surprise you that God gives them what they want, even though it is going to hurt them in the long run? (Discuss)

Q – Why then does God give them a king? (He gives them the choice to choose, just like in the Garden of Eden).

Q – Will everything be alright then if God is allowing it to happen? (Not necessarily. There will be a lot of struggle ahead that could have been avoided).

Round up (2 minutes)
Sometimes we would do well to learn from other people's mistakes and be intentional about ensuring that the same thing doesn't happen to us. Other people's mistakes can often serve as a warning to us and may save us from a lot of pain.

And like Israel wanting a king, there might come a time when we will want something that will do us no good in the long run. Insisting on getting what we want, when God sees a wiser way may mean he wants us to avoid a painful choice. This may even affect our connection with God for years. Our trust of God is at its strongest when we are asked to give up something that might not seem all that wrong, but that God says won't benefit us. Trust like this is always rewarded with better things.

(Point out the diagram on the whiteboard/flip chart "Good, better, best"). Say: Sometimes getting the best plan means we have to sacrifice the "good" and the "better" in order to have God's best for our lives. This is the outcome that will lead to us being happiest and most fulfilled in our lives.

Pray (As long as it takes!)

59) King Saul is tested

Icebreaker 1 - Where's Wally or Waldo (5 minutes)
See if you can get hold of some Where's Wally pictures. Separate the group into smaller teams and give them one of 4 sheets of Where's Wally pictures. Once a team has found Wally in the first sheet, they bring it to you, show you where he is and then you can give them the next sheet. The team who finds him in all 4 sheets wins. Maybe have a time limit, in case Wally becomes elusive!

Icebreaker 2 – Copycat clap (5 minutes)
Get the youngsters to sit in a circle and choose one person to go out of the room. Then select a person inside the room for the rest to copy. Invite the person back into the room to stand in the middle. All the youngsters in the circle will start clapping. The person everyone has to copy can change the clap beat and rhythm at any time. The others then have to follow by copying the new rhythm. The person in the middle has 3 guesses to find who everyone is copying.

Introduction (2 minutes)
Recently we've been following Samuel the prophet, how the Ark of the Covenant was taken, but returned by the Philistines when they realised they couldn't handle it. Samuel does well as a prophet, but his sons are a nightmare and the Israelites ask for a king to lead them. This is against the will of God, but God allows Israel to have a king. This means they get God's good plan for them rather than his intended best plan.

Now the time has come for God to point out to Samuel who is to be Israel's first king called Saul. He's not to be confused with the Saul who got blinded and became Paul.

Teaching 1 (15 minutes)
READ 1 Samuel 9:1-3,

Q – How does the Bible introduce Saul? (He is impressive and without equal and very tall).

Q – Saul is from the Benjamite tribe; the smallest of the tribes and from the least of all the clans of Benjamin. Why do you think God chose him? (God was looking for a humble man who would rely on him, rather than being proud because of his status).

Q – In what way do you think Saul was without equal? (It might refer to his height and physical appearance. It might also describe what

Lord Sugar might describe as "acumen." Acumen is the ability to make good judgements and take quick decisions).

Q – Why do you think God might have chosen a very tall person at this time? (Because another very tall person is about to enter the story in a few chapters... Goliath).

So the story goes on and Saul is looking for some lost donkeys. He ends up hearing about a prophet, and goes to look for him instead so that the prophet can tell Saul where his donkeys are. God has obviously got something to do with Saul's missing donkeys... he's about to meet Samuel. Saul is a big guy, sharp minded and quick, and humble too. The perfect choice for a king... only what's his heart like? What's he like at waiting for stuff...

Discussion – Waiting (9 minutes)
Imagine it was your birthday recently. You had lots of birthday cards... you know the ones you open, where you are hoping with something more than a nice message inside... maybe something in note form will fall out...

Well imagine you did really well and got loads of money. So you did some online shopping and saw something you really wanted... maybe a piece of tech... a new mobile, a tablet, a camera or something really cool. Next you persuaded your folks to use their credit card to buy the item and all you are concerned about now is when it is going to arrive.

Then the email comes through. The delivery is to be today by courier. You don't want to be out when they call... What if they were to lose it before you could have it redelivered? So you decide to wait in. It's a lovely day outside, but you're stuck indoors. And you wait... in your pyjamas, hoping it will be in the morning. You try not to spend your time waiting, but whenever there is a vehicle outside or a door slamming, you race to the window to see if it is your delivery, each time it isn't.

Then there's a van outside, but they deliver to next door... So you check your email, make sure the info you gave was correct, and check that it's arriving today... Then that moment happens.... You need the toilet. No-one else is in the house... what if the delivery arrives when you are on the bog?

You wonder what you can do... hold it in? Or leave the bathroom door open to listen for the doorbell? Well you can't bear it any longer. You go to the toilet, but shut the bathroom door in case someone returns home. But you are listening... what's that noise? Was it just another car door?

You're done in the bathroom, you go downstairs and there is a note on the doormat... you missed your delivery, you can re-arrange delivery for tomorrow...

Q – Has anyone had a situation of waiting for something and not knowing if or when they might turn up? Tell us about it... (Discuss)

Q – Describe some of the emotions that you are feeling, having been unavailable for just 5 minutes and that is the time they choose to deliver? (You might feel disappointed, angry, let down and sad that you don't get to test out your new gadget on that day).

Q – Why is waiting so difficult? (Because we are used to having things immediately, or when we think we need them.)

Q – Have you ever waited for something from God, for example an answer to prayer? (Discuss)

Q - What things go through your mind when you are waiting? (Has God heard? Will he answer? Has he said no? Is he going to help?)

We're going to continue with King Saul and see what it can be like sometimes to wait for God. Waiting can tell you a lot about a person, it is often found in people of very good character. Let's see what Saul's character is like...

Teaching 2 (10 minutes)
READ 1 Samuel 13:1-14 (possibly 1 Samuel 10:8 has some meaning here)

Q – Now that Israel has their King, they get ready to attack the Philistines under Saul's leadership. What unusual thing does Saul do in verse 2? (He sends some soldiers home).

Q – Why do you think he did this? (He probably felt this was a small attack. Maybe he was planning a series of small attacks on the Philistines to gradually take ground. Then he could call on the soldiers as substitutes later on in the military campaign).

Q - Do the Philistines respond as expected? (No. They assemble a massive army in response).

Q – Why is the trumpet blown in verse 3? (To call for help in the battle).

Q – What would you think about it all if you weren't needed at first and now you were needed? (You would expect that things were going badly).

Q – How would you feel about going in to battle under those circumstances? (A bit concerned about the outcome).

Q – What did the men of Israel find when they got to the battle front line? (The battle wasn't going well at all).

Q – Comment on the numbers of Philistines. (A lot).

Q – What do you think "as numerous as the seashore" means? (A vast number it's like when we use the suffix "illion" and add a letter like "z" and say there were zillions of ants – a vast number that you didn't officially count).

Q – Saul has made a big error in judgement, and now the Philistines are getting lary. He then sends out messengers throughout Israel to get fighters to help out. What word does the end of verse 4 use to describe those who were summoned to Saul? (People. Not necessarily soldiers, but people against the Philistine military).

Big though this mistake is, Saul is in danger of making a bigger one by trying to cover up his mistake so as not to make things worse. Sometimes when we are desperate to find the solution to our mistake as quickly as possible, we can do some silly things to make it better or to try and cover up our mistake.

Q - Whilst we read about the numbers of Philistine troops assembling, Saul is waiting for something. What is he waiting for v8? (So in the back of Saul's mind is the fact that he is waiting for Samuel the prophet to arrive and make the sacrifice to God before the battle).

Q – Everyone is looking to their leader for the answer. Saul is waiting for Samuel to arrive. It's just like the delivery situation... he's desperate and he can't wait any longer. Why

do you think God allowed Saul to face that situation? (God was testing him to see how obedient he could be as king).

Q – What do you think might be going through Saul's mind whilst he is waiting? (Has Samuel forgotten? Has he been kidnapped or killed? Is he coming at all? Has God deserted me?)

Q – I'm sure you've asked God for something, and you're waiting for the answer. It's easy to feel similar to Saul... "Is God going to answer?" "Is the answer no?" "Is God even there and listening??" What would you say to someone struggling with those questions? (Sometimes the only way we can show God that we trust him is to set aside worry and let God take away our concerns. Then we know he will direct the outcome in the right way).

Q – What was Saul's excuse for not waiting for Samuel? (He saw the men scattering, Samuel was late and he was concerned that the Philistines would attack).

Q – What was the problem with Saul offering the sacrifice? (Only a prophet should offer the sacrifice, though a king could if a prophet was present).

Round up (2 minutes)
If you've ever seen Mr. Bean on the TV you'll be familiar with situations where he makes a mistake and goes to correct it in the wrong way, making it a whole lot worse! Like sneezing on a piece of artwork by a famous painter and his attempts to clean it up with turps, ruin it forever.

We find three problems with Saul's response: He was okay to wait, but only up to a point. He was prepared to disobey God's word through Samuel, thinking if he did the ritual he would defeat the Philistines. If he ticked the box, God would do his thing.

Did he actually trust that God had the whole thing in hand? No.
Was he obeying God? No.
Was he prepared to wait for God as long as it took? No.

He was an impressive man, but there was something wrong with his heart connection with God. So God was looking for another king whose heart would be after God. Sometimes God wants to see that we trust him in the waiting. He knows what we need and will provide in his timing.

Pray (As long as it takes!)

60) Jonathan's bravery in God

Icebreaker 1 - Signs (8 minutes)
Have the youngsters sit in a circle with space for someone to stand in the middle. Then get each young person to think up a (nice) hand signal to do (for example playing air guitar, brushing your hair, a simple thumbs up, a dance move or anything else). Make sure that people's signs are sufficiently different from each other not to be confused.

Then one of the group members must volunteer to stand in the middle of the circle and close their eyes whilst a person is chosen to start the group off. Once the person standing in the middle has opened their eyes, the person chosen to start the group off begins by doing their signal when they are ready, followed by someone else's hand signal (though they mustn't take all day!).

The aim is to do this whilst not being detected by the person standing in the middle (without them seeing). The person in the middle has 3 chances to catch someone doing their signal and correctly identify them before they finish doing the second hand signal.

It is really fun watching people get away without being detected! When someone is detected they get to take the middle spot. To keep the game going at a good pace, people who take too long to do their signal will be eliminated and therefore chosen to stand in the middle.

Introduction (2 minutes)
Today we're going to read another incredible story. Recently we've been reading about godly men who had unruly sons. Now the focus is on King Saul's son who is a good man. His name is Jonathan. Jonathan takes an amazing risk which turns into an amazing opportunity... all because he saw something... signs of an opportunity where God was working.

Teaching 1 (15 minutes)
READ 1 Samuel 13:16- 23, 14:1-23,

So we pick up from last week where Saul's army went to attack the Philistines. He decided he had too many and sent some of the soldiers home. Things went badly and he had to send out a call for more to join the battle later on. He was told to wait for Samuel, but he lost patience in waiting and now things are going from bad to worse.

Q - In the first bit that we read the battle has progressed. What is happening in verse 17 & 18? (The Philistines are retaliating by sending out small groups to attack Israelite villages).

Q - What important piece of equipment did the Israelites notice had suddenly become scarce? (Weapons).

Q – Where do you think the weapons had gone? (They had been lost in battle, the soldiers who fled and hid had left theirs behind).

Q – Why couldn't they get more weapons? (The Philistines who ruled over them had made sure that there were no blacksmiths in Israel to make the weapons).

Q – What do the Israelites use instead of weapons? (Farming equipment).

Q – Who is the last person you would go to in a battle to make your weapons from? (The enemy).

Q – Who do they go to, to sharpen their farming equipment/makeshift weapons? (They went to the enemy; Philistine blacksmiths).

Picture the scene (3 minutes)
You might picture the scene: An Israelite walks into the Philistine blacksmiths with an axe.

Israelite: "Excuse me. I would like to make use of your tool sharpening service."

The Philistine jokes: "Yep. I can do that for you. As long as it's not for a sword. Ha ha!"

Israelite laughs: "Ha ha, no. The wife wants me to do some landscaping on the farm. She says some trees are blocking the light to her kitchen. So I thought, yeah a couple of trees won't take long, only to find my axe is blunt!"

The Philistine goes: "Okay that'll be a third of a shekel"

Israelite: "Really? That much??? Okay. Can you make it extra sharp then?"

Then no sooner has the man left with his sharp axe, than another Israelite wants a tool sharpened... something about digging out some tree roots and blaming his wife. Then business gets a little busier for this Philistine blacksmith and suddenly everyone is doing extra work on their farm and the guy in the Philistine blacksmiths was like, "hang on a minute, what's going on here??"

Q – Why do you think the Bible mentions the cost of the sharpening? (To make the point that the Philistines were charging high rates, knowing that the Israelites didn't have blacksmiths of their own. It's difficult to know how much it was as a shekel differed in value depending on what metal it was and values at the time, but maybe one third of a shekel could be half a day's wage or more).

Q - Who are the only two people to have actual battle weapons? (King Saul and his son Jonathan).

Q – Why didn't God just defeat the enemy by sending some freak weather or something? (God works with us in partnership, in faith. Faith takes a response from us to get what we need).

Q – What thought pops into Jonathan's head? (To go and attack a Philistine outpost).

Q – What is King Saul doing? (Sitting under a tree).

Q - Why do you think Jonathan suddenly has the idea to attack another Philistine outpost? (There appears to be a stand-off, with battle lines drawn and the Philistines now sending out raiding parties. One such raiding party went from an outpost leaving a lot less soldiers to guard it. Saul is holding back from attacking, seemingly unable to take the risk, but Jonathan sees the potential of God's opportunity).

Q - What do we call people who see the potential of something not yet achieved? (Visionaries).

Q – Who gives Jonathan his support? (Jonathan's armour bearer)

Q – What's the job of an armour bearer? (To carry the weapons and to fight).

Q – What do you think Jonathan means by the term "these uncircumcised men"? (These uncircumcised men means unrighteous and ungodly men).

Q – Do you think Jonathan would have gone ahead if his armour bearer hadn't been up for it? (Probably not).

Q – Why is it important for people to support visionaries with practical help? (Otherwise nothing significant would get done).

Q – Why is faith compared to taking with a risk? (Because you don't have all the answers of how it is going to turn out. You have to trust that God will fill in the answers and act!).

Q – What does Jonathan do to confirm that he is on the right track? (He does all that comes to his mind. And what comes to his mind is to see the reaction of the Philistines when they spot him).

Whenever you have a vision, asking God to confirm the way to do things along the way helps to keep you on the right track. It's not enough to know the vision and go for it, you have to stay connected to God and do things his way along the way.

Q – So when the Philistines saw Jonathan and his armour bearer, what did they assume had happened? (They assumed they had been soldiers who had retreated and had been in the hole too long and were maybe weary).

Q - So they call Jonathan up, maybe not expecting that he would, after all they had the higher ground. What do you think it means, "The Philistines fell before Jonathan, and his armour bearer followed and killed behind him"? (That Jonathan quickly attacked the men, leaving them injured for the armour bearer to finish them off, so they could take the outpost back).

Q – What happens next?? (Panic!!)

Q – Jonathan's openness to God's vision and his willingness to risk himself to do it has made the way for a greater win. Jonathan only responded to a small idea and now the Philistines in the outposts and attacking armies have turned to panic. What does Saul ask for when he hears the noise? (He asks for two things: to find out who is missing and to bring the Ark of the Covenant).

Q – Take a look at verse 19. What do you think is going on there, where he says to the priest "withdraw your hand." (He's like, "actually I've changed my mind. I can't wait for the Ark of the Covenant to be brought, let's go fight people!").

Q – What's the difference between Jonathan's actions and the actions of Saul? (Jonathan's mind-set is on the possibilities that God has set before him. He's connected with God, he's decisive when he gets God's confirmation, and he's dependant on for his safety. Saul makes decisions and then has to change them. He depends on things more than God).

Round up (2 minutes)
When we first meet Saul in the Bible, we are told he is impressive. He seemed to be smart and quick witted, however he lacks a dependence on God. In the heat of battle we see his impressiveness melt away.

Jonathan on the other hand demonstrates the faith steps of a visionary. He is dependent on God, but is also ready to go for it, trusting that God will save him if he is wrong. God will work amazing things through people who are dependent on him, people who are ready to risk it in faith and do something positive for him and his kingdom.

Pray (As long as it takes!)

61) Saul doesn't learn

Icebreaker 1 – Guess the famous person (8 minutes)
Using post-it notes write down names of famous people (one on every note). Then get a volunteer to stick the note on their forehead without seeing what the name is. The volunteer must then go up to each person in the group who will say one word associated with that famous person. The volunteer must guess the name of the famous person on the post-it note. Examples of famous people you could use:

David Cameron, The Hulk, Richard Branson, Wayne Rooney, Taylor Swift, Princess Leia, The Queen, Enid Blyton, Michelle Obama, Chewbacca, Black Widow, Spiderman, Andy Murray, Prince George, Adele.

Icebreaker 2 - 10 best excuses for not doing your homework (8 minutes)
We have a list of the 10 best excuses for not doing your homework. Get the youngsters into teams to see if they can guess the top 10 list:

My dog ate my homework
I don't remember there being any homework
I thought it was in my bag, but I must have left it at home by mistake
I didn't understand the homework
Technical difficulties (My computer crashed, or printer ran out of ink)
Emotional trauma (My cat died)
I think I was off ill when the homework was set
I've been busy volunteering outside of school
I've been so ill over the past few days that I couldn't do it
My bag was stolen with my homework in it.

Introduction (2 minutes)
Last week we saw King Saul of Israel at war with the Philistines and an amazing victory through his son Jonathan who attacked twenty soldiers by himself and his armour bearer, causing a panic in the Philistine army. This was a victory by God's hand.

Now there's another threat, one God had it in his mind to defeat, which was the Amalekites. They were descendants of Esau, a nomadic tribe of people who were brutal and unrelenting. Earlier on in Israel's history, the Amalekites attacked the people of Israel, soon after they fled Egypt with Moses (see Deuteronomy 25:17-19). At that time the Amalekites slaughtered the weak and those who were lagging behind. Now is the time for God's people to eliminate the threat of this tribe for good.

Teaching 1 (15 minutes)
READ 1 Samuel 15:1-35,
Q – So Samuel gives Saul some pretty specific instructions. What are they? (They must attack and wipe out the Amalekites).

Q – Why does he start by saying "I am the one the Lord sent to anoint you king over his people Israel"? What is he saying by that? (He's saying. I'm speaking to you with God's authority, for God's people. So listen carefully!)

Q – What is the reason God gives for this attack? (It was God's revenge for their attack on the people of Israel as they left Egypt. The Amalekites killed off the stragglers and those at the back of their travelling convoy. Israel wasn't a threat to them; they just wanted to pass by. However the Amalekites still attacked. This was the first of many attacks).

Q – Why is God allowed to take revenge, but we can't? (God is all knowing so he isn't ignorant of the facts. He is able to do justice. He is without pride, bias or evil intent. We are all accountable and answerable to God. Instead revenge is God's to do on our behalf).

Q – The obvious question is why would they have to kill them all, women and children too? (In verse 33 we see this is what the Amalekites had done to the Israelites. But more importantly if they didn't kill the descendants of the Amalekites, they would one day grow up again and take their revenge on the people of Israel. Who wouldn't want to kill those who killed their fathers? They would always oppose Israel and be a danger to others).

Q – Saul sends word to the Kenites a nearby tribe to evacuate, because at the same time that Israel were fleeing Egypt, the Kenites showed them kindness instead of attacking them. How does the attack go? What happens? (Israel wins. But instead of following all the instructions God gave through Samuel, Saul captures the opposing king and keeps some livestock and stuff).

Q – Why do you think Saul captured the Amalekite king instead of killing him? (Pride. It would look good in front of others).

Q – Why do you think it was important for Saul to look good in front of his people? (In the previous battle, his son Joanthan was the hero, which followed Saul's mistakes against the Philistines. As Israel's first king he wanted to look the part and be celebrated)

Q – What is the problem with Saul capturing the Amalekite King? (2 problems: 1. The Amalekites have survived. 2. He disobeyed God's instructions).

Q – How else did Saul disobey God's instructions? (He allows the sheep and cattle to be taken as plunder).

Q – What were Saul's reasons? (See verse 21 and 24)

Q – Were these actually good reasons, or simply excuses Saul was coming up with to get out of trouble? (They were excuses. First he blames his soldiers and then he says they were to sacrifice to God. He was actually king and could command his soldiers to whatever he wanted).

Q – What would have been better than sacrificing to God? (To obey what God had said – see verse 22).

Scenario on the spot - Milkshake attack (5 minutes)
Take a look at verse 24. It's quite easy to find ourselves carried along by the group and end up doing the thing we didn't mean…

Tell the youngsters that you would like them to imagine the following thing is about to happen to them, and to think instantly what they would do… because you might put one of them on the spot and ask what they might do (though they have the right to say "pass").

Picture the scene. You've been to McDonald's and you're walking back finishing off your milkshakes with your friends from school. As you cross over on a bridge, one of your friends spots someone you know from school, walking below. The group have taken a dislike to this person after you had an argument with this person. One of your friends suggests that you all lob the last of your milkshakes at them. Before you know it you are being expected to hand over your milkshake to be used as ammunition. You're in the moment, what do you say?

Q – How would you act afterwards? (Discuss. Maybe go and check on that person/apologise).

Q – As a leader what is wrong with what Saul says in verse 20? (The leader has to take responsibility for those he or she is leading).

Q – Sometimes excuses are like invented reasons for us to avoid facing up to the truth. Why are excuses unhelpful for us? (It hides the source of the problem. Sometimes we have to deal with a wrong attitude that we have on the inside, rather than blaming things that are not to do with us).

Q – What if we don't deal with our wrong attitudes and keep making excuses? (The same sort of problems will keep happening).

Q – What happens when we stop making excuses? (We realise who caused it. The truth will set you free!).

Round up (1 minute)
So this is King Saul. Leader of the nation of Israel, saying that he was afraid of the people he had authority over. He's blaming his soldiers and trying to impress the people, rather than facing up to his fears. If only he would put God first, he would see things work out.

It's really easy to make up excuses. Maybe we have excuses for why we haven't spent time with God, or why we said or did something we shouldn't have. It took King Saul a lot of persuading to see that he was responsible and had done wrong before God. We have to be truthful about our excuses; otherwise the same things will happen again and again. The moment we own up and do things differently, these recurring problems will begin to lessen.

Much like someone who won't own up to the real reason for not doing their homework, we're in danger of ignoring the truth: that we are responsible and we can do something about it.

Pray (1 minute)
Invite the youngsters to pray this prayer in their heads:

"Father God, please show me where I've been making excuses in my life, whether it is my behaviour, my actions, my thoughts or my words. I choose to take responsibility and ask you help me to change my ways. In Jesus' name!"

62) David and first impressions

Icebreaker – The Minister's cat (5 Minutes)
This is a game to sharpen the minds! Get the youngsters to sit in a circle. Someone chooses a letter of the alphabet with which to describe the minister's cat. So for example if the letter "S" was chosen, the first person might say "The minister's cat is smelly cat," then the next person might say "The minister's cat is a silly cat," and so it goes round. If someone can't think of one or repeats one already said, they are out and have to fold their arms to indicate that they are out.

Additionally, to keep the tempo up you might want to get the group to clap in rhythm, but quietly enough for people to hear what was said.

Face impressions (5 minutes)
Maybe you think you know your friend's face? Sometimes our first impressions or perceptions of what a person looks like aren't actually what they look like at all. So get the youngsters to pair up with a person sitting next to them and study their face for 30 seconds. Then turn back to back and ask them the following questions.

> Are the lobes of their ears attached or unattached?
> What colour are their eyes?
> Describe the colours in their hair.
> What words did their top have?
> Were they wearing glasses? If so what shape were the frames?
> Was their hair tied back or not tied back?
> Did they have freckles?
> Does their face have dimples?
> Were they wearing braces?

Introduction (5 Minutes)
Last week we saw King Saul not paying attention to the way God had directed him. Saul has made the same mistake once too often and God has chosen a new man to be king. He has found a man after his own heart (1 Samuel 13:14). You will know this guy when you see him...

Teaching (20 Minutes)
Read 1 Samuel 16:1-13
So the last verse of chapter 15 reads "And the Lord was grieved that he had made Saul King over Israel."

Q – Why does God now tell Samuel to fill a horn with oil?
(Samuel is a prophet in Israel, and when God chooses a new king; the prophet has to pour oil over him).

Q – What is Samuel nervous about? (He's worried that the current King Saul will be annoyed, and send someone to kill him for an act of treason).

Q – Does God answer Samuel's question if Saul will kill him? (Yes and no. He tells Samuel what to do, but he doesn't say whether this will stop him from being killed).

Q – Why do you think God doesn't give Samuel the direct answer that he wants (is Samuel going to be added to Saul's hit list)? (God gives him direction for the next step; the rest is to trust God knows what he is doing).

Q - In the New Testament Jesus was asked 183 questions. Guess how many of those questions he answered with a direct answer? (3).

Q – Why do you think that is? (Because people were asking him the wrong question! They got the answer they needed though!).

Q – What do you think God is expecting Samuel to do then? (To obey and to trust that God has things covered. Nothing takes God by surprise!)

Q – So Samuel is hoping that king Saul is not going to find out that he is up to something. What happens when he arrives in Bethlehem that puts him at risk? (Samuel is spotted and the elders of the town go out to meet him).

Q – Why are the elders trembling? (They see Samuel's presence as either good news or bad news, as they know his reputation).

The elders fear the worst, in which case word about Samuel's presence will spread quickly.

Q – Now God's help will come in handy. What did he tell Samuel to do? (Get a cow and say I have come to make a sacrifice to the Lord. Or in other words let's have a sacrificial meal together).

The sacrificial meal turns the atmosphere to one of calmness and friendship (probably a fellowship offering) and also gives Samuel the opportunity to test which of Jesse's sons is to be the new king.

People arrive at the feast. The first one to arrive at the feast is Eliab, God's plan is coming together...

Discussion Starter
Two stories about first impressions (10 minutes)
Story 1 - Swedish visit
Picture the scene. Your school has invited a class from Sweden to stay in your town for a week. You have been chosen to buddy up with a Swedish pupil. You are told to wait in the car park with the others who have also been chosen.

As the coach pulls up you can see the happy faces of the Swedish school people. As they get off the coach there are some who look beautiful, cool and popular and others who don't. You find out that you don't get to choose who you want to buddy up with, and you are paired with one who doesn't look so cool.

Q – Why do you think if we are given a choice we would rather be paired with someone who looked nicer, since we haven't even met them before? (Discuss)

Q – People say "You will never get a second chance to make a first impression." Is that a good thing or a bad thing? (Tell us why).

Story 2 – French pen pal
Your school has been running a French pen pal project in which you have been taking part. You have been writing to a French person called Michelle, and you have never seen them before. You have developed a really close friendship and you are excited about meeting them for the first time.

As the coach pulls up you can see the happy faces of the French school people. As they get off the coach there are some who look beautiful, cool and popular and others who don't. As the names are called out it turns out that Michelle is one who doesn't look so cool.

Q – Why do you think that this time it makes no difference what they look like? (Discuss).

Back to Samuel and Jesse's sons...

Q – What are Samuel's first impressions of Eliab and what physical description does the Bible give? (see verses 6-7) (He thought, "This guy is impressive, he looks the part and he is tall. It must be him.")

Q – Why is there a problem in judging a person by what they look like? (Looks can often be deceiving).

Q – Is it true that if someone has nice hair and stylish clothes and looks confident that we want to be more friendly with these people? (Discuss).

Q – Why is it we often decide whether we like or accept someone because of their appearance? (Discuss)

Q – Why does none of this matter to God? (Because having style is meaningless when it comes to facing hardships, or being a good friend, or doing what is right).

Q – What are the character attributes that God looks for in a leader? (A good character who is loyal, trusting, honest, genuine, persevering, caring, patient, obedient, with a loving heart towards God. All those good things and others! It wasn't his abilities God was looking at, but his attitude).

So God chooses people by looking at the heart. Just like your French pen pal. You already know what they like and don't like, their dreams and what they think about stuff. You know their heart even before you have seen their face. God knew David and saw that David wanted nothing more than to know God more. What God found in David was a man after his own heart.

Q – Now that David has been chosen as king, do you think people will forget about his small insignificant appearance? (No people will still underestimate him – Goliath for one!).

Q – What does this tell us about how God sees you? (When others take the mickey or reject you, he knows you better than you know yourself and he loves you).

Round Up (5 Minutes)
So we've seen that God chooses people to serve him who sometimes seem unlikely candidates for the role. So if you think you're an unlikely candidate, don't worry about that. He sees what you are truly like. And even in your life so far he's working on you, so that you will be prepared for what is ahead.

People often place an importance on the wrong things. We're used to judging on appearances, seeing people looking good, judging a book by its cover. The trouble is people spend a lot of time and money trying to be cool and emulate and be like those we see on the telly. We never see the hours that celebrities put in at the gym, the money spent in the beauty salon or with the stylist.

Looking good is fine, so long as we don't make that the most important thing in our lives. If we judge other people on first impressions, then we'll get it wrong. This could result in the type of friends that we have, not being the "kind encouraging" types we need them to be.

God looks at the heart. Those around us shape us. Let God be your friend and let him shape your character as he talks to you in those quiet times. Because he wants to say something to you and he wants to prepare you for the life you haven't yet lived. Maybe this time together has inspired you to want to spend more time alone with God. Just like a pen pal you can get to know him better any time you want.

Prayer (As long as it takes!)

63) David beats the bully

Icebreaker – Deathball (5 minutes)
Get the youngsters to sit in a circle with one player in the middle. Using a ball (preferably soft) they have to throw the ball to another member in the circle without the person in the middle getting the ball. The person in the middle can also get the ball by tagging a player who is holding the ball.

When starting off a player cannot pass the ball to someone on their immediate left or right. However, once play has started this is okay.

Lastly, if you throw a ball that wasn't touched by someone and isn't caught, only you and the middle person can race to get it!

Video clip – Bart the General (5 minutes)
Today we're going to be looking at the issue of bullying. We could all do with some good advice on bullying. So show a clip from the Simpsons episode "Bart the General" (season 1) where Bart's mum and dad give Bart some advice after he has been attacked by a bully.

Discussion Starter (8 minutes)
Picture the scenario: You sit down in your form room before the register is given and a friend of yours tells you that they have just been bullied. You ask what has happened, but they don't want to tell you.

Q – How would you get your friend to tell you what happened?

Q - What would you do next? (Discuss)

Q – What concerns might your friend have? (That telling others might make things worse).

Q – What could you do to help with those concerns? (Promise to walk with them around school until the bullying dies down).

Q – If you did help your friend, what concerns of your own would you have? (That you might also become a target of the bully).

Q – Take a look at Ecclesiastes 4:9-12. How could this verse relate to the situation we have been talking about? (Getting someone to help you will greatly increase your chances of dealing with the problem successfully. It might be to invite someone to walk with you to bring more security as you walk round school. Asking for God to be the third person involved in this problem. Ask for his inspiration on things like which route to take home, who to tell, for courage to say the right thing to the bully).

Introduction (1 Minute)
Today we're going to read about the most famous bully in the whole Bible. Any ideas who he is? It's Goliath. We often find that bullies have size on their side, whether it's a big body, big head or big mouth! Well Goliath had all of these and managed to make a whole army scared of him.

We're going to consider how a bully operates and how you can operate around a bully.

Teaching (20 Minutes)
Read 1 Samuel 17:1-58

Q – Where does this story take place? (A valley called Elah amongst a hilly area called Socoh, which is over 15 miles from Jerusalem).

Q - Why do you think both armies are camped on opposite hills with a valley in between? (Often the most advantageous military position is to fight from a higher place. This region was a strategically important one for access to other areas of the country).

Q – How many days had the two armies been facing up to each other without fighting? (Forty days).

Q – So there is a stand-off between both armies, with no-one attacking each other. Why do you think this is? (Both armies seem well matched, and well positioned, but maybe both armies were as scared of the other).

Q – Why do you think that Goliath is described as a Champion? (Maybe he had taken part in fighting competitions).

Q – We can see that Goliath is intimidating the Israelite army. What is intimidation? (He is using threatening behaviour, causing fear in order to persuade the Israelites to do what he wants them to do).

Here Goliath is using typical bullying tactics. He is creating a culture around himself that intimidates those around him. His threats cause the Israelites to think the only option is to do what he says.

Q - What was Goliath's deal? (Whichever side loses has to serve the other).

Q – Why do you think Goliath offered the deal? (The idea was to avoid huge deaths and casualties in a horrible battle).

Q – What is the problem that King Saul has? (He doesn't have anyone big enough or brave enough to fight Goliath).

Goliath has controlled the situation reducing it to a scenario that he knows he will win. Bullies are strongest when they play to their strengths. See if you can get the youth to write a list (flip chart) of when they think a bully feels strongest.

- When there is no-one stronger than them.
- When authority figures are absent.
- When what they are doing is kept a secret.
- When no-one will challenge them.
- When they can control the surrounding environment.
- When people are afraid of them.
- When they have a group to support them.
- When people play by the bully's rules and submit to the bully's culture.

Bullies are good at using intimidating tactics to control a situation. So if these are the times that the bully feels strongest, does that mean that when the opposite is true they are at their weakest? (Contrast these answers with those on the flip chart).

- When there is someone stronger than them, they'll be less vocal.
- When an authority figure is present, they'll avoid trouble.
- When what they are doing is made known, they'll avoid drawing attention to themselves.
- If someone is assertive and speaks firmly confronting what they are doing, they'll lose their influence.
- A bully needs the attention to control the environment. If the attention is on something else, the bully will lose his platform.
- When people don't let their fear of the bully stop them, they can overcome the bully.
- When the group of individuals being bullied become a group themselves they will be the stronger entity.

When people look beyond the bully's rules, the bully loses control and they refuse to get bullied quietly. When they step outside of the box of what is expected they will catch the bully off guard, making the bully vulnerable.

Sometimes we just don't have the resources to counteract every bully's strengths. King Saul didn't have a stronger person in his army to fight Goliath. He needed God's strength. He didn't have an authority figure that could arrest Goliath (and Goliath's mum probably wasn't going to be a help). And without a helpful authority figure Goliath didn't need to rely on secrets. Yet God is the ultimate authority, whom people must be accountable to.

However, Saul did have someone who would challenge Goliath. Someone who didn't let his fear of Goliath stop him. David wrote "Even though I walk through the valley of the shadow of death I will fear no evil" Maybe he wrote this about his time standing in the valley against Goliath?

David's bravery then brings courage to the Israelite army who then charge in once David has lopped off Goliath's head.

Q – So after the battle, do the Philistines honour what Goliath promised and become Israel's servants? (No).

Q – What do they do? (They run).

When David gives his reply to Goliath he rejects the culture that Goliath is imposing. Goliath's culture is to say that they must fight his way (expecting a sword fight) and that the losers must put down their weapons and become slaves. David turns up with sticks and stones and rejects Goliath's deal, declaring that a victory over the Philistines has been given by God.

Q – Was that deal ever going to work anyway? (Discuss. Probably not. It just helped start the battle, giving the winner's side an advantage. David uses the plural "you" though).

Q – Why do you think that David selected 5 stones? Was it in case the first 4 shots missed? (It is thought that Goliath had 4 similar sized brothers and that David was prepared to take them out too).

Q - So did the stone kill Goliath? (Probably not).

Imagine if David was a footballer. He approaches Goliath, selects a stone flings his sling. The stone goes flying towards Goliath and hits him in the top corner of his head. Down goes Goliath, to a gasp from the Philistine army and cheers from the Israelites. Does David run over to the corner flag and do a dance? No because Goliath may only be stunned. So he runs the 50 yard dash to Goliath before the armour bearer can get there (no armour to slow David down!), he takes Goliath's sword and severs off Goliath's head to secure the victory!

Q – How do the fearful Israelite army respond? (They chase the Philistines to Goliath's home town. Imagine being there and hearing the result!).

Round up (5 minutes)
So David's bravery has brought courage to others. Saul didn't have the physically biggest or strongest guy on his side. He didn't have the Police to help settle the dispute. He wasn't able to expose Goliath in the news. But he had a boy/man who would stand up against Goliath, deciding to fear God rather than fear Goliath.

Bullying can be stopped. We don't suggest you start using a sling-shot or anything. Instead God has the exact weapons that you need to defeat a bully. There are people you trust, those in authority, friends to support you – use them! He has courage to give you to say "No" and wisdom to know when to confidently walk away. He has angels to protect you and a voice to be loud.

He also gives you humour. If they say "Give me your sweets" you can say "OK, but my cat licked them earlier so they don't taste very nice."

He's also given you prayer. So you can talk to him about it all. He hears every word, suffers with you and will give you a way out when you need it.

Prayer (As long as it takes!)
Take the opportunity to pray with anyone who has been bullied. Remind them who God says they are and how God sees them. Ask for his help with current bullying situations and strengthen those going through it.

64) David acts with integrity

Icebreaker 1 - Catchphrase (8 minutes)
Using the attached sheet get the youngsters into teams to see if they can decipher the catchphrases! And remember, say what you see!

Discussion starter – All's fair in love and war (8 minutes)
Split into groups of 3 discuss the phrase "All's fair in love and war" which means any behaviour is okay if you are contending for a lover or fighting in a war.

All's fair in love and war is a principle that many people live by today where they think some things in life are so important, that you are allowed to resort to unfair means in order to get what you want, even if it hurts someone else.

Imagine the scene. Two friends (we'll call one Emily and the other Georgie) of a similar age fancy the same lad (we'll call him Fin. He is good at swimming and into Star Wars). Georgie manages to ask Fin out. However that same day Emily was thinking of asking him out. As time progresses Emily falls in love with Fin, though it is Georgie who is going out with him. Emily is conflicted; she has been friends with Georgie for ages, but she really wants to be with this lad.

So one day Emily asks to borrow Georgie's phone. Emily discovers that Georgie is meeting Fin in town tomorrow. So Emily texts Fin to change the place and time of the date with Georgie. Fin turns up and Georgie is nowhere to be seen. Fin is upset and cross with Georgie for not turning up, but Emily is there to swoop in and console Fin. They have a nice time together and as a result Fin goes out with Emily instead.

Q – What do you think of Emily's actions? (Discuss)

Q – How is this going to affect Emily's relationship with Georgie? (Discuss)

Q - Are there any circumstances where "all's fair in love and war" can be true? (Discuss)

Q – Can you describe the nature of love? What's love like? (The phrase "all's fair…" makes out love to be something it is not. Love is not something that is selfish. God demonstrates his love by being the opposite, by being selfless).

Introduction (1 minute)

We pick up the story with the current King of Israel King Saul pursuing the promised King David in order to kill him. David has been in hiding in the desert, fleeing from place to place, hideout to hideout, even risking his life by going to the enemy, the Philistines for safety. King Saul has been less than a good king, disobeying God, ignoring his instructions and giving in to huge bouts of anger. He believes he won't stop until David is dead.

Today we are going to see that there is a cost to following God. Times where we are faced with having to give up what we want to do, in order to choose God's better way and do what he wants us to do.

Teaching 1 (10 minutes)

READ 1 Samuel 24:1-22, 2 Samuel 5:1-4

Q – Do you remember how old the Bible describes David when he was anointed and killed Goliath? (Saul says to David when he goes to fight Goliath that he is just a boy; though he may be using language that exaggerates the facts. A boy became a man at the age of 13; but he could have been older. He may have been too young to fight in the army, as you had to be at least 20 years old - Numbers 1:3).

Q – And how old was David when he became king? (Thirty years old).

So we can safely say that David probably had to wait more than 10 years, from when he was first anointed as king by Samuel to the time that he actually became king.

Q – After all this pursuing and fleeing, how does David come into contact with King Saul? (Saul needs a wee. Actually it was more likely a number 2, how else would David have had time to sneak up on him?? David approaches and cuts off a corner of his robe and retreats).

Q – What is the conversation that David has in the back of the cave with his men? (They see this as God's opportunity to kill Saul, but David tells them off for suggesting it. It's a bit like when your folks tell you off for being naughty in the library or church when you're supposed to be being quiet. So trying to be quiet they tell you off in a sort of whispered cross voice!).

Q – We know David has been called to be king. We also know that King Saul has rejected God and is not leading God's people

faithfully. He has waged war against David and threatened to destroy him. So why did he think it was wrong to kill Saul? (He didn't think it was good for someone to kill another person whom God had called and appointed. It would seem like going against God's choices).

Q – Can someone describe how David would feel having been waiting to be king for such a long time and then finally the opportunity is there? (Maybe he was wondering whether it was ever going to happen).

Q – What do you think might have happened if David had killed Saul? How would this have affected the process of him becoming king? (Having killed the current king, it may have started up a time of unrest with people loyal to Saul causing problems).

Sometimes by doing things our way (because of impatience or selfishness) it can get us what we want; however the circumstances may not be as favourable. By letting God do it in his timing, we can enjoy the blessings that his timing brings).

Q – Have you ever wanted something so bad and not got it. Then after the initial disappointment, you came to actually be glad that it didn't happen? (Discuss. It's possible to be blind to our bad actions and attitudes when we want something so badly. We can become obsessed in such a way that makes the guy we fancy better than they actually are. Falling in love with the idea rather than the reality is a very real pitfall!).

Q – David uses the saying "From evildoers come evil deeds." What do you think that means? (He didn't want to be around evildoers so he mustn't be like them).

Q – Why does David call Saul his father and Saul call David his son? Is this a Darth Vader/Luke Skywalker moment? (Jesse was David's father. However, Saul had been like a father figure to David in better times. They still had a relationship. By speaking to each other in these terms they were restoring that relationship).

Q – David was so close to the moment of becoming king. But it is not yet. How do you think David is feeling at this moment? (He is probably glad that he didn't kill Saul. First he didn't have to answer to the 3,000 soldiers waiting outside. Second he had managed to make peace with King Saul. Third, his integrity was intact. He had acted honorably when he did not kill Saul).

Round up (2 minutes)
Jesus talks about taking up your cross and following him. That whoever wants to gain his or her life must lose it. Sometimes in life, doing what God wants us to do doesn't always make sense at the time. But it is in giving up what we have and what we want that we find life.

Using devious or selfish means to get what we want can taint what God wants to give us anyway. When we give up the opportunity to God we often find he gives back to us so much more than we had in the first place.

Pray (As long as it takes!)

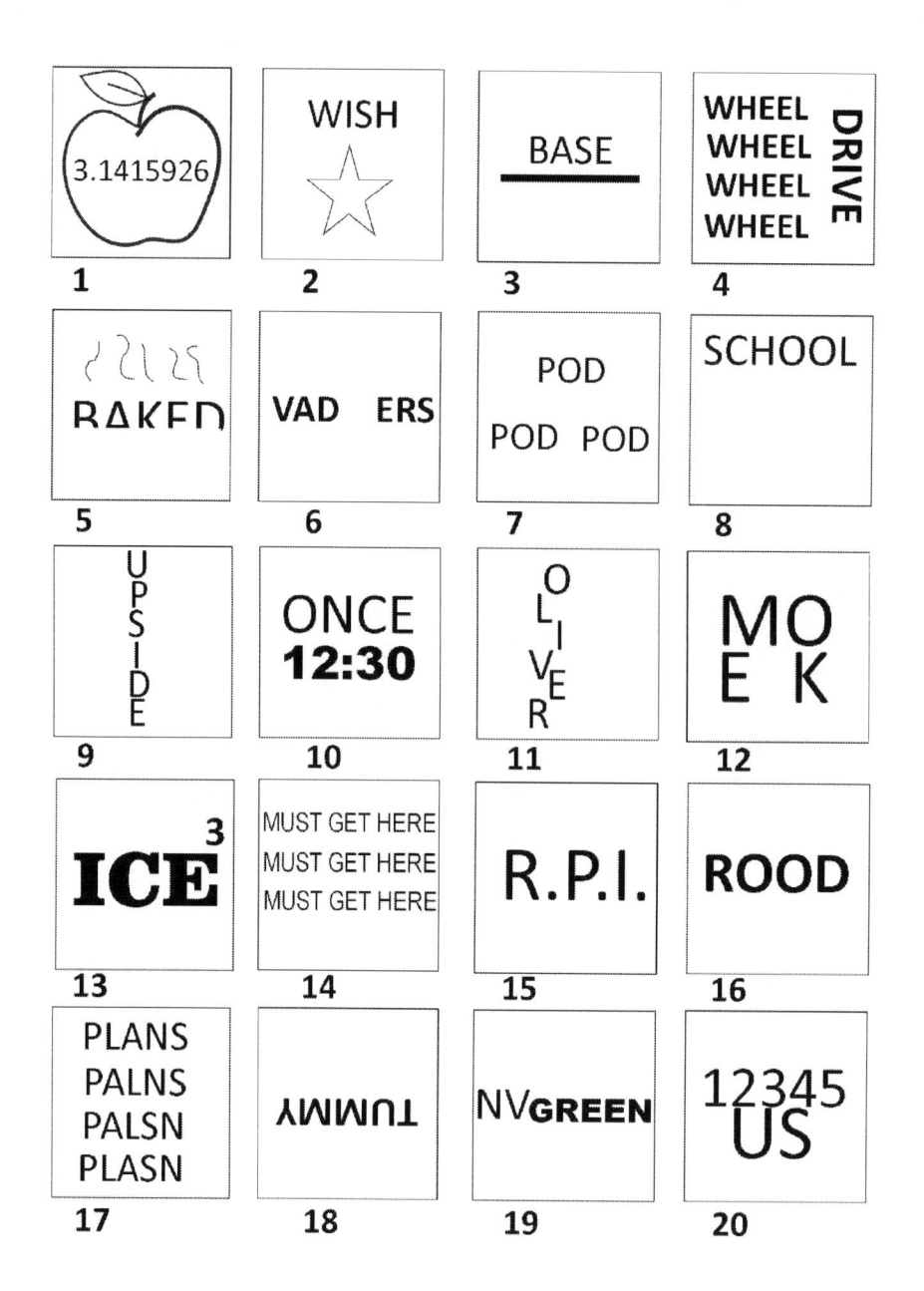

🍎 3.1415926	WISH ★	BASE ___	WHEEL WHEEL WHEEL WHEEL DRIVE
1	2	3	4
ϱϨϨϨ BAKED	VAD ERS	POD POD POD	SCHOOL
5	6	7	8
UPSIDE (vertical)	ONCE **12:30**	OLIVER (vertical)	MO E K
9	10	11	12
ICE³	MUST GET HERE MUST GET HERE MUST GET HERE	R.P.I.	ROOD
13	14	15	16
PLANS PALNS PALSN PLASN	TUMMY (upside down)	NVGREEN	12345 US
17	18	19	20

Catchphrase Answers
1) Apple pie
2) Wish upon a star
3) Base line
4) Four wheel drive
5) Half-baked
6) Space invader
7) Tripod
8) High school
9) Upside down
10) Once upon a time
11) Oliver Twist
12) Okay by me
13) Ice cube
14) The three musketeers
15) Grave mistake
16) Back door
17) Change of plans
18) Upset tummy
19) Green with envy
20) Count on us

65) Saul goes off the rails

Icebreaker 1 - Would you rather?? (3 minutes)
Tell the group you want to get to know them more. So you are going to give them two options and they must decide which option they would prefer.
Would you rather...
... eat dog food or cat food?
... win by cheating or lose while playing fair?
... wait a year to have an iPhone or have a new android phone now?
... feed a snake or a tarantula?
... be embarrassed in front of friends or strangers?
... holiday at the seaside in England or in the snow of Switzerland?
... have a year's supply of Haribo, or a year's supply of Cadbury's choc?
... be lost in the jungle or the desert?
... go to church on a Sunday morning or a Friday evening?
... sit n learn or stand up and teach?
... have superhuman strength or be able to fly?
... train for one year and win the bronze medal or train for 4 years and win the gold?
... travel back in time or forward in time?
... give sweets to trick or treaters, or have an egg thrown at your house?
... be given a haunted house for free or have to pay £200,000 for a house that isn't haunted?

Discussion starter – Ghostbusters (5 minutes)
A Ghostbuster has been called to a "haunted" hospital following reports by staff of a cloaked figure roaming the wards and corridors. The spooky sightings at the new Royal Derby Hospital have prompted NHS bosses to summon an exorcist, The Sun claimed.

Senior manager Debbie Butler sent an email to staff, informing them of a plan to bring in a priest to rid the hospital of paranormal activity. She wrote: "I'm not sure how many of you are aware that some members of staff have reported seeing a ghost. I'm taking it seriously as it is affecting some members of staff and the last thing I want is staff feeling uneasy at work. I don't want to scare anyone any more than necessary, but felt it was best I made you all aware of the situation and what we are doing about it.

"I've spoken to the Trust's chaplain and she is going to arrange for someone from the cathedral to exorcise the department."

The £334 million hospital is located on the site of the old Derby City General Hospital, which was built in the 1920s over part of a Roman road. Ms Butler added: "I understand that some of you will probably be worried or scared about this. If any of you wish to discuss this, feel free to contact me at any time."

Anglican priests usually need to seek permission from a bishop before performing an exorcism. A spokesman for the Bishop of Derby told the newspaper: "Any case such as this is put to the Bishop. He would seek proper advice before taking action. A spokeswoman for Derby Hospitals NHS Trust said: "We take information from staff seriously and are working with the hospital chaplaincy to put people's minds at ease."

Q – Does anyone here believe in ghosts? (Discuss. But yes they are real).

Q – What do you think ghosts are? (Contrary to popular belief, ghosts are not people who have died, they are demons who know a lot about humans and can give information in order to impersonate a dead relative. If anyone has ever had encounter with a supernatural being it's important to discern the source – is it God or not).

Q – Where do you think ghosts come from? (The spirit realm. They are fallen angels).

Q – What do you think the Bible has to say about contacting spirits and ghosts? (Not to!)

Introduction (1 minute)
Bible has its fair share of unusual stories of things that seem a bit bizarre and maybe surprising. We're going to look at one such story from the life of King Saul.

We pick the story up where Saul has been pursuing David in an effort to kill him. David has somehow managed to join a Philistine settlement with his men without causing too much trouble. There are more battles on the Horizon. Strangely a man called Achish the Philistine king asks David to fight in the battle on the side of the Philistines as his bodyguard. Yet this is no football match, it is a battle against King Saul and the Israelite army.

Teaching 1 (10 minutes)
READ 1 Samuel 28:1-25

Q – What things are happening to put King Saul under pressure? (The Philistines are in the mood for a fight. They have moved their army close, so there is a physical threat that needs to be dealt with).

Q – Who is not around that King Saul needs to talk to? (Samuel the prophet has died).

Q – Why is it a problem that Samuel is dead? (Saul can't hear God and needs help to know what to do to win the battle).

Q – What are the emotions that Saul is having that are adding to the pressure? (He felt physically afraid. Fear saps your energy and leaves you feeling weak and unable to think).

Q – Of all of the things happening to Saul, what is the worst? (His relationship with God was broken).

Q – Why is this a big problem for Saul? (God is the only one who can help him and he is realizing that without God, he is nothing).

Q – Can any of you tell me why God has left King Saul, the leader of his people? (In previous situations, Saul did not obey God when leading God's people. Then when he realised he had messed up he was only sorry because of the consequences, rather than his wrongdoing).

So Saul is under pressure. An army was ready to attack and he wasn't sure the Israelite army could win. Also Samuel, Saul's link to God was gone. Now Saul was fearful and panicking and he had no relationship with God to help him through.

Discussion - Pressure (5 minutes)
We all experience pressures of different kinds and at different times. Often a limited time frame and a deadline is a strong factor in making us feel stressed.

Q – What are the pros and cons of being under pressure? (Pros: it focuses the mind to achieve the task in hand. Cons: you only have a limited time to produce a solution)

So pressure can do things to us, if we are feeling overwhelmed it's easy to make the wrong choices.

Teaching 2 (10 minutes)
So King Saul's reliance appears to be on Samuel rather than God.

Q – Who does Saul go to see? (A psychic or medium)

Q – What do they do? (They contact the spirit world for knowledge and power).

Q – Is it right to consult a medium or psychic for information from paranormal sources? (No, it is not okay. Whether or not they can gain accurate information; it does not mean that the source of that information is trustworthy or reliable).

Q – But something very unusual happens. Normally a demon would manifest with information on the dead. However, that doesn't happen. Explain what happens when the Witch consults the spirits? (The dead prophet Samuel actually shows himself and gives a message from God).

Q – Someone reading this might then say "I can consult a medium, because God talks through them." Why is this the wrong conclusion to come to? (This event only happened once in the Bible. There are no other similar occurrences. You can't come to that conclusion through one text in the Bible. The Bible quite plainly says that we shouldn't consult mediums).

Those are the facts, but that doesn't get to understanding "why" Samuel appeared and why we can't consult mediums.

Q – Can anyone say why God caused Samuel's dead spirit to manifest and communicate to the medium, when it was contrary to what God had commanded? (God had commanded it so that people wouldn't be deceived by demons. God was not allowing Saul to hear from a demon, but rather God was speaking a final word of judgement on King Saul and his leadership of Israel).

King Saul is in rebellion. People turn to all sorts of things when they are rebelling against God. Oftentimes it's something God has said not to do.

Q – Why do you think God says to not do some things in the Bible? (Because he wants to protect us from the harm those things can do to us. But also he wants to provide a safe way of living that invites his blessing).

Are ghosts real?
There are many spirits and none of them are good apart from the Holy Spirit, who is part of God. He is more powerful than any evil spirit or demon.

Ghost stories
I'm sure we have all heard ghost stories. Often they are linked to a story of someone who died, maybe in tragic circumstances.

Q – Why do you think ghosts appear in connection with someone who has died, like a story in the past? (The demons want to draw you in to be curious to find out more. It is possible for an unhealthy curiosity in demons to get caught up in interacting with them. They work on fear and are not good or friendly. They want to be served and paid attention to).

Leviticus 19:31 "Do not turn to mediums or seek out spiritists, for you will be defiled by them. I am the LORD your God." The warning is for those who would be curious about these things not to get tangled up in it all as it will be harmful for you.

The story goes of a Scottish Christian lady (Miss Taylor of Greenock) who woke up with a start in the night to see a Shadowy figure at the foot of her bed that looked like Satan. She took one look at him and said "Och it's only you," and turned over and went back to sleep! We are God's children and protected by him.

Q – So is it okay to read books and watch films like Harry Potter? (Discuss)

Q – What if those books provide actual spells and practices that witches actually use? (Discuss)

Q – Do you think that there are any subtle false teachings in those books that people might unknowingly take on board? (Discuss. Do they have any examples?)

Q - So if we were to have a show of hands. In the Harry Potter books white magic is good and black magic is bad. In the real world where these things actually exist, do you think that statement is true or false? (It is false. There is no "good magic" because it comes from the same source which is demonic).

In Halloween (the witches' favourite day of the year) children go around saying the words "trick or treat." This literally means "demanding with menaces" this is the nature of evil. To control by the use of power.

Round up (1 minute)
For some people, hearing about ghosts and paranormal activity will make them either scared or curious. Both reactions are understandable but can be harmful. We are told in James 2:19 that the demons know there is a Living God and they shudder in fear.

As God's children you are protected by him. It is possible to step out from under his protection by getting curious about the paranormal. This can lead to very scary situations. It is also possible to take on beliefs about the paranormal without knowing it.

The Bible also says that all who call on the name of the Lord will be saved. Prayer is a more powerful weapon in the spirit realm than we can ever imagine. You are protected by angels every day!

Pray
Thank God for his protection and his provision over our lives.

66) David a heart after God

Icebreaker 1 – Song birds (10 minutes)
Separate the group into 3 or 4 teams. Tell them they have 3 minutes to think up as many songs as they can with the word "heart" in them. Get them to write them down, but not let the other teams know what they are.

Once they have had enough time, the first team must sing the line of just one song which has the word heart in it. The next team must do the same (and the next), but they must not repeat a song already used. Each team has 5 seconds to begin singing. When a team runs out of songs, repeats one (or tries to make one up!) that team is out. Continue with the other teams until you have a winner.

You can repeat the game with other words like "worship" or "love" or anything relating to today's theme!

Discussion starter – The word heart (8 minutes)
Q – So the word heart is in a lot of songs. But what exactly is that word trying to communicate? (A love, inner affection, emotional desire, hopes and dreams?).

Q – Have you ever heard people say "I've got a heart for..." something? Whether it's music, art, fashion, people in poor countries etc. What do you think they are trying to communicate? (That their motivation, their love or desire makes that person or thing their priority in life).

Maybe you as the leader would like to share something that you have a heart for...

Q – Whose got a heart for something? Can you tell us what it is? Why is that thing important to you? (Discuss).

Introduction (1 minute)
The events leading up to what we are about to read could have been in any movie. King Saul, jealous about David's ability to fight (and generally be better than him), leads Saul to pursue David. David makes it to safety in some caves. By a God-incidence Saul needs to use the facilities and enters the cave David is in. Well to cut a long robe short, David makes peace with King Saul by not killing him. Saul continues to get himself into trouble by consulting a witch for God had rejected him as king and chosen David instead.

It says of David, God has sought out a man after his own heart. Well king Saul dies painfully in battle and David becomes king. Now there is some unfinished business. The Ark of the Covenant, where God's Holy presence stays, is about to be brought to the city of God, Jerusalem. David's heart's desire is to worship God and honour him. Unfortunately the people of God have picked up some bad habits…

Teaching 1 (10 minutes)
READ 2 Samuel 6:1-23

Q – Can anyone explain what the Ark of the Covenant was? (It was a golden box with carvings of Cherubim (like angels) on it. It contained the 10 commandments, but more importantly it was where God allowed his holy and powerful presence to be).

Q – Can anyone recall any amazing things that happened involving the Ark of the Covenant? (The Israelites needed to cross the river Jordan. When they brought the Ark of the Covenant to the water's edge the water parted like when they crossed the Red Sea. Also when the Philistines captured the Ark of the Covenant, they experienced serious health problems and returned it to the Israelites).

Q – Why do you think King David was bringing the Ark of the Covenant to Jerusalem? (This was to be the main city in Israel, the place where God's temple and his presence would be).

Q - What went wrong? (The Oxen stumbled and the Ark of the Covenant nearly fell off the cart).

Q – Do you know what the people were doing wrong? (They were copying the way the Philistines transported the Ark of the Covenant, rather than the way the Lord had told them to).

Q – Do you know how the Ark of the Covenant should have been carried? (There were holes on either side of the Ark of the Covenant when poles slid in, in order to be carried on the shoulders of Levites).

Q – Do you think we do anything in church that offends God that people have assumed is okay? And we're not talking about our own personal preferences! (Maybe needlessly using mobile phones during the worship?)

So they did not show due diligence in how God wanted to be honoured and worshipped. They came to God with assumptions, rather than checking out what might be required. Here are the instructions for handling the Ark of the Covenant: READ Numbers 4:5-6, 15, 18-20

Q – Why do you think it made God so upset for Uzzah to touch the Ark of the Covenant? (They were treating God like the idols of other nations).

Q – Why was it so important to get it right? (When the Ark of the Covenant was made, there were some very specific instructions that had to be followed that were honouring to God. This was not simply some box. It was where the presence of God went).

So after some soul searching David made some corrections on how to handle the Ark of the Covenant and then they go again...

Q – What are the differences between this time and last time? (There is no cart. The Ark of the Covenant is carried on poles. There were sacrifices being made).

Q – What is David wearing? (A linen ephod).

Q – What is a linen ephod? (It is a similar garment that Samuel wore as a boy, not the same size though! It was the basic attire of a priest).

Q - What is noticeable about what David is not wearing? (He is not wearing his kingly robes).

Q – Why do you think he wore a linen ephod and not his kingly robes? (David was performing the duties of a priest by sacrificing a bull, which a king could do under certain circumstances).

Q – How does this show his heart? (It showed his desire to worship God).

Q – Why did he wear what he did? (Ephod was a simple garment of a priest, not a king. As a person being humble before God).

Q - So David's wife has a lot to say about his dancing and what he was wearing. What is she complaining about? (She is complaining about what he was wearing and the manner in which he was dancing).

Some people have said that because she used the word disrobing in front of common servant girls that this means David didn't have any pants on. An Ephod was like a small dress that the priests wore with gaps down the side from the waist down.

However, priests were also supposed to wear under-garments if they were to approach God's presence Exodus 28:31-43. After the last mistake with the cart, David would not have been taking any chances. It is likely that Michal was using sarcasm and being snobby. It was more likely that she was upset because he wasn't wearing his kingly robes, making him like any "commoner."

By wearing the Ephod David was showing that he was a worshipper of God first, a servant of him before he was a King.

Q – Why might there be dancing in some churches but not others? (Cultural differences could be one reason!).

Q – Does it mean if you don't dance, you aren't as devoted? (No).

Q - What is the most important attitude in worshipping God? (That the worship comes from the heart).

Q – How can we best show our heart to God? (By forgetting those around us and focusing on God in our worship).

Round up (1 minute)
When the heart is stirred it shows on your face and what's real inside begins to show. Does that mean we should dance? There are a lot of reasons why we might not feel comfortable dancing in church, but that when we're on our own those inhibitions have gone and we can dance freely.

Sometimes it's difficult when others are around to shake off a feeling of self-consciousness when others are around and people are looking. However worship isn't for those people. It's not for an audience it's just for God.

Pray (As long as it takes!)

67) David's big mistake

Icebreaker - Bargain Hunt goes arty (15 minutes)
There's a bit of printing for you this week. You'll need to find pictures of paintings and print one painting out for each of the following values (just postcard size). Also print out a piece of paper for each person with these values on them:

1 - 20 million
1 – 8 million
2 – 5 million
3 – 2 million
3 – 1 million
4 - ½ million
2 - Forgery

On the reverse of the painting write a value. Note there are more paintings of a lower value; ie. there are 4 paintings that you can price at ½ million, 3 paintings at 1 million, 3 paintings at 2 million, 2 paintings at 5 million, 1 painting at 8 million and 1 painting at 20 million. There are also 2 paintings that you must write on the back as forgeries.

Each player is allowed to choose one painting to sell (without looking on the back to see the value). Once they have selected their painting, they can look at the price (without showing anyone else during the game). That person must then attempt to talk up their painting and its value before auctioning it off to the rest of the group.

Each bidder can bid up to 20 million, but once they have bought a painting they cannot bid any more. No actual paper money is used; it's all done by money transfer (numbers on a piece of paper). Once a painting is sold, a leader needs to make a note of the profit margin gained or lost by the seller and the buyer.

The aim of the game is to make the best profit margin by buying one painting and selling one painting, so the value of the painting is not counted. By the end of the game every person must have bought and sold a painting.

If you have a large group, it's worth teaming people up into groups so that you have time for the teaching!

Introduction (1 minute)
Ever had the feeling when you want something and you can't have it... but that doesn't stop you, so you try everything in your power to get it...

Discussion starter (10 minutes)
Which of these crimes deserves the worst punishment?

1) Stealing - McDonald's in a pickle over cheese slice firing

A Dutch branch of McDonald's was wrong to fire a worker for giving a colleague an extra piece of cheese on a hamburger, a court ruled on Tuesday.

"The dismissal was too severe a measure," the district court in Leeuwarden in the north of the Netherlands said in a written judgment. "It is just a slice of cheese."

A written warning would have been a more appropriate punishment, said the court, which ordered McDonald's to pay the worker the salary for the remaining five months of her contract, a total of €4,265.47. The company was also ordered to pay court costs.

The worker was fired at a McDonald's branch in the northern town of Lemmer in March last year for giving a colleague on a break a more expensive cheese burger instead of the hamburger she had paid for. McDonald's maintained she had broken the rules, which prohibit any free gifts to family, friends or colleagues.

2) Injustice - Man gets parking ticket after 30 seconds

A motorist was furious to return to his car and find a warden issuing a parking ticket only 30 seconds after he'd parked there. Twenty nine year old Andrew Oxley had found a space in Exeter Central Train Station car park and had gone to pay for a ticket. On his return he found a warden writing out a £75 penalty fine.

The female warden, from Premier Parking Solutions (PPS), was taking a photograph of his car and warned him that failure to pay within seven days would see the fine jump to £100. PPS has been accused of overzealous ticket issuing before. PPS was recently criticised for handing a £75 fine to a man in the same car park that had left his car for four minutes. He too was paying for a ticket at the time.

In this case Mr Oxley is refusing to pay the fine, and is willing to take the matter through the courts. His appeal to PPS has so far yielded no response and PPS has not commented on the case. Mr Oxley said: "The only thing I can say is that I must be the only driver in Exeter to be done for parking for leaving his car for a matter of seconds. I've worked it out that PPS are demanding £3 per second."

3) Lying - Fake war hero

A man who wore unearned medals at an Armistice Day parade has been given a community order, after admitting his crime. Roger Day of Church Street, Earl Shilton, Leicestershire, was arrested attending the parade at Bedworth, Warwickshire, on November 11.

The 61-year-old who had worn 17 medals on his suit was charged under the Army Act of 1955. During a brief hearing at Nuneaton Magistrates' Court on Tuesday he pleaded guilty to unlawfully using military decoration. Day, who was exposed as a fraud, when parade organisers became suspicious, was told he must complete 60 hours of unpaid work over the next 12 months.

He was also ordered to forfeit the 17 medals and pay £40 costs. Pinned to Day's lapel had been the Distinguished Service Order and the Military Cross, in addition to campaign medals stretching from World War II to the Gulf, three SAS badges and an SAS beret. Military experts said it would have been "impossible" for one man to have been decorated with so many honours.

Q - Are these just harmless wrong doings or are they crimes deserving punishment? (Discuss)

Q - Which of these 3 crimes deserves the harshest punishment? What do you think that punishment should be? (Discuss)

Q - Have you done any of those 3 things during the past week? (Discuss)

We're going to look at a person in the Bible who has done all of these things and so much worse.

Teaching (15 Minutes)
Read 2 Samuel 11:1-27

David was having an off day...

Q – It's spring time now. People tend to do certain things in the spring... spring cleaning, DIY, going out, buy a kitten. Verse 1 says in those days at spring-time the kings don't do DIY on castles, or have a clean. Instead, they go off to war (whether protecting their land or attacking enemies). What does verse 1 say King David did and what does this suggest to us about David's frame of mind? (It seems that David was having an off day. Instead of fulfilling his leadership responsibilities and considering his Nation's defence, he was feeling a bit lazy).

Q - So King David sees Bathsheba in the bath. Do you think this was wrong? (Discuss. David was just enjoying the view from his castle. When his eyes came upon Bathsheba in the bath it wasn't wrong. He just noticed her).

Q – What was wrong then? (Not looking away, instead looking for more and taking it further).

Q – How should King David have responded? (It would have been better to have immediately looked away and gone and done something different. Finding an alternative distraction like playing a worship song, going for a run, talking to a friend, just anything to stop himself from being drawn in).

Q – Obviously we don't have a castle and people don't tend to bathe on their roofs in our country, but can you think of any ways in which we might be faced with a similar scenario? (Our computers, tablets and smartphones are the new castle roof tops. We can be innocently working when something catches our attention, maybe someone without much clothing on).

Scenario (2 minutes)
Imagine the scenario... Maybe you're tired, you're in exam times and you have some coursework to complete. You haven't seen your friends for a while and you should be studying. But instead of getting down to it, you think you'll just check Facebook. All your mates are studying and there's not even one person to chat to. As you're on there you notice a funny clip from YouTube that someone has put on their newsfeed. You check it out. But then at the end of the clip come up options for other clips. And you notice something sexy, that you decide to check out.

Before long you're on the wrong side of YouTube, looking at things that won't do you any good and a couple of hours have passed and you haven't looked at your work and now it's late.

You go to bed and wake up in the morning in a panic. Suddenly you remember what you haven't done. You make up lies to explain why your work hasn't been completed.

The fact is that when we are feeling tired, lonely, or bored, the enemy has you in his sights and will use this moment when you are weak to take you down. What starts with feeling a bit down can lead to temptation. This can then lead to doing wrong things and then trying to cover them up.

Temptation
Sometimes the pull of temptation for these things can last for a while after you have made the decision not to do it. The enemy can nag at your mind and say "Remember what you saw? You'll really enjoy yourself if you take a longer look." Of course this is a lie. It is one step towards an addiction.

Well David doesn't look away. Instead he sends for Bathsheba and seduces her. He sleeps with Bathsheba. Then when she becomes pregnant he gets her husband drunk to try and cover it up and when that doesn't work, he arranges for Uriah to be killed in battle.

Q – What do you think David's conscience is like after this? (He doesn't even realise he's done something wrong).

Q – What do you think makes us so blind to temptation? (When you are tempted by something, all you can see is what you want to do. The enemy uses temptation to combine with the strong desires within us, in order to pull us into doing wrong).

Temptation is like a drug dealer
Temptation always suggests to us that whatever we shouldn't do is going to satisfy us inside. It says that doing it will be exciting, like an amazing thrill. Unfortunately, temptation is like a drug dealer. It nags away at you to give it a try, until you give in. The thrill of it seems pretty good, but the after affects aren't so good. But then temptation comes back, and the second time it's a bit easier, the thrill is still there, but the guilt doesn't seem so strong.

Next time, temptation doesn't need to knock on your door, you want more so you go looking for temptation; and before long, you're an addict. Your soul feels deadness, numbed to guilt; in fact your soul doesn't care for much. You're now controlled by your habit and become a different person. Your attitude has changed. Like the man with the medals, you don't want people to see the real you.

Once King David had seen Bathsheba once do you think he forgot about her? I think he would have seen her several times since. I reckon he'd also have gone for several more walks on his rooftop in the chance of seeing her again. He wouldn't have been able to stop thinking of her.

Teaching 2 (10 minutes)

READ 2 Samuel 12:1-14

Q – So Nathan speaks to David about his terrible actions. Why does Nathan tell King David the story about the little sheep? (He sees that King David is blind to his own actions and needs to be shown things from an outside perspective).

Q - If we see a fellow Christian behaving in a way that is dishonouring to Jesus, should we go and tell them? (Discuss).

Q – How should we go and tell them? (It is very easy to judge others and to misunderstand what is going on. Also even if we are right, the Bible tells us in Romans 2:4 that it is God's kindness that brings people to repentance, to saying sorry. So if we feel we must, then think how you would like someone to deal with you if the role was reversed, and go and do likewise).

So just like an addiction, the consequences of his actions don't turn out well. He kills a man; he loses his child, his sons end up behaving like him and worse. And there are all these repercussions to letting those temptations get the better of him.

Round up (2 minutes)
A little girl once said "When the Devil comes knocking on my door. I don't answer it. Instead I send Jesus to answer it." The Bible says "come near to God and he will come near to you. Resist the devil and he will flee from you" (James 4:8).

The answer in this is to recognise that although temptation may seem exciting, it actually becomes poison to our soul. So instead of umming and arring about whether you want to do what you're being tempted, override those thoughts by saying "no." By ignoring the thoughts, distracting yourself with other things you are resisting the devil and he will go away. But also come near to God. Tell him "the devil is knocking on my door!! Send him away please!!"

By doing this you will save yourself so much strife in life.

Prayer (As long as it takes!)

68) David's Thankfulness

Icebreaker - Air guitar champion (5 minutes)
You may need a prize to motivate people for this one, if your youngsters are a little shy! Tell them you are going to do an air guitar competition. Get two youngsters to go head to head and play a suitable rock n roll track that has a good electric guitar solo. If you can't find anything "Rain down" by Delirious? will work!

If you have an inflatable guitar all the better! Play about 20 seconds of the track and get the youngsters to imitate playing the electric guitar. The winner is the one with the most applause.

Discussion – Thanksgiving (5 minutes)
A woman was walking in a park in the American town of Sante Fe, when she came across an envelope on a park bench. The delighted woman found $100 inside with a handwritten note saying: "Hello. Yes, this is for you. Money comes into my life and I am grateful for it. This is my way of expressing my gratitude. We live in an infinitely abundant universe. There is much more than enough for all of us. Enjoy! A friend."

Q – What is the most memorable "thank you" that anyone has ever said to you? (Discuss)

Q – How does it make you feel when someone says "thank you" to you? (Discuss)

The thank you note... (5 minutes)
Birthdays are great. We look forward to them every year. What is not to like? Everyone treats you nicely you get cake, and cool stuff to eat, you get presents, parcels or cards through the post, cards often with money in... it's a great day to be alive, your birthday. But if there's one down side to having a birthday it's after everything is opened. Probably at the end of the day, your mum or your dad will say "Don't forget to remember who got you which presents, because you'll need to send everyone a thank you message.

In days gone past when they didn't have text messages, you actually had to get your writing set out that you got for your birthday and write about 20 letters, which meant 20 pages of thank you for the flannel and scarf set that you sent me for my birthday. Well I dreamed of becoming more organised and efficient in sending thank you letters, so I came up with this system...
(See end of notes - Thank you for the... tick box advice form).

Have one of these printed out for each youngster. As a fun activity, get the youth to complete the form using made up names and gift ideas, ticking boxes and adding comments to make for funny reading.

Unfortunately I never put this into practice; I just didn't bother doing letters anymore.

Q - Ever had a bad present? What is it you were given?
(Discuss).

However when it comes to being thankful to God this is something that is ever so important. God's gifts and help are so amazing. Unlike some people's presents, he gives us exactly what we need.

Teaching (10 minutes)
READ 2 Samuel 21:15-22, 22:1-7

Q – Did anyone notice the reference to Goliath here? Can anyone explain what is meant in verse 19? (And the question then comes up "who killed Goliath???")

Who Killed Goliath?
Some people might say "Ah ha! I told you! The Bible does contradict itself. You just read that Elhanan killed Goliath, but we know it was David!"

Let me explain how things have got confused. The literal translation is "And the giant, the among of sons who was in Gob with the Philistines and struck Elhanan the Jaare of son Oregim the Bethlehemite Goliath the Gittite and wood his the spear of like (was) beam the weaver's."

So first there's an idea of the job translators have to do in making sense of ancient texts, when the order of the words seem to be mixed up. Back to the question... earlier in the Bible it tells us that David killed Goliath in the valley of Elah in Socoh. But here we read of Goliath being killed at Gob (modern day Gezer).

The problem comes with the word "Bethlehmite." To cut a long story short it appears that the translators got this mixed up with the name of Goliath's brother who is called Lahmi.

The word Bethlehmite is actually split into 3 parts "bet" and "hal-lah-mi" and "et." "Et" is a prefix for a noun (people, place or thing). "Bet" appears to have been confused from a previous word.

If you remove "bet" you are left with hal-lahmi or Lahmi – which is the name of a person who was Goliath's brother and not Goliath. Also if you were to look at 1 Chronicles 20:5 you'll find this name Lahmi properly translated.

So this is actually Goliath's brother.

Q – Why do you think Ishi-Benob was so intent on killing King David? (Because he was a relative of Goliath, who was very popular because he was big and wanted revenge).

Q – Think back to the David and Goliath story. How many stones did David pick up when he went to fight with Goliath? How is this significant? (Goliath had 4 other relatives, probably brothers and David went wisely prepared in case they came after him following Goliath's defeat).

Q – What happened to David during the battle? (He was exhausted from all the killing).

Q – And why do you think he became exhausted? (Because he was getting on in years).

Q – What did his friends promise him? (That he would never fight in battle again. It was time for David to retire from the front line of battle.)

Q – If you consider what age David was when he killed Goliath, and what age he is now, what does this tell us about Goliath's brothers? (They were *still* after David! Even after all those years).

Q – How did David respond to his fortunate escape? (He is very thankful. But not only does he thank God for rescuing him then, he goes on to thank God for all of his goodness to David. It also feels like a retirement speech).

Q – Why is it important to thank God for the good things he does for us? (It's part of our ongoing relationship with him. Part of our worship is to give heart-felt thanks not just for what he gives us, but also who he is and what he's like. We thank him because he is good).

Thanking God also reminds us of his provision and of his nature to look after us as a loving Father. Thanking God does us good too!

Q – Have you ever had an experience of seeing a spoilt child? Why is it that this is such a bad character trait? (Some people who have everything given them with no hardships, or having to earn anything can be very selfish, uncaring and get easily upset when they don't get their own way. But those with thankful hearts are often kind, generous, understanding of others and are not so driven by possessing things).

Scenario (2 minutes)
Sometimes it takes an extreme situation to help us to see exactly what we have to be thankful for. Imagine you had to live for two weeks without the internet. Imagine your electricity was turned off and all that you had was gas for cooking and heating. Imagine you could only eat jacket potatoes with cheese and beans for dinner.

When everything was given back to you, you may well have a new appreciation for the things that you didn't have access too. Rather than complaining that his fighting days were over, King David appreciated all that God had given him. Learning to live a life of thankfulness is a very good character trait to have!

Round up (2 minutes)
Let's go back to my "thank you" letter. If I sent out that letter people might get the feeling that I don't really mean my thanks. They may even think I'm being sarcastic. A thank you goes beyond the value of the gift. It actually expresses an appreciation for effort that the person has gone to, to find us an appropriate gift.

It's all about relationship. When we begin to think about what that person has done, looking online or in the shops, spending their hard earned money, and taking the time to wrap it for us, we begin to understand the kindness that has motivated that gift. And as we appreciate the lengths that God has gone to for us, we begin to see his provision in all sorts of unexpected ways.

If we can see all that God has done and is doing on our behalf, then we would never stop thanking him for his goodness to us!

Pray (As long as it takes)

TH1 – THANK YOU ADVICE FORM 1

From: Me
       10 Country Lane
       Ashtown
       Midway
       MD22 4DT

Dear Aunt/Uncle/Cousin (delete as appropriate) _____

Thank you for the _____

that you gave me for Christmas/my birthday/Easter/other celebration (delete as appropriate)

It was very/slightly/almost (delete as appropriate)   Tick box

Interesting	☐
Useful	☐
Nice	☐
Exciting	☐
Thoughtful	☐
Just what I always wanted	☐
None of the above	☐

I hope you had a lovely Christmas/Easter/other celebration

Me

© Julia Louise Hope Photography

Amy Walters Art & Design

Christian Graphic Design Artist

FURNACE

Amy created this logo for Paul Martin's Furnace youth group in 2015.

For enquiries and commissions e-mail amywaltersart@gmail.com

Available now at Amazon.

INSPIRE – A resource for busy youth workers - VOLUME 2
Volume 2 continues where volume 1 left off with another 28 Old Testament sessions, beginning with King Solomon asking for wisdom. Additionally it has 32 New Testament sessions, taking the same format as the Old Testament sessions.

Volume 2 also contains 24 pages of icebreakers for easy reference at the back of the book. Great for when you're in a rush and just need inspiration for an icebreaker!

Digital copies are available through Amazon Kindle.
Simply download the app and purchase Kindle copies on Amazon to be used on any device.

Printed in Great Britain
by Amazon